GUIDING GOD'S MARRIAGE

Guiding God's Marriage

Faith and Social Change in Premarital Counseling

Courtney Ann Irby

NEW YORK UNIVERSITY PRESS
New York

NEW YORK UNIVERSITY PRESS
New York www.nyupress.org

© 2024 by New York University
All rights reserved

Please contact the Library of Congress for Cataloging-in-Publication data.
ISBN: 9781479822140 (hardback)
ISBN: 9781479822157 (paperback)
ISBN: 9781479822171 (library ebook)
ISBN: 9781479822201 (consumer ebook)

This book is printed on acid-free paper, and its binding materials are chosen for strength and durability. We strive to use environmentally responsible suppliers and materials to the greatest extent possible in publishing our books.

Manufactured in the United States of America

10 9 8 7 6 5 4 3 2 1

Also available as an ebook

For Todd,

who has been both my partner and colleague through this journey.

CONTENTS

List of Figures and Tables   ix

Introduction: Preparing for Marriage... An Institution in Crisis?   1

1. Historical Shifts in Christian Lessons on Marital Success   25
2. What Is Christian Premarital Counseling?   50
3. Constructing a Good and Godly Marriage   77
4. Teaching Gender (and) Differences in Marriage   104
5. How Do You Feel about Sex and Money?   134
6. What Did We Learn? A Structure for Couples' (Pre)marital Emotion Work   161

Conclusion: Working toward the Good Marriage   189

Acknowledgments   207

Notes   211

Bibliography   235

Index   247

About the Author   255

LIST OF FIGURES AND TABLES

Figure 2.1. Johari Window   61

Figure 3.1. Covenant Image from Exploring Your
    Relationship Retreat   83

Table 4.1. Explanations of Gender and Difference in
    Premarital Education   111

Figure 5.1. Fulfillment Curve from St. Sebastian   153

Introduction

Preparing for Marriage . . . An Institution in Crisis?

As the only person sitting alone, I stood out in the audience of engaged couples waiting for the Exploring Your Relationship Retreat to begin. Along with eight couples, I sat quietly in anticipation in a small conference room at a rural evangelical retreat center. Even though the room had a wall of windows that looked out over a small field, we faced the opposite direction and were positioned instead toward a raised dais seasonally decorated with fake fall leaves and Christmas lights. Whereas everyone else sat next to their fiancé(e) at tables that made up two half circles, I had my own small desk off to the side by the door, which coincidently also positioned me closer to the snacks. Having no one to quietly chat with, I instead reviewed the itinerary in the packet of provided materials for the upcoming weekend. I noticed that our first evening would be low-key, with only two sessions, one for welcome and the other for orientation. The next day, however, was scheduled to start promptly at 7:00 a.m. with a breakfast and not end until after 7:00 p.m. Tomorrow's sessions would include topics such as "Stages of Love," "Heal the Hurts," "Sexuality," "Love Languages," and other more substantive issues.

My focus on the packet of materials was broken as the three married couples who led the program took their seats at the elevated table. Before any introductions, they drew our attention to a short video playing on an overhead projector to their side. Much like the technology being used, the video itself had a 1990s vibe. Filmed on a simple set of a couch with a telephone on a side table as a prop, a woman in a brown plaid jacket complete with shoulder pads dramatically acted out her relationship with a man in a comedic manner that elicited laughter from the live audience. Sitting quietly in the dark room, all of us silently watched this fictitious couple first be drawn together and then eventually challenged by their personality differences. Initially, the woman called someone to describe how she loves how organized and methodical the man is, and he similarly explained in his own phone call that he loves her spontaneous and carefree nature. The video revealed how over time, these characteristics that they once loved soon became sources of conflict. The tensions escalated as the man began to see the woman's spontaneity as disorganization and recklessness, whereas she started to perceive his commitment to organization as controlling. The video concluded with each character making more phone calls to complain about their partner but ultimately realizing, through these one-sided conversations, that some of the partner's critiques were probably valid assessments of their personality. In the end, the man and woman both realized that despite their differences, they agreed on at least one thing: their love for each other. Despite expecting there to be a discussion after the film ended, Paul, one of the group leaders, offhandedly commented, "The film is a way to start on a light note" before he proceeded with introductions.

When it was finally my time to speak, I quickly stated my name and explained "I'm studying premarital counseling programs and will simply be here to observe and learn with you all." Unexpectedly, Paul took a moment to lend his support to my research, noting how important it is because "marriage is under assault." At first, I wondered whether this was a veiled comment about the debates on marriage equality. However, he continued to explain, "I hope her work will help to prepare people for marriage." I would come to realize that although some leaders may be privately concerned about the perceived threats of feminism, "blending" of gender roles, or gay marriage, premarital counseling is organizationally designed to contend with one threat: divorce. In fact, it has become practically impossible to contemplate marriage without also considering divorce.

Programs such as the Exploring Your Relationship Retreat operate as religio-therapeutic ministries that offer couples a community intervention during the transition to marriage. Over a short span of time, "premarital counselors" are tasked with distilling and transmitting what they view as the most pertinent information about how to act, how to feel, and what to believe in marriage.[1] By drawing on their own relationships, social scientific insights, popular self-help texts, and religious teachings, they create lessons and exercises that they believe will help couples identify and prepare for future challenges. These programs, therefore, offer insights into how religious communities have responded, interpreted, and repackaged recent cultural transitions in marriage. As it turns out, mundane concerns about communication styles and conflict management emerged as more salient than politically polarizing rhetoric or sometimes even theological lessons. The prescriptive advice about what marriage is and ought to be became narrowly focused on working with individuals to create unions that premarital counselors imagine have what it takes to survive. Yet, embedded in these lessons about ordinary concerns are broader messages about gender, faith, intimacy, and social change.

Ultimately, this book is about people asking, and answering, the question, "What makes a good marriage?" The seeming simplicity of this question asked by so many people actually masks its own history of controversy, anxiety, hope, and challenges to individuals, communities, and the nation. Over the past century, the characteristics of a good marriage have shifted from one that didn't end in divorce[2] to one where both partners are individually happy and fulfilled.[3] Yet, at any moment, the ideas about a "good marriage" are not static or universal but are often contested. The last hundred years have seen dramatic changes to the institution of marriage—the rise of dual-earner households, delayed first age of marriage, increased access to contraception, passage of no-fault divorce, reimagined scripts for division of labor, and of course, marriage equality—all of which has created less predictable patterns of marriage. Although the place of marriage in society may have become less of a given, it continues to be a primary access point into adulthood for Americans broadly and a means of sanctification for Christians specifically. For both the Catholic and evangelical Protestant communities that I studied, marriage was seen as critical to one's spiritual development and an important institution into which people shouldn't enter lightly. In particular, I regularly heard that Christians, unlike secular people, are supposed to take marriage more seriously and that their faith should result in a unique commitment to the relationship. I, therefore, ask a further question: "What is the connection between a 'good' marriage and a 'godly' one?" Nearly every Catholic and evangelical premarital counselor with whom I spoke argued that God calls Christians to have a "covenant marriage," which they viewed as healthier, holier, and happier because it requires each partner to be other focused. Yet, they also consistently acknowledged that Christians aren't immune to divorce and sometimes may even do so at higher rates. For many, this anxiety and uncertainty about how to have a good marriage motivated not only their participation in these programs but also efforts to cultivate a marital work ethic.[4] This book tells the story of how Christian communities developed and continue to offer premarital counseling as a form of emotional, spiritual, and relational socialization. It argues that their teaching of what I call the *covenant rhetoric* offers an interpretative framework to make sense of this increased contingency in marriage culture, establishes "feeling rules"[5] to emotionally identify a successful and loving relationship, and sacralizes relationship skills to ensure people work against the threat of divorce.

Something Borrowed: A Cultural Approach to the Study of Religion and the Good Family

An array of social sciences, including psychology, sociology, demography, and public health, have all sought to understand "religion's role in maintaining or undermining a stable family life."[6] At the heart of much of this work have been questions about whether religion is correlated with healthier practices or happier outcomes in the home. For example, religious involvement has been associated with reduced rates of premarital sex[7] and increased marital satisfaction and commitment.[8] However, it has also been associated with declined use of contraceptives among adolescents,[9] authoritarian parenting styles,[10] and a complicated relationship with domestic violence.[11] An underlying assumption in this type of work has been that "declines in the institutional vitality of the family will be associated, other things being equal, with declines in religious vitality."[12] Whether intentionally or not, this stance offers an overly simplified conception of "family" and "religion" by assuming static and universal views of each institution and the relationship between them as either negative or positive. Yet, as sociologist Kathleen Jenkins observes, "family and religion are fluid social institutions produced by multiple beliefs and practices."[13] By employing a cultural perspective, we can better identify the complexities and contradictions that shape identities and interactions that people mark as religious and intimate.

A cultural approach is less concerned about "what's best" for the family or church and instead pursues questions of meaning making: "how meaning-making happens, why meanings vary, how meanings influence human action, and the ways meaning-making is important in social cohesion, domination, and resistance."[14] Replacing studies that long sought to measure growth or decline in American religion, cultural approaches in the sociology of religion emerged and reconceptualized religious authority as contested.[15] Sociologist Penny Edgell has identified three goals for a cultural approach to the study of religion: (1) identify the institutional context that fosters religious expression in a historical moment, (2) adopt a practice-oriented approach to religious identity and experiences that recognizes them as socially embedded, and (3) consider how discourses enable religious repertoires to shape social relations of power.[16] From this perspective, she further contends that we must investigate how religious institutions produce and transmit "religious familism"—the "ideology about what constitutes a family and what a good family should be like."[17]

The cultural approach best fits the study of marriage preparation for several reasons. Although I am often asked whether participating in these programs can save a marriage from divorce or at least improve future marital quality, this question misses the point. First, it is unrealistic that a single weekend or six weeks of evening classes could create a distinctive enough impact on relationships to measure. Even if I had tried to conduct a longitudinal study to learn about the long-term effects, it is not clear at what point it would be appropriate to collect data again. After all, as sociologist Kathleen Gerson has pointed out, "family life is a film, not a snapshot. . . . [It is] not a stable set of relationships frozen in time but a dynamic process that changes daily, monthly, and yearly."[18] As the premarital counselors themselves contend, all marriages go through stages that are marked by different needs, issues, and strengths, which means the impact—positive or negative—of their classes could vary at different points during a marriage. Second, the family unit is not cohesive but is made up of a differentiation of experiences and sometimes divergent views of the same events. Feminist scholars of family life have long observed that treating the family, or marriage, as a consistent experience shared by all parties will marginalize some voices and possibly mask inequalities.[19] In sociologist Jessie Bernard's classic study, she argued that in each marital union, there are really two marriages—his and hers.[20] Since that time, researchers have continued to illustrate how treating "the family" or "the household" as the basic category of analysis obscures the unequal bargaining power in decision-making about household labor, childcare, where to live, and more. Thus, any impact from participating in marriage preparation will vary both by time and person because marital quality is not static.

So why study premarital counseling if we cannot determine whether it will save individual marriages? The overly simplified cause-and-effect question about marriage preparation misses what the practice reveals about the contestation of religious authority, the negotiation of social scripts for intimate relationships, and the sacralization of therapeutic and emotional regimes. As a practice that has spanned decades and transcends religious communities, premarital counseling offers a unique window into how religious communities respond to, package, and transmit religious familism. In other words, Christian premarital counselors' "problem" to save marriages from divorce is not my own. I am less interested in whether these programs "work" but rather explore what the work of the programs reveals about marriage, religion, and how people construct relational goals and pursue a good and happy life. By reframing the question in this way, I argue that the power of the covenant rhetoric emerges more from how it establishes ways to *feel* in a Christian marriage than through the lessons' direct instructional content.

Something Old, Something New: Learning Therapeutic Love in Christian Marriage Preparation

An integral part of being a Christian includes the "ability to feel and display the 'right' emotions at the right times."[21] Within a religious context, "right" implicates more than social competency and contains a moralized connotation. By elevating the stakes to sin and salvation, faith communities produce "religious emotional regimes"[22] that order emotional lives by connecting members to a sense of transcendence that purports to be truer, more satisfying, and at times, more natural. Interestingly, however, people often tend to overlook and downplay the role of emotions in their lives. Sociologist Scott Harris notes that emotions are often disregarded as inferior because they are seen as irrational or merely treated as physiological responses that people automatically feel with little to no control.[23] For example, romantic love is regularly viewed as a private and mysterious feeling that can overtake an individual to make them act irrationally, impulsively, and unthinkingly.[24] Yet, cultural expectations exist for how one *ought* to love—whom to love, how to showcase love, ways to identify the feeling in oneself and others, and what to do once someone realizes they are in love. To explain how these feeling rules work, sociologist Arlie Hochschild uses the applicable example of a bride reflecting on her conflicted emotions on her wedding day.[25] As the woman recalled, "My marriage ceremony was chaotic and completely different than I imagined it would be. . . . I was depressed. I wanted to be so happy on our wedding day. . . . This is supposed to be the happiest day of one's life."[26] Hochschild highlights that a tension exists between what the bride believes she should feel at her wedding and her own actual emotions. The mismatch, or what is sometimes called emotional deviance,[27] points to how her own feelings are in violation of the cultural and internalized expectation that one should feel happy at one's wedding. In fact, emotion norms further guide the bride by denoting *when* to feel excited about getting married (e.g., the appropriate age), *whom* she should love (e.g., a kind partner and not an aggressive one), and *how strongly* she should feel love for this person (e.g., with only a "moderate degree of abandon"[28] to ensure she doesn't lose herself in the relationship). As this example indicates, however, feeling rules exist as part of a broader emotional regime that structures individuals' interior worlds in a manner that reflects and (re)produces inequalities.[29] A closer examination of relational norms about who can show love and how people are expected to do so in American history reveals how this seemingly "natural" and ephemeral feeling has been structured by gender, sexuality, religion, race, and social class.

While colloquially, people use the phrase "traditional marriage" to refer to the 1950s model of a homemaker and breadwinner, social historian Stephanie Coontz argues that in the *real* traditional marriage of preindustrial society, love was too fleeting to serve as the basis of an institution as important as marriage.[30] Instead, people across social classes were more likely to treat marriage as a political and economic transaction. The rise of industrial capitalism fundamentally transformed the relationship between work and family by ultimately converting the home from a site of production to a site of consumption that was "separate" from (paid) work.[31] In the process, the way of life for a small set of white, upper-middle-class Americans became *the* ideology of family life.[32] Love, historians have observed, emerged to "bridge" the bifurcated social worlds of public sphere versus private sphere, men versus women, and work versus home.[33] Love increasingly became seen as "complementarian," supposedly uniting two parts (men and women) into their destined whole (marriage). The problem, however, is that this "love bridge" was predicated on opposing views of the meaning of love because of the underlying social hierarchy within gender complementarianism.[34] For white, class-privileged men, love was irrational because it was the opposite of the independence and autonomy that structured their lives in the public spheres of work and politics. In contrast, love was rational for white, class-privileged women for whom it was the only way to fulfill their roles and obligations as well as to access goods and resources. Rather than serve as a "bridge," feminists have long "recognized the centrality of the concept of 'love' to familial ideology, to the maintenance of heterosexual monogamy and patriarchal marriage."[35] Ideologies of romantic love therefore, sociologist Chrys Ingraham argues, reinforce and naturalize a "heterogendered division of labor" that expects women to subordinate their own needs to men's desires.[36]

Yet, this hierarchical and often paternalistic conception of love began to be replaced in the twentieth century with what I call a therapeutic love that is about the fulfillment of an inner self.[37] Sociologist Ann Swidler has noted that the media continues to reflect these "love myths," where an individual faces an all-or-nothing choice about whether to pursue a partner who is entirely different from themselves.[38] In contrast to this type of intense and overwhelming love found in the movies, however, the people she interviewed often described "real love" as something that grows slowly and sometimes uncertainly, which requires people to learn to assess a relationship on the basis of compatibility and the type of traits that they believe will make a good partner. Love, thus, relies on therapeutic practices of sharing about one's inner feelings and desires and requires working on one's self to ensure one is ready for, open to, and competent in love. Sociologist Jennifer Randles notes that this type of "skilled love" emerged as part of a broader rationalization of romance.[39] Over the past century, love, relationships, and marriage have been subjected to the rigors of science, where experts claim that impartial techniques will reveal "healthy" practices. Although the shift to therapeutic love disrupted the ways that relationships are gendered, the legacy of romantic inequality remains. As we will see, experts' advice has often reflected the cultural understandings of love, gender, sexuality, and social class dominant at their time.

The transformation of "real love" to a cognitive process that people can learn to properly monitor and control[40] is part of a broader therapeutic culture. The term captures the influence of both the "formal knowledge systems" in professional disciplines, such as psychology, and the genre of self-help that dominates popular culture.[41] In *Rethinking Therapeutic Culture*, English scholar Timothy Aubry and literary historian Trysh Travis observe that "we have made the individual psyche the primary object of our attention. We treat its improper functioning as the principal source of society's ills and see its balance and well-being as the ultimate goal of our strivings on this earth."[42] Building on the work of sociologists such as Robert Bellah, Frank Furedi, and Eva Illouz, their volume highlights the ways Americans are preoccupied with their emotional well-being and have come to define their sense of self by their interior feelings. On the one hand, this therapeutic ethos is individualistic in how the needs and desires of the self are seen as more important than social roles, obligations, or institutional demands. It becomes the responsibility of the person to treat the self as a project, as they constantly and creatively strive to be better and happier. On the other hand, this self-work often relies on the advice and cultural logics provided by "experts" who offer their knowledge as a guiding intervention. In addition to the therapists or even talk show hosts who offer self-help advice, politicians' and economists' neoliberal policies also espouse a similar ideology of personal risk and responsibility.[43]

Prominent scholars of therapeutic culture, however, would have us believe "that America has traded its soul for its psyche, has swapped religion for therapy, and has given up faith in God for a faith in inner selves."[44] Yet, much of this scholarship relies on analyses of cultural discourses and has not examined how religious leaders and laity within, across, and outside of congregations actually interpret, use, or live out a therapeutic ethos.[45] As will become clear, Christian premarital counseling illustrates how religious communities have been active in shaping and spreading the therapeutic ethos, including a vision of therapeutic love. For example, the covenant rhetoric emphasizes the belief that working on one's self and relationship is paramount and that love (in marriage and from God) is worth striving for, and it has transmitted these ideas through a wide network of religio-therapeutic programming.

The study of premarital counseling provides a unique opportunity where many of the taken-for-granted norms of love as well as of a "good" marriage are articulated. By design, marriage preparation programs intervene in a liminal moment where people are shedding one role and preparing to acquire a new one. As Hochschild observes, "When roles change, so do rules for how to feel and interpret events."[46] We culturally recognize the significance of this transition in our shifting language that moves from boyfriend/girlfriend to fiancé(e) to bride/groom to husband/wife.[47] A range of experts have observed the ways that this transition can often take people by surprise. Social historian Stephanie Coontz observes that "no matter how well you think you know your partner beforehand, the first years are full of surprises, not only about your spouse but about yourself."[48] Furthermore, Gary Chapman, popular author of *The Five Love Languages*, has observed that "the kind of loving, supportive, mutually beneficial marriage . . . will not happen simply because you get married."[49] So what makes this transition so challenging? And what does it reveal about how we learn to love and why we get married in the United States?

Prescribing the "Good Marriage": A Short History of Marital Advice

For the past 150 years, historians have identified myriad ways that marriage has changed; yet, perhaps surprisingly, a consistent theme appears to be a fear about the stability and longevity of the institution.[50] In her book *Marriage, a History*, Stephanie Coontz begins by pointing out that "for thousands of years people have been proclaiming a crisis in marriage and pointing backward to better days."[51] Although the potential "threats" have been numerous—contraception, gay marriage, cohabitation, single mothers, teenage pregnancy, women's employment, and feminism—the one that has regularly animated Americans' attention over the past century has been divorce.[52] In fact, as historian Kristin Celello argues, concerns about divorce are central to understanding the history of marriage.[53] Throughout the twentieth century, a deep-seated anxiety about divorce reinforced Americans' desire to strengthen their relationships to be more satisfying.

Beginning in the 1920s, Celello documents how a diverse group of "experts" began to conceptualize a marital work ethic in response to growing fears about divorce and what they perceived as a crisis in American marriage. The nineteenth-century view that marriage was a duty had been replaced by the increasingly popular view of a "companionate marriage"—the belief that the institution should be based on love and would be most successful if both parties fulfilled their roles. Religious leaders and experts, however, feared that men and women would begin to expect too much from their relationships. Historians such as Kristin Celello and Rebecca Davis have documented how these fears about romantic love and the companionate marriage motivated experts to craft programs to intervene before those trapped in seemingly loveless marriages sought divorces.[54] Davis chronicled how marriage counseling began in the 1930s as an "experiment in social reform" to help engaged couples avoid disappointment and married couples manage their existing conflicts. Despite this seemingly individualistic focus, experts were motivated by communal responsibilities and saw their role as creating social anchors in society. Celello notes how many of these early efforts at marriage education often contained vague messages of what one should do to work on a marriage, but it was clear that the labor was expected to fall almost exclusively on women. The pressures placed on women to maintain marriages and deter divorces intensified by mid-century as experts, religious leaders, and the government became deeply concerned about "war marriages." The fears that young men and women were getting married because of a "now or never" mindset provided them a national stage as media and the government sought their insights into how to make any relationship work.

Building on the prominence they had gained during World War II, experts reached new audiences of apprehensive wives during the postwar era. With the "message that it was their job to create marital happiness and stability after years of economic and social upheaval,"[55] Celello documents how wives' expected relationship work became increasingly demanding and more specific, including to be highly aware of their family's physical needs, promote their husband's career, and be responsible for the psychological well-being of the home. In fact, experts regularly argued that no problem, including infidelity or abuse, was so severe that a marriage couldn't be saved. They additionally claimed that the wife must recognize her own culpability and actively work to ameliorate these situations. Davis notes that although women most often initiated trips to marriage counselors, once the couples participated in the therapeutic practice, men articulated their own frustrations about the evolving demands of the marital bargain: serving as an emotional partner and become more involved in child-rearing, housekeeping, and sexual intimacy.

By the 1960s, clients had become dissatisfied with the decades-long advice offered by marriage counselors that lowering one's marital expectations would create domestic bliss. Although the belief that marriages require hard work had permeated the American culture, the view that getting and staying married is the primary achievement of women began to be questioned.[56] The consequences included some, such as Betty Friedan, calling for women to stop sacrificing their own desires in an effort to fulfill the complementarian roles of the companionate marriage. She instead encouraged women to become independent and to separate from their role as a wife and mother. Furthermore, a paradigm shift occurred in marriage counseling. The "adjustment" frame that called for spouses, especially wives, to accommodate to the marital roles was slowly replaced with a "self-actualization" perspective that argued that self-fulfillment is critical to marital health.[57] Similar ideas were also being espoused in popular publications, such as *Ladies Home Journal*, and by the 1960s, marital advice became dominated by three key themes: self-development, flexible roles, and open communication.[58]

Reflecting on the twentieth-century changes to marriage, sociologists Claude Fischer and Michael Hout observed that "standards for a good marriage rose and escapes from a bad one became easier."[59] By the 1970s, people were living longer, which meant that divorce had overtaken death as the primary means of marital dissolution.[60] The numerical tipping point is only one sign of a "marital watershed," which led to the decline of a "marriage culture" in the United States.[61] The idea that one must get married, that the relationship should last forever, or that divorce should be a last resort had been slowly replaced by new ideas about intimacy and what makes a good marriage. By 1985, all states had replaced fault-based divorces that required "guilt" and "innocence" in the proceedings with no-fault divorces that allowed for "irreconcilable differences," which privileged individuals' needs over the obligations of social roles.[62] Even marriage counselors began to shift their view on the institution and their metric for determining success—marriage became seen as "an ideal site for personal empowerment"[63] that should be built on "a model of mutual emotional, financial, and sexual gratification."[64] Thus, Coontz argues that "the same values that increased people's satisfaction with marriage as a relationship had an inherent tendency to undermine the stability of the institution [because] the very features that promised to make marriage such a unique and treasured personal relationship opened the way for it to become an optional and fragile one."[65]

The new understandings of marriage meant that it also began to occupy a different position in the life course. Sociologist Andrew Cherlin has argued that the importance placed on emotional satisfaction and romantic love coupled with the rising therapeutic belief that people should cultivate their own sense of self led to the "deinstitutionalization of American marriage."[66] In other words, the social norms that defined people's behaviors in marriage weakened, creating more variability and options. Under the "companionate marriage," the emphasis on roles helped to ensure conformity across the life course, with people following a predictable pattern of whom and when they married, had children, bought homes, determined who stayed home, set the division of labor, and so forth. By the 1960s, however, young Americans began to postpone marriage in favor of activities that cultivated the self's potential, such as completing college or starting one's career. Sociologist Frank Furstenberg and his colleagues contend that the transition to adulthood became more nebulous at this time.[67] Adulthood has long been seen as when one establishes emotional and economic independence from one's parents. In recent decades, this threshold has taken longer to accomplish, which subsequently has elongated the transition to adulthood. Starting in the late 1960s, young adults found that what it takes to locate a secure full-time job became more challenging and required them to spend at least their twenties investing in themselves.[68] As both men and women strived to attend college and develop professionally, they often have postponed marriage and childbearing but not living together.

An "individualized marriage" emerged, Cherlin argues, to replace the companionate marriage.[69] Under this new framework, marriage is expected to be simultaneously a partnership that can function as one *and* a relationship where two individuals can cultivate their own selves. The expectations of a "good marriage" were personalized with people now evaluating their relationships on individualistic and emotional criteria, such as personal satisfaction. No longer was happiness expected to emerge from pleasing one's spouse or raising children; instead, people ask themselves, "Am I getting the personal satisfaction I want from my marriage? Am I growing as a person?"[70] The new model of marriage, changes to divorce law, and prolonged transition to adulthood coalesced into an altered meaning and context for marriage in the twenty-first century. People now have more choices available in their personal lives, and thus when they form relationships, they anticipate personal growth and deep intimacy.[71]

Overall, even though marriage continues to be desired, these changes have made marriage less necessary. It's no longer the only context in which people choose to live together, have sex, or raise children. Even more fundamentally, marriage is no longer the only way to regularly access the production of goods, such as food and clothing. People simply do not need marriage to survive or to form loving families.

So why do people still get married? According to Cherlin, marriage has become "a marker of prestige" and "a status one builds up to."[72] Whereas "it used to be the foundation of adult personal life; now, it is sometimes the capstone. It is something to be achieved through one's own efforts rather than something to which one routinely accedes."[73] In other words, people want a *good* marriage and are willing to wait to find not only the right person but also for the right time when they are financially stable and emotionally secure in themselves and in the partnership.

The challenge, however, is that people are striving for marriage within an "insecurity culture," which includes, among many other challenges, persistent job precariousness and rising costs of living.[74] As a consequence, scholars have noticed that a "marriage gap"[75] has emerged that has widened the socioeconomic and racial divide of who marries.[76] Although Americans almost universally aspire to marriage, this vision of what makes a "good marriage" has created classed barriers and "ideologically associated [it] with middle-class advantages, namely, finishing college, being securely employed, making decent wages, and owning a home."[77] Working-class couples and those living in poverty not only struggle to meet these personalized thresholds for *getting* married, sociologists have further observed how cultural logics for how to *stay* married presuppose that it is an individuals' responsibility but mask the structural and material factors that can make this task easier. For example, sociologists Sarah Corse and Jennifer Silva observed that to try to "insure themselves against the possibility of marital complacency, conflict, and dissolution" middle-class men and women turned to weekly therapy appointments, building a relaxation room, going out on "date nights," and other forms of "private insurance" that are too costly for working-class couples.[78] These strategies reflect a therapeutic ethos that myopically positions problems, and their solutions, as rooted within individuals who are "responsible for their [own] well-being, emotional health, and self-realization"[79] without attending to the structural forms of inequality and privilege that couples are embedded within.

Building on a century of changes to the public and private meaning of marriage, contemporary Americans are left with the paradox that the institution is more satisfying but less stable.[80] In other words, the "good" marriage is made possible because emotional fulfillment is now the primary goal, but maintaining an emotional connection between partners requires work, time, skill, and possibly, financial resources. For many Christians, this paradox represents a crisis for marriage because the institution is a key site for people to fulfill their religious calling and become fully fledged adult members of their community.[81] On the one hand, this marital anxiety has motivated efforts to legally ensure Christian views that marriage should be an indissoluble, heterosexual union structured by male headship.[82] This view has manifested in a variety of broad-based political efforts in the form of a "marriage movement" that is often concerned with what an "other" is doing, such as promoting marriage to low-income families, only teaching abstinence education, and challenging marriage equality.[83] On the other hand, this marital anxiety has a more diffuse cultural impact for the Christian communities themselves and their members who are hoping for this indissoluble, heterosexual marriage. During premarital counseling, these Christian communities find themselves intervening, responding, and engaging with people at a liminal time where engaged couples are not yet married but forming ideas that can normalize what the institution is, what it should be, and its moral significance.

Organizationally Studying Christian Marriage Preparation

Ethnographic research is "the study of groups and people as they go about their everyday lives"[84] and has generally been distinguished by sustained and lengthy time spent in the field to allow researchers to obtain a deep understanding of locals' own meaning. Yet, this approach to ethnography often presupposes a longevity of the intended object of observation. The problem, as sociologist Krista Paulsen notes in her call for an "ethnography of the ephemeral," is that "many socially important institutions, scenes and events are of limited duration."[85] Premarital counseling represents both a sustained practice within certain communities and a brief experience for the couples who participate in it. To examine the liminal and persistent dimensions of marriage preparation, I designed a mixed-method approach that included archival research into organizations that helped to popularize Catholic marriage preparation, content analysis of historical and contemporary texts used in evangelical and Catholic curriculum, observations of Catholic and evangelical premarital counseling, and finally, interviews with those who offered and participated in a variety of programs.[86]

Since the topic of families can be plagued with nostalgic and often inaccurate claims about what "used to be," I began by conducting a social history of premarital counseling. The differences in how evangelical Protestants and Catholics developed these programs shaped my strategies for data collection. The centralizing mechanism of the Catholic hierarchy and the existence of multiple social movements that sought to promote marriage preparation within the Catholic Church helped to produce a wealth of archival data.[87] For example, I listened to old recordings of parish programs offered in the 1950s, read internal memos debating how to adapt the programs, and more. In contrast, the lack of a central structure among evangelical Protestants and the existence of fewer organizational archives among them resulted in a dearth of this type of data. During the same period, however, both evangelicals and Catholics embraced self-help literature resulting in extensive relationship books published (and presumably read by members) within these communities. The analysis of evangelicals relied on these primary sources to learn about shifting views and practices over time. Although written for a variety of audiences, many of the books were designed to help pastors counsel couples and included questionnaires used for assessment that I could examine.

While I continued to rely on textual analysis of relationship guides to triangulate data, I approached my contemporary data collection as what I call an *ethnography of a practice*.[88] To theoretically and methodologically shift away from studying "how people live their lives with one another in particular places"[89] to studying what participating in a temporary practice reveals about community, emotions, and religious familism required that I reimagine some of the benchmarks in qualitative work. I started with standard ethnographic procedures: immersing myself in research sites, learning by actively participating in activities, and establishing informative relationships with people.[90] The key difference is that I did not focus on learning the routines of congregations but instead the nuances of a shared practice that transcends individual religious communities. While I immersed myself in research sites, each time period was brief but the locations more numerous.

To explore how religious communities attempt to intervene and prepare couples for marriage, between 2012 and 2015, I employed an open recruitment strategy that involved contacting congregations and paraministry organizations to see if they offered premarital counseling and whether someone would be willing to speak with me and/or allow me to observe. This approach introduced me to a variety of organizational forms of premarital counseling and provided insights into the resources and community concerns that impacted programming and frequency. In the end, I conducted thirty-nine interviews with pastors, clergy, married lay couples, and Christian therapists who offered marriage preparation in fifteen Christian communities in the Pacific Northwest. Unlike the predominance of Catholicism in the Northeast or Midwest or evangelicalism in the South, the Northwest region has been described as the most "unchurched" area in the country.[91] Despite Christians accounting for about 61 percent of people (twice that of the approximate 31 percent of the religiously unaffiliated), the participants perceived themselves as living in an overwhelmingly secular place.[92] While waiting in the lobby of an evangelical congregation to speak with a pastor, a church staff member described the area to me as "the mission field." In contrast to this characteristic evangelical zeal, the Catholics I spoke with expressed a level of hesitancy about how best to engage the typically young, engaged couples seeking their services without turning them off religiously. In either case, the pronounced sense of the "secular other"[93] may have intensified but also clarified premarital counselors' lessons on what makes a marriage *Christian* and how they understand God's plan for having a happy and healthy relationship.

From this open recruitment strategy, I came to learn that two organizational forms dominate contemporary marriage preparation: individualized counseling sessions and collective classes typically held in congregations or at retreat centers. Of the thirty-nine interviews, twenty-six were with premarital counselors who conduct personalized sessions, small-group mentorship teams, or those who facilitated couples' use of workbooks.[94] In some cases, the individualized approach occurred because a congregation conducted weddings too infrequently to offer large classes, but in other cases, professional therapists conducted sessions for clients or congregations employed a small-group structure to create personalized opportunities for engaged couples to learn from married members of the church. The remaining thirteen interviews were with members of the leadership teams of the four collective programs that granted me the opportunity to attend their classes along with premarital couples.

Recognizing that interviews would not provide me with the experience of marriage preparation, I also conducted ethnographic observations of two evangelical sites ("Cosmopolitan Church" and "Exploring Your Relationship Retreat") and two Catholic parishes ("St. Sebastian" and "St. Bernadette").[95] For each religious tradition, one site was urban and the other was located in a nonurban area (under one hundred thousand people). Unlike the individualized counseling sessions that tended to occur with a therapist or clergy member, the collective programs were led by married couples. The Catholic programs rotated the leadership each week, which allowed for one evening where a religious director and/or priest spoke with the couples. In contrast, the evangelical leadership teams stayed consistent but tended to include a couple where one spouse was either a pastor or a therapist. At all the sites, the leadership were white, college educated, married couples, and often had young children. With the exception of the Exploring Your Relationship Retreat, which was held over one weekend (Friday evening to Sunday afternoon), all of the other programs met on a weekly basis for nearly two months.

Since the programs encouraged couples to take notes during their talks, I easily recorded the leadership's lessons as well as their interactions and responses to couples' questions. At a later point, I expanded on these jottings to create extensive field notes that captured how the teams leading these programs wove together their personal experience, Christian worldviews, and social-scientific insights to craft a narrative of relationship success (and failure). As much as I wanted to understand the reception of discourses, I took extra precautions to ensure the confidentiality of the premarital couples by recording general field notes about the audience, their reactions, questions, and stories. The frequency of engaged couples speaking varied by the program, leadership style, and session. Whereas the retreat included only one session where the couples could ask questions, the weekly programs typically included time for small-group activities. Since I attended the programs alone, I never intruded on any "couple time" where they were expected to have private discussions. I did, however, join small-group discussions and completed individual activities that were assigned, such as answering worksheets, taking personality tests, reading assigned resources, and journaling on the materials. Occasionally, for some of these activities that occurred outside of class time, I would ask my husband to do them with me to gauge the type of conversations that we could have as a couple.

My own limited experiences working through the materials as a married woman and listening to the lessons as a sociologist trained in gender, families, and religion admittedly provided a "researcher perspective." I quickly learned that this positionality oriented me to focus on the *content* of the lessons, but in speaking with the couples, I came to realize that they found the *process* of spending time together more meaningful. To obtain this "couples' perspective," I conducted dozens of informal field interviews and thirty-one semi-structured interviews after the programs concluded.[96] From listening to the questions asked to the leadership and casually speaking with the couples during breaks or as we waited for a session to start, I noticed that the emotional culture varied between the evangelical and Catholic programs. The Catholic programs had a laidback feeling where engaged couples completed the tasks asked of them but did not actively seek additional insights and the leadership team met this tenor with more informal lessons from their own marriages and time raising families in the parish. In contrast, the evangelical programs had an underlying intensity and anxiety on the part of both the attending couples and leadership. For example, the questions during the lessons on sexuality were fraught with questions about "how far is too far?" and how to handle sexual shame that may result as couples (fail to) negotiate these pressures. The evangelical leadership teams also tended to reveal more about their personal challenges in marriage and emphasize how hard one must work to stay in love long term. It wasn't until I had attended programs from both traditions that I realized their impact on my own emotional state—in leaving the evangelical programs, I noticed that I nervously wondered if I was doing enough to be a "good" spouse because the expectations and number of relationship strategies felt overwhelming, whereas I walked away from the Catholic programs with less clarity about specifics but with a greater sense that it would all work out.

There were also differences between evangelicals and Catholics who attended the programs. The Catholic programs tended to be smaller (six or so couples), whereas the evangelical programs were larger (ranging from ten to twenty couples). The fewer Catholic couples likely reflects both the fact that they are less prevalent in the Pacific Northwest and that couples *only* attended to get married in a Catholic church. In contrast, both dating and engaged couples participated in the evangelical programs and, I came to learn, regularly participated in more than one. Across the sites, however, the couples were typically heterosexually partnered young adults in their twenties to early thirties. While marriage equality passed during my fieldwork, none of the programs had enrolled a gay or lesbian couple.[97] For the Catholic programs, there was no discussion about whether this would change, but at the evangelical sites, some of the younger members of the leadership teams quietly mentioned to me that it might be an issue they would need to wrestle with in the future. Whereas the participating couples' educational backgrounds, types of profession, and race varied by site, white individuals with at least some college education dominated all the programs, reflective of the marriage gap in the United States.[98] The urban programs skewed more professional than the nonurban programs, which also had more racial and class variation. Approximately a quarter of participants at St. Bernadette were Latino/a and about 20 percent at the evangelical programs identified as Black or Asian American.[99]

Unlike many ethnographies within the sociology of religion, this book does not provide an intimate or in-depth look at the everyday patterns of communal religious life. The practice of marriage preparation exists outside the daily lives of the collective communities and the religious individuals that populate them to offer each an intentional, set-apart time in which to reflect on the meaning and significance of specific dimensions of everyday life. It thus provides an ideal site to explore how religion operates as a regime that creates "a structured emotional repertoire that guides how adherents feel about themselves, one another, and their wider circumstances."[100] This book argues that evangelical and Catholic marriage preparation programs put forward a vision of a good marriage in the form of the covenant rhetoric. Its call of oneness—between spouses and with God—represents more than a religious way to think about marriage, it operates as a way to identify, feel, and manage therapeutic and godly love. By taking seriously the power of emotions in people's lives, this book challenges the simplified narrative that views the emergence of a therapeutic culture as evidence of secularism and a distancing from religion.[101] Likewise, it contends that even as Christian communities have called for "traditional marriage" to combat what they view as threats to the privileged position of heterosexual marriage, they have also more broadly participated and stabilized cultural shifts in how Americans conceptualize the "good marriage" as a lifelong project characterized by therapeutic love.

Organization of the Book

The following chapters introduce the reader to Christian premarital counseling—how the practice spread in congregations, the various forms it takes, the religious and relational lessons contained within, and finally, how engaged couples reflect on their experiences. Following the structure of a cultural analysis of religion,[102] chapter 1 begins by providing the institutional and historical context for the development and changes to premarital counseling in each faith tradition. Starting with the postwar era when Catholic family movements first began to spread marriage preparation across parishes and evangelicals adapted the practice of pastoral counseling from their mainline counterparts, I consider who offered counsel on behalf of their religious communities and what they taught couples would help to improve their relationships. I chronicle two parallel stories of religious communities wrestling with what a successful Christian marriage should be against a backdrop of rising divorce rates and secularism. These cultural anxieties about keeping young people married and faithful led religious leaders to develop a widespread therapeutic practice that would sow the seeds for the covenant rhetoric and reimagine the spiritual authority of laity. The sociohistorical examination importantly enriches the overall analysis by allowing readers to immerse themselves in the concerns, fears, and hopes of decades of Christians who have used this practice to comment on the state of intimacy and faith.

Chapter 2 shifts to draw on my ethnographic research of contemporary marriage preparation practices. To provide the broader practice-based and contextual analysis demanded by the cultural approach, it presents the field of premarital counseling that emerged across the fifteen religious communities and interviews with independent Christian therapists. Concerned that the allure of a wedding may overshadow more realistic assessments about the marriage potential of a relationship, clergy, lay married couples, and therapists employ two organizational forms of relationship education: collective classes where groups of couples learn together and individualized counseling sessions personalized to a couple's particular situation.

Chapters 3 through 5 focus on my research with the four collective classes I observed to complete the final cultural analysis goal of interrogating how discourses of the good and godly marriage produce religious repertoires for emotions, gender, sexuality, and finances. Chapter 3 considers in-depth the intersection of religion and therapeutic culture by describing how the premarital counselors constructed a covenant rhetoric to distinguish between the unitive goals of a Christian marriage and what they view as selfishness in the "contract" marriage in secular culture. Yet, an ambivalence about the self—its needs and desires—emerged in premarital counselors' efforts to prevent divorce because their lessons on how to work on a marriage were predicated on therapeutic self-work. Chapter 4 explores the tension of difference embedded within the covenant rhetoric expectation of unity and oneness. Specifically, it interrogates when and how gender differences emerged as part of the construction of an ideal, healthy marriage. Despite the general orientation toward gender complementarianism among both traditions, I found that programs were equally likely to privilege psychological differences as gender differences. Chapter 5 shifts from the calls to work toward a covenant marriage to instead explore the relationship issues that married couples often argue about: sex and money. Even though these lessons could have offered gendered advice or been strictly informational, I instead found that instructions emphasized emotional socialization about identifying and managing individuals' desires toward the goal of creating the shared foundation required in a covenant marriage.

Chapter 6 shifts the locus of analysis from cultural transmission to reception by investigating why couples participate in and what they take away from marriage preparation. Drawing on the interviews with couples whom I met while attending the four sites (and who also sometimes participated in other programs), I move away from teachers and lessons in relationship education to the intended student. Whereas evangelical couples routinely attended these programs early in their relationship and often more than once, Catholic couples waited until a wedding date and venue had been selected. Despite this tendency for evangelical couples to conceptualize the religious practice as a resource and for Catholic couples to treat it as a requirement, those belonging to both Christian traditions more clearly remembered the significance of the process and struggled to recall specific content. Finally, the conclusion returns to the question of what discourses about a "good marriage" reveal about cultural expectations of faith, intimacy, and emotions. Specifically, it considers the question of "family change" by pulling together the threads of cultural changes in the institution of marriage within American society with the community practices that guide couples through their own life course transition.

1

Historical Shifts in Christian Lessons on Marital Success

In 1956, Father Mathias Fischer of St. Pascal Parish in Chicago oversaw one of the many Pre-Cana Conferences, the earliest form of Catholic marriage preparation, that were increasingly becoming popular for engaged couples. After the opening prayer ended, Father Fischer introduced himself and exclaimed, "Welcome to the Cana Conference each and every one of you. We're very happy that you are interested in your own marriage, and the sanctity and the holiness of marriage, that you've come to make this conference with us. . . . You are about to enter a marriage and, primarily, marriage is the gift of love—the highest gift that you will give to any other person in this world."[1] After acknowledging and extending a special welcome to any non-Catholics present, he continued by providing a little background on his own ministry and how his interest in marriage preparation emerged. Recollecting his days as a young priest working in a particularly poor neighborhood of Chicago in the 1930s, he recalled, "During those Depression days, one of the great, wonderful things that happened in the neighborhood at that time was the wedding. It was always a great event, as it should be because a marriage is a community affair. When two people get married, they marry into a community. They are beginning a new cell in a community."

Father Fischer continued by explaining that his understanding of love and marriage was deeply informed by the ability of people to create such beautiful unions during a time of such little material wealth. Yet, one specific wedding also spurred his early thinking that couples needed to be better prepared for marriage. "On this particular Saturday, a very funny fellow was getting married. He's quite serious now. But everything was funny to him. Even his wedding day was funny." As the light laughter from the crowd subsided, he elaborated, "And, I'll never forget the scene. The wedding was over and the recessional had begun and the couple turned to leave the altar and come down the aisle. Well, the bride, her little feet were scarcely touching the floor. She was literally on cloud heaven floating down the aisle. And my friend was shuffling alongside." Again, the description of the begrudging groom elicited laughter from the crowd, and once more he continued, "Everything went fine until they got to the vestibule of the church, where I was standing. And, instead of rather tenderly and reverently giving his bride her first little marital kiss. He runs away from the bride, and he comes running up to me, and he throws his hands up into the air, and he says 'My gosh Father! What have I done?'"

After yet another bout of laughter, Father Fischer shifted to enlighten the gathered couples about why Pre-Cana is important and how participating in the program would help to prepare them for their future marriages. "It isn't because we want to prevent such a scene at your wedding day that we give Pre-Canas, but I'm sure that the question must be in the minds of many of you—just what is a Pre-Cana conference? What are we supposed to do?" Answering his own question, he explained, "First of all [it] is a conference between the two of you. What you begin this afternoon will end only when you die. We are trying to set up between you and your beloved a communication that will draw you closer and closer together and make you the one flesh that Christ talked about. The important work at a Pre-Cana conference is not done by the priest, or the doctor, or the lay couple, the important work is done between the two of you. We want to teach you how to talk things over, how to share with one another, how to take problems together and solve them, how to get everything possible out of marriage, and God has put many good things in marriage. We want to teach you how to become saints, for this is your vocation. For we will try to tell you through the course of the afternoon, this is how you are going to get to heaven, by being a good husband, by being a faithful wife."

By the 1950s, when Father Fischer was extolling young, engaged couples in Chicago about the virtues of marriage, his voice was one of many that had emerged to promise new levels of companionship and intimacy for married couples.[2] During the postwar era, different types of "experts" surfaced to offer advice on how to be happy and successful in marriage—women's magazines, religious ministries, and marriage counselors—each worked within their own fields but agreed that through hard work, people could find fulfillment in the home. For the most part, the bar for success was straightforward: avoid divorce.[3] Yet, in their efforts to protect couples against divorce, they began to transform the idea of what constitutes a "good marriage." By stressing the need for communication, mutuality, and partnership as we see in Father Fischer's opening statements, a good marriage began to transition from fulfillment of obligations to the cultivation of personal gratification.

This chapter offers two parallel stories of how Christians' fears about divorce motivated the creation of religious ministries that infused theological visions of marriage with nascent therapeutic insights from the burgeoning field of relationship science for how to have a successful marriage. As evidenced by Father Fischer's introduction, the growing chorus about the importance of working on one's marriage was seen as holding this and otherworldly consequences. The sacralization of working to create a good marriage became interwoven with one's personal sanctification. As with advice offered by secular experts, however, much of the work was expected to fall disproportionately to women and presumed a white middle-class lifestyle. Yet, as we will see, the Christian belief that marriage represents believers' access to personal salvation also created an opening to expect men to engage in the emotion work of maintaining a relationship. This chapter, therefore, helps provide insights into the historical origins of the *covenant rhetoric* that would come to conceptualize Christian marriages as healthier than the secular contract model due to their relational focus, even as they promoted individualized self-work. In doing so, it also provides an organizational analysis of the ways Protestant and Catholic subcultures produced divergent models for premarital education and, in the process, illustrates how "the history of therapeutic practice cannot be disentangled from the history of Christianity."[4] By contrasting Catholics' broad-based efforts to create a collective ministry to prepare couples for marriage and evangelicals' adoption of individualized counseling practices, we will see how each community responded to the shifts in the meaning of love and the self in American religion and family.

Teaching Conformity to Marriage: Christian Premarital Counseling, circa 1940s–1960s

Many of the soldiers returning home from World War II were reuniting with wives to turn their attention to the postponed task of creating homes and the families to fill them.⁵ Yet, this likely highly anticipated reunion often did not go smoothly, leading to a peak in divorce rates in 1946 and 1947.⁶ Despite being poised on the precipice of what people today consider to be the golden decade of marriage, the institution was a central feature of social anxieties of the time.⁷ Fearful that young people were rushing to the altar without considering the gravity of their decision or the sanctity of the institution, movements developed among both religious communities and secular experts to educate and protect marriage. From the perspective of several Catholic family movements, such as the Cana Conference Movement and the Christian Family Movement, which we will examine in this chapter, American families were under an assault by secular forces that encouraged individualism over commitments like those found in marriage.⁸ Likewise, the budding field of marriage counseling, which evangelicals slowly began to incorporate into their own infrastructures, reached new levels of popularity during the postwar era with people increasingly turning to professional assistance.⁹ In each case, preparing engaged couples emerged as a potential mechanism to stabilize American marriages. This stability, experts and religious leaders believed, would be accomplished by couples conforming to the clear gendered division of labor and distinct roles of a heterosexual, companionate marriage.

Catholic Movements Prepare Couples for Marriage to Combat Secularism

On April 16, 1946, in the midst of a year that would eventually mark a national high in American divorce rates, the first Pre-Cana Conference was held in Chicago.¹⁰ As a branch of the broader Cana Conference Movement that served married couples, Pre-Cana developed to translate similar principles as its parent organization to engaged couples to help them obtain a holy and happy marriage. This first event occurred because Patty Crowley, a local lay leader in the Christian Family Movement, wanted her sister to be better prepared for marriage than the cursory education occasionally offered by parish priests. Along with some friends, she scoured approximately a dozen parishes to locate enough interested newlywed and engaged couples.¹¹ From these inauspicious beginnings, Pre-Cana rapidly spread across the United States. By

1950, thirty-one dioceses across the country reported hosting Pre-Cana with an estimated 27,500 in attendance in that year alone and an average of 131 persons per conferences.[12] The Archdiocese of Chicago, in particular, reported that by 1951, nearly 75 percent of Catholic marriages were preceded by participation in Pre-Cana, amounting to couples attending one of nearly a hundred conferences offered each year across their parishes.[13]

Pre-Cana operated organizationally and ideologically within the broader Cana Conference Movement that imagined itself as a means to combat the threat of secularism.[14] Speaking at a weeklong conference of Cana leaders, Alphonse Clemens, a sociologist involved in the movement with his wife, characterized the larger vision of Cana as an effort to "re-Christianize" marriage.

> Every aspect of marriage and family must be reintegrated with Christ. Cana must deal with nothing less than the totality of family life if it is to rout secularism. You might rout a certain degree of secularism by getting people to Communion more frequently. But these people might still continue to be quite secularized in their recreational habits, in their economic habits, in their lovemaking habits, and in many other aspects of marital life.[15]

To alleviate this problem of a secularized household, the movement focused their efforts on improving Catholic homes. Cana joined the legions of voices during the postwar era that sought to reinstitute the importance of home life as well as to help couples ensure a smooth domestic adjustment to the gender roles that experts asserted were necessary for every happy household.[16] Cana leaders articulated these recommendations within a spiritualized frame, however, that linked mundane household tasks to the vocation of marriage. Doing so required reimagining the understanding of spirituality within the Catholic Church at the time.[17] Unlike the universal connotations of the term in contemporary usage, among postwar Catholics, "spirituality" tended to be applied to the celibate priesthood. By arguing that "marriage is a special vocation," the leaders of Cana hoped to expand theological discussions on spirituality to combat the tendency to view marriage as an inferior vocational trajectory (compared with Holy Orders).[18] With the awareness that "marriage is a difficult vocation," however, Cana sought to also help couples determine how to be happier in the institution as a means to ensure their own sanctification.[19]

Cana leaders optimistically envisioned Pre-Cana as well-positioned to address these issues because they saw engaged couples as blank slates on which to imprint the correct practices and beliefs. Whereas married couples attended Cana Conferences because their marriages "needed brightening up,"[20] the clergy and laity who coordinated Pre-Cana hoped that an early intervention could "get marriages off on the right foot."[21] Confidently imagining Pre-Cana as both a type of remedy and vaccination, one priest hopefully observed, "Until the children of our Cana couples come to us, Pre-Cana must reach back to supply what has been lacking in the home."[22] While covering similar topics as the husband-wife conferences, Pre-Cana approached the subject matter from the viewpoint of the needs of couples not yet married. It operated within an informational frame that involved a series of talks—given by priests, married lay couples, and Catholic doctors—on basic principles of how to love in a manner that produces "happiness and perfection in marriage."[23] The leaders who coordinated Pre-Cana believed engaged couples attended the conferences anxious and excited for these insights. Between wanting to know more about what marriage would be like and how to ensure that they would be happy within their own, Cana leaders envisioned engaged couples as "eminently ready to be challenged to embrace the highest ideals."[24]

The primary challenge that priests identified involved reeducating couples on the meaning of love and marriage. Believing that marriage had become "a strictly personal affair with couples almost selfishly seeking their own happiness," they sought to replace this perspective with a vision of sacrificial love.[25] Their theological discussions of God's vision for marriage and the importance of this sacrament were subsumed in broader discussions of the meaning and practices of love. Even as they presented love as a bridge and solution to most problems in marriage, they cautioned it could be enacted incorrectly, resulting in conflict, unhappiness, and potentially, divorce. At a Chicago Pre-Cana Conference, engaged couples learned "if marriages are not successful, it is largely because most people no longer know how to love."[26] Learning to love according to God's design, therefore, frequently became the goal of the priests' talks.

The priests' presentations on God's intentions for human love were predicated on gender differences as well as complicated by them. On the one hand, priests detailed how men and women lived such separate lives from each other that it made it difficult to forge connections. These "daily divorces" frequently meant that husbands and wives did not understand or appreciate what the other person did with their day, how they contributed to the household, or the sacrifices they made. One priest explained how after a long day of work, husbands could be left "fed up with people," whereas wives had spent the same day alone "yearning for loving companionship."[27] The rigid sex role division idealized within postwar homes operated as a barrier to marital intimacy. One priest even chastised men who say "I can't understand women" as usually "using this as an excuse for not trying."[28] On the other hand, the recognition of how the modern structure of gender roles inhibited happiness in marriage did not preclude viewing gender differences as part of God's plan for the home. Presenting men and women with different "natural endowments," priests taught that men's more aggressive nature helped them in their job as a provider and women's devotion served them well in their calling as a wife and mother.[29] God, they argued, created love to bridge these differences while also pulling men and women into marriage. To successfully overcome the combination of these "natural" gender differences and the predominant family arrangement, love had to be other-oriented. As the lecture notes for one priest detailed, "If each will take care of the need of the other, [then they] will find one's own need met."[30]

In intimately linking happiness with sanctification, priests normalized a particular mode of faith and model of a heterosexual relationship. As a priest explained, "You cannot succeed in marriage unless you accept marriage and its responsibilities fully as God intends you to."[31] Rather than offer an interactional conception of marriage based on its meaning emerging from what individuals bring together, priests presented universalistic and externalized definitions of marriage that required couples to conform to be happy and capable of fulfilling their spiritual calling. They described the meaning of marriage as a given and deviation was not encouraged. In teaching that "happiness and holiness equal the same thing," priests articulated a worldview that conceptualized home life falling under the authority of the Church. Yet, this also operated in tension with a view that vested laity with the right and responsibility to cultivate these on their own terms.[32]

Pre-Cana, in fact, organizationally offered married lay couples the opportunity to authoritatively speak on matters of faith and to represent the Church to other couples. The Cana Conference more broadly prided itself on being a movement for and by laity, specifically dedicated to their own vocational needs. In Pre-Cana, married couples had the responsibility of articulating theologically sensitive insights. One manual stressed the power of this practice for engaged couples, explaining,

> To many of the audience the spectacle of lay people talking about spiritual matters will be a revelation. This will make particularly cogent the emphasis on marriage as a vocation, a complete way of life, with its own possibilities for sanctity arising out of the very nature of the calling, and not in spite of it.[33]

Complementing the more abstract discussions on how to live and love spiritually, married couples offered insights into "marriage in practice."[34] As opposed to an unmarried priest, these lay couples could present "a picture of the gradual adjustments in marriage which lead to unity and stability."[35] In addition to answering any questions from the engaged couples, they discussed their personal experiences with topics such as in-laws, finances, creating a religious household, communication, whether a wife should work outside the home, leisure, sex, gender roles, and conflict. In their manuals, directors of Pre-Cana suggested that married couples minimize abstractions and generalizations in their talks but also avoid presenting too much about their unique, and likely haphazard, experiences of finding out what works in marriage. In other words, married couples were supposed to balance their lack of expertise with simply being married.

To round out their premarital education, Catholic doctors provided sex education to engaged couples often by discussing "the general physiological aspects of marriage," such as anatomy, fertilization, menstruation, pregnancy, contraception, and any type of abnormalities.[36] To address common problems in sex, doctors would hold breakout sessions for men and women separately to provide an ostensibly easier context to ask questions and tailor conversations on topics such as frigidity, ovulation, and sexual adjustment "to masculine or feminine needs and interests."[37] One manual cautioned the doctors to adopt a "frank reverence" as they provided talks on "sex, maleness and femaleness, in its broadest and most Christian sense . . . with authority as a Catholic and a doctor."[38] Pre-Cana leaders believed doctors could assist in the reeducation of engaged couples by "help[ing] the young people shed their false notions about sex and see it as the Church sees it."[39] Warning that much of the sexual problems in early marriage emerge from ignorance and fear, these talks provided engaged couples with religiously informed knowledge on the basics of sex education. A critical part of this agenda included explanations on the problems of contraception. At this time, however, some priests discouraged them from recommending the rhythm method and instead instructed doctors to counsel couples to engage in chaste periods of marital abstinence.[40]

Collectively, priests, lay married couples, and Catholic doctors presented engaged couples with an education of what to expect in marriage and how to understand their marriages within a Catholic framework as a spiritualized practice. As part of a generalized anxiety in the Church, a central goal of the programming was to spiritualize the laity as a bulwark against secularism. Yet, to accomplish this goal, religious leaders also needed to help couples have happier marriages to ensure that households did not break up. As with their counterparts in secular marriage counseling, modern marital tension was interpreted through a gender lens that attributed a failure to comply with marital roles as the root of most problems.[41] Pre-Cana, therefore, sacralized the prevalent idea among experts that marriage required hard work by linking its success to couples' future salvation. Unlike marriage counseling, which few couples at this time attended,[42] or women's magazines, which translated this ethic to women only,[43] Pre-Cana annually reached thousands of men and women about to be married. It provided a whole new generation of young people with an ideal of a successful marriage that involved love manifesting in deep intimacy and communication, even asserting that gender roles must not keep couples from this goal. Likewise, it presented the next generation of Catholics with a view of spirituality as their own responsibility and the importance of developing it outside the bounds of the church.

Evangelicals Slowly Embrace Premarital Counseling

In 1959, the mainline Protestant magazine *Christian Century* reprinted a letter from *Pastoral Psychology* detailing a man's regret and disappointment about his sixteen-year marriage. Blaming the officiating minister for offering little guidance and not inquiring more into the tenability of the relationship, he implored pastors to make premarital counseling a greater priority.[44] In fact, during the interwar period, a group of predominately mainline Protestant clergy had become interested in applying insights from the burgeoning field of psychology to their work ministering to congregants.[45] Unlike the Catholic marriage preparation practices that emerged from the efforts of family movements of the postwar era, evangelical premarital counseling would eventually develop in the late 1960s and early 1970s in relation to this broader Protestant practice of pastoral counseling. As such, the organizational structure and motivations differed substantially between these similar activities.

By the postwar era, Protestant clergy had established a professional network of pastoral counselors with their own journals and seminary curricula.[46] Although it included a variety of denominational backgrounds and ministers who worked in a range of settings, most of them were liberal and mainline Protestants. Given the cultural preoccupation with marriage during this time, it is not surprising that many pastoral counselors began to reflect on how best to intervene in the domestic sphere. In addition to the multitude of articles published on premarital counseling in *Pastoral Psychology*, this developing field of experts wrote manuals designed to help church leaders cultivate effective counseling practices. Far from the collective efforts of Pre-Cana, these writings focused on teaching pastors how to practice this task by themselves. Despite the occasional suggestion that pastors consider joining with other churches to develop marriage preparation programs, greater attention was paid to instructing pastors in the art of effective and personalized counseling strategies.

For example, in 1958, Granger Westberg, a professor of religion and health at the University of Chicago, wrote *Premarital Counseling: A Manual for Ministers*, which was distributed by the National Council of Churches.[47] In his first chapter, "Why Premarital Counseling?" he articulated a less activist-oriented motivation for preparing couples than the leaders of Pre-Cana:

> The family is the legitimate concern of all ministers and they ought to devote their lives to its improvement. When an automobile is in need of repair we naturally go to a mechanic whose life is spent working with cars. When people have concerns about their family life, either before or after marriage, they should quite naturally seek out the clergyman.[48]

He encouraged ministers to think of the sessions as "premarital conversations" and to consider conducting them in informal settings like one's own home. To provide tools for these conversations, he included an example of a quantitative questionnaire. The twenty-nine-item survey instrument included questions designed to compare a couple's backgrounds, assess their level of religiosity, and learn about their parents' approval. Each potential answer was weighted with the more desirable responses earning more points, resulting in "well-matched couples" earning higher overall scores. Couples with greater commonalities generally earned more points, such as both people being a believer (50 points), attending the same church (50 points), and coming from the same cultural background (20 points). However, if there were to be differences, they tended to support heteronormative gender role ideology. For example, one question awarded fifteen points if the couple had the same level of education, ten points if the man had more education than the woman, and zero points if the woman had more education than the man. Westberg believed the results from this survey could help a minister stimulate conversation with a couple. To help pastors recognize the value of a "conversational exchange," he also provided excerpts of potential discussions with couples on a variety of topics, including personal backgrounds, economic and cultural problems, religion in the home, vocation, and sex. In each instance, the minister did not lecture on the subject matter, as was customary of the priests at Pre-Cana, but instead acted as a counselor who helped guide the couple to talk and discover their own realizations about the relationship.

In her study of the history of marriage counseling, Rebecca Davis argues that in emphasizing the *science* of their profession, counselors could assert the superiority of their advice over common wisdom.[49] In practice, these claims to objectivity often legitimized preexisting prejudices. Although less explicit in its articulation than Pre-Cana about what marriage *should* look like, mainline Protestant premarital counseling practices also operated from the perspective that marital happiness and success more likely occurs when couples conform to authoritative and external views on marriage. Mainline Protestant pastoral counselors used social scientific insights to construct a more implicit construction of a healthy Christian marriage but one equally based in strict gender roles, heterosexuality, and the indissolubility of a Christian marriage.

During the time that pastoral counseling developed among mainline Protestant clergy, their counterparts within conservative Protestantism had become more culturally withdrawn and separatist. After the modernist-fundamentalist conflicts of the early twentieth century that culminated in the Scopes trial, a pervasive antagonism toward scientific knowledge permeated conservative Christian communities.[50] With few exceptions, psychological insights and counseling practices were treated with suspicion.[51] In this state of relative isolation, fundamentalist Protestants began to develop their own infrastructure of knowledge production and dissemination, including universities, publishing presses, and radio programs.[52] Starting in the postwar era, a group of self-proclaimed "evangelicals" within this community began to imagine a relationship with secular culture that would maintain fundamentalist orthodoxy but replace its isolationism with an engaged theology.[53] Whereas fundamentalists emphasized eschatological concerns such as the second coming of Jesus, evangelicals centered concerns about the Christian family, believing that "a vibrant evangelical Christianity could survive so long as evangelicals maintained truly Christian homes."[54] By the 1960s, this new ethos would help evangelicals to create their own separate network of "Christian counselors,"[55] but during the 1950s, a few lone voices began to blaze this path and offer therapeutic insights to couples on the precipice of creating Christian domiciles.

Wayne E. Oates wrote *Premarital Pastoral Care and Counseling* specifically to help Southern Baptist pastors recognize their responsibility to instruct engaged couples.[56] Considering the practice from the perspective of the religious community, he argued that as part of the "fellowship of Christians," congregations owe their members premarital instruction and that pastors must remember that they represent their church when they oversee weddings. For example, he maintained that pastors should only agree to marry practicing Christians because otherwise, the church would be "consciously yoking two people together unequally."[57] He also believed that preparing young couples for marriage would help to instill in them a responsibility toward the church and avoid the common problem of "losing them." As opposed to the attempts at scientific neutrality among his mainline Protestant peers, Oates organized his advice on premarital counseling around pastors' roles within their churches: preacher, worship leader, teacher, organizer, and administrator. Under "preacher," for example, he listed a series of scripture references for "New Testament teachings on relationships within the family" to help pastors "develop a careful exegesis on the biblical materials on the husband-wife relationship."[58] His manual lacked any quantitative measures or case studies in conversational dynamics. Instead, he imagined the "counselor" as a teacher responsible for instructing couples in appropriate actions and beliefs.

In contrast to the clergy-centric advice, Clyde Narramore began to translate psychological insights more broadly into the conservative Protestant subculture. Even though he was not trained as a psychologist, his popular radio program, *Psychology for Living*, was an early influence in showing evangelicals that psychological frameworks were compatible with Christianity by presenting "the talking cure" as a biblical concept endorsed by Jesus.[59] In addition to his radio program, he wrote numerous books, including *Life and Love: A Christian View on Sex* and *The Psychology of Counseling—for All Who Are Engaged in the Art of Counseling*.[60] Whereas the latter was oriented to Christian ministers and counselors, the former was written to help young people answer such pressing questions as "How can I be sure I'm in love? What does the Bible say about sex? How does the body develop and function? How can I be certain of happiness in marriage?"[61] Similar to the talks provided by the Pre-Cana doctors, the book offered the reader basic sexual education, with chapters dedicated to physiological development in young men and women, pregnancy and childbirth, and a Christian view on sex.

While most of *Life and Love* focused on sex, one chapter—"Looking toward Marriage"—discussed a Christian view on marriage to give young adults "a firm foundation on which to build a happy life."[62] Counseling them on how to discern when love is strong enough to serve as a "safe foundation for a permanently successful marriage," he stressed the importance of "common interests, mutual ambitions, devotion to Christ, and a similar background."[63] He warned, however, that without maturity, shared interest and love would be insufficient conditions for marital success. To help discern this about oneself or one's partner, the chapter provided guidance from studies on happy marriages and vignettes of young couples to impart: the importance of marrying the "right" Christian, God's intention of blessing couples with a sexual relationship, and keys for successful financial planning. As an example of the type of self-help book that would dominate evangelical publications in following decades, it used an accessible writing style aimed at nonexperts to translate a therapeutic message that linked faith with individual happiness in relationships.

As opposed to Pre-Cana's origins as a social movement activity to combat secularism and re-Christianize American society, evangelical premarital counseling developed as a depoliticized project among Protestant intellectuals. Despite the overall similarities in their efforts to prepare couples for a happy and holy life, these two practices emerged among different sets of interlocutors. For the most part, all the works by mainline and evangelical pastoral counselors were written by individuals with graduate degrees and who were often associated with universities. For example, Narramore had an EdD from Columbia University and would go on to found a foundation and graduate psychology program now located at Biola University.[64] The writings reflected the isolationist tendencies of conservative Protestants at this time who sought to establish their own parallel infrastructures. Evangelical psychology indicated less concern about fighting secularism but rather turned inward to their own communities.[65] Within these contexts, the advice focused on ensuring that young Christians remained faithful and married someone from a similar background, normalizing views of not only religious homogamy but also implicitly race and class. These early small-scale efforts at evangelical premarital counseling sowed the seeds for the growth of the cottage industry of self-help books on relationships, sex, and gender. By the 1960s, evangelicals had more fully embraced the practice of pastoral counseling, which they acquired from their mainline colleagues, and had begun to disseminate self-help literature as means to offer counsel that considered individuals' souls and psyches.[66]

Teaching a Self-Reflexive Marriage: Christian Premarital Counseling, circa 1970s–2000s

By the 1970s, the currents of change became more pronounced and a new style of marriage had begun to emerge, which in turn reimagined the motivations for divorce as well.[67] Although themes of self-development and the importance of communication had been present in these previous decades, they had been largely channeled toward fulfilling the roles of the companionate marriage. The view that marriage is "a partnership in which two functioned as one" began to make way for the new idea that it is "a relationship in which two people maintained their individual selves."[68] Under this framework of an "individualized marriage," the notion of a good marriage also began to change with profound gendered consequences that called men and women to both pursue their own self-fulfillment.[69] While the marital work ethic persisted, feminists' challenges to women's role in the home began to destabilize the expectation that it was largely the wife's responsibility and they called for men to share in the labor.[70] This renewed and increasingly more therapeutic calls to work on one's marriage occurred against a broader backdrop of changes to paid labor. Starting in the 1970s, the economy began to shift from the manufactory jobs that dominated industrial capitalism to the service industry and "knowledge work" of late capitalism.[71] While white middle-class families would find it more challenging to maintain their desired lifestyle on one income, class-privileged white women also entered the labor force because it afforded them personal opportunities in these new types of work.[72] All these torrential changes required a response from religious leaders. Although still remaining largely organizationally distinct, both Catholic marriage preparation and evangelical premarital counseling began to alter their lessons, which also impacted the transmission process. Rather than directly teach about the roles one ought to hold and how to feel about them, the lessons employed more therapeutic rhetoric and became more directed toward explorations of the self and internal emotional states.

Catholics Reorganize and Reenvision the Purpose of Marriage Preparation

In 1971, the Cana Conference of Chicago celebrated its twenty-fifth anniversary amid what they felt was a general sense of excitement and confusion in the Catholic Church.[73] Unlike the confidence among postwar Pre-Cana leaders, who envisioned marriage preparation as an instrumental tool in the transformation of the Church and secular culture, the subcommittee that met in 1971 to discuss the implications for the programming in the Archdiocese of Chicago had a more jaded assessment.[74] In response to their main question, "What expectations should we have for Pre Cana's effect?" a consensus agreed on "very little impact, limited expectations."[75] During the quarter century they had offered this program, divorce rates had continued to rise, and it appeared that family life had only become more unstable. Scaling back their goals, they explained, "Pre Cana, hopefully, can provide a climate in which the couple can talk to each other." Despite this less-than-optimistic evaluation of the effectiveness of the program, marriage preparation became the primary focus of the Cana Conference of Chicago during the next three decades and even began to be required prior to any Catholic marriage.[76]

In dioceses across the country, however, new forms of marriage preparation emerged to compete with Pre-Cana. Engaged Encounter, in particular, became highly popular and its programming reflected the increasing emphasis on the authority of the individual. Engaged Encounter inverted many of the underlying assumptions in Cana about how to transmit knowledge to couples and the best way to make an impact on marriage. Whereas Pre-Cana manuals emphasized *teaching* with leaders authoritatively presenting the correct way to have a Catholic marriage, Engaged Encounter sought to cultivate *learning* with leaders facilitating conversations in couples. While covering similar topics—the state of marriage in the modern world, sex, the sacrament of marriage—a manual from 1976 provided very few examples of the content to be presented on these issues.[77] Privileging "self-knowledge" in both the leaders and engaged couples, Engaged Encounter shifted discussions of a good marriage away from accomplishing an external goal toward an internal journey of reflection and communication. The approach also circumscribed the role of priests because they could not offer peer mentoring on marriage or model the desired pattern of open communication.

As the alternative and more lay-centric model of Engaged Encounter spread across the country, some dioceses, such as Chicago, began to consolidate their authority over Catholic marriage. In contrast to the sense of mutual affirmation between priests and laity during postwar Cana, a growing sense of separation, and even antagonism, began to characterize this relationship in Pre-Cana. Priests began to complain that discussing faith with engaged couples before their wedding had become "a source of unspoken tension."[78] Feeling like they served as "an interrogator" who represented an "unnecessary roadblock on the way down the aisle," priests critically evaluated their role in the process of getting married.[79] Whereas some questioned whether they should even continue to be involved, the Archdiocese of Chicago eventually chose to follow other dioceses across the country and established a centralized and mandatory "common policy" for marriage preparation. In 1979, the Archdiocese of Chicago published their *Pastoral Guidelines for Marriage Preparation*.[80] Compared to earlier decades of lay leadership, this manual unambiguously privileged the role of priests in the process. Despite recognizing marriage preparation as a "shared ministry" that can include participation in the preexisting lay coordinated programs, the diocese contended that "the Church gives the main responsibility for preparing couples to the parish priest."[81] In response to one priest who questioned this shift by asking, "What has happened to the teaching that couples have the natural right to marry?" they reaffirmed the priest's authoritative role by explaining that "while people have a natural right to marry, they don't have a natural right to the *sacrament of marriage*."[82] Marriage, thus, had become increasingly differentiated as priests and laity diverged in their views on the institution.

This period of introspection regarding the purpose of marriage preparation also brought about a significant expansion in programming. The Archdiocese of Chicago realized that if they were to require participation for all couples seeking to get married in their parishes, then they would need to better serve the diversity of their parishioners. Acknowledging the racial/ethnic diversity of Chicago Catholics, and to a lesser extent the emergence of alternative family trajectories such as remarriage, the archdiocese developed their own Pre-Cana Conferences that catered to specific populations such as couples entering second marriages with children, older couples (over 30), Hispanic couples who spoke Spanish, Hispanic couples seeking a convalidation (church approval of a civil marriage), Hispanic couples who spoke English, and African American couples. In each case, the same content was somewhat revised and presented by a team of married couples recruited from the specific community in an effort to better reflect their particular situation. Most dioceses across the country may have offered marriage preparation at this time, but few had this range of "special" programs. For those that did offer alternative conferences, they were more likely to be in the case of a marriage that occurred after an annulment or during a pregnancy.[83]

By the 1990s, the Archdiocese of Chicago had to revise their *Pastoral Guidelines for Marriage Preparation* because the reliance on priests had become untenable. The original version from 1979 had not only placed greater expectations on the parish priest to conduct individualized meetings with engaged couples to determine whether they *should* marry but the expansion of Pre-Cana programs in the 1980s had also created more work. During this time, married lay couples began to dominate more of the teaching in Pre-Cana, although there remained an expectation that priests should be present to witness and provide some contribution. A report from 1984 estimated that 99 percent of Pre-Cana programs in the archdiocese continued to have a priest present, but by the 1990s, this number had significantly declined to only 20 percent of programs.[84] The territorial tone that had pervaded the first manual was now replaced with a more conciliatory feel. Although priests continued to have a "serious responsibility" to engaged couples, their basic role had been redefined to "extend support and help a couple in their decision to marry."[85] No longer was a priest instructed to act as an arbiter over numerous sessions to assess the legitimacy of a marriage, but instead, he was encouraged to try to get to know couples over a few brief meetings. Additionally, the lay couples who had to take a more active role in marriage preparation programs were encouraged to acknowledge the "new issues confront[ing] couples."[86] From recognizing the presence of interfaith couples to being aware that couples may be living together, they were advised to make it clear "we are not here to judge you, but we are here to ask you to think about your up-coming marriage in terms of the *sacrament of marriage* and the permanent commitment that you will be asked to [make to] one another."⁸⁷ Although priests had hardly relinquished authority over marriage, they had loosened their grip again and even encouraged a greater role for Catholic laity to speak on marriage. Compared with the religious leaders' worry about spiritual laity during the postwar era and the compartmentalization of the lay perspective in the 1970s–1980s, marriage preparation at the end of the twentieth century revealed that laity had located some space from which to authoritatively speak on their vocation. The variety of curricula also illustrates that the concept of a good marriage had expanded and had been adapted to minister to changing family structures and settings.

Evangelicals Embrace the Therapeutic Culture Industry

In the 1973 inaugural issue of the *Journal of Psychology and Theology*, Clyde Narramore's nephew, Bruce, penned a treatise on how to improve relationships between the church and therapeutic culture.⁸⁸ While he considered how "the rapid growth of the psychological sciences and professions may . . . be viewed as an encroachment on the ministry of the church," he believed integrating biblical and therapeutic knowledge would provide "a comprehensive understanding of the human part of God's creation."⁸⁹ After years of the (evangelical) church being dominated by fears of the psychological realm—their science, their view on humanity, their emphasis on emotions, and their discussion of sex—he contended that "Christian counselors" needed to help bridge these worlds. Although the tensions between Christianity and psychology would continue to be debated through the 1970s, in the end, therapeutic practices and discourses would become an integral part of American evangelicalism.⁹⁰ For example, by this time, "churches developed entire institutional spaces within their communities to offer specifically Christian care of the self, emphasizing small-group ministries to treat addictions and promote self-esteem."⁹¹ Shedding much of their previous resistance to psychology, the next few decades witnessed the growth of a cottage industry of evangelical therapeutic advice from both professional counselors and lay authors focused on family life.⁹²

During the early years, this group of self-identified "Christian counselors" felt as if they straddled two worlds and had to defend themselves in each.⁹³ Following the model of their fundamentalist predecessors, they created an extensive alternative infrastructure of academic journals, universities, and professional associations. Major evangelical universities, such as Biola and Fuller Seminary, offered graduate degrees in psychology. They differed from the separatism of fundamentalism, however, in that they did not withdraw from the secular professional world of psychology and counseling in the process. The universities ensured they were accredited, and individual practitioners looked to secular professional associations, such as the American Psychological Association or the American Association for Marriage and Family Therapy, for certification.[94]

In the process, evangelicals also worked to distinguish their approach from their mainline counterparts who practiced pastoral counseling. For example, Fuller's School of Psychology specifically set out to provide a PhD in clinical psychology that integrated theological insights rather than training individuals in pastoral counseling.[95] Historian Susan Myers-Shirk describes how this oppositional relationship also aided the development of a "conservative moral sensibility" that privileged the authority of scripture and God's transcendence, as well as maintained a belief in the inherent sinfulness of human nature.[96] From the perspective of the mainline pastoral counselors who had cultivated a "liberal moral sensibility" that emphasized the importance of cultural context, human relatedness, and personal autonomy, evangelical counselors appeared overly narrow and disrespectful of people's needs. In fostering their view as distinctive from mainline Christians, these evangelical "Christian counselors" helped to redeem psychological knowledge by translating its insights into an acceptable and less threatening discourse.

Evangelical Protestant counselors differed from their mainline or Catholic brethren because they were predominately psychologists or therapists and less often clergy.[97] Some may have offered premarital counseling within their individual practices, but churches continued to serve as the primary location for this work and sometimes provided people with their first foray into counseling.[98] Pastors across the country likely conducted premarital counseling by only relying on their own theological understanding of marriage without turning to therapeutic insights, but over time, it became more difficult to not engage these views. The development of counseling and psychology degrees in evangelical seminaries introduced more pastors to these ideas. Additionally, evangelical Christian counselors continued the tradition of translating professional and academic insights directly to pastors by writing manuals on how to conduct premarital counseling.

For example, a professor at Biola and a licensed marriage and family counselor, H. Norman Wright, wrote *Premarital Counseling: A Guidebook for Counselors*.[99] In addition to describing how the changing state of marriage has made this ministry even more necessary for churches, he provided an incredibly detailed discussion of how to conduct sessions and provided various resources. Generally, he recommended that couples be required to attend a minimum of six sessions, which should include time to meet with each partner individually. He personally incorporated an opportunity for his wife to join in the final session by having the engaged couple over for an informal dinner at his house. The book more closely resembled the premarital counseling guides of the postwar mainline pastoral counselors than the earlier evangelical ones. At almost four times the length of Westberg's book, however, it included substantially more detail. For example, in the chapter on "Resources to Use in Premarital Counseling," Wright reviewed multiple types of quantitative assessment, which he required couples to complete in advance of their first meeting with him. As opposed to the twenty-nine-question survey Westberg provided, Wright recommended using the assessment tools that had become widespread by this time, such as the 125-item PREPARE *and* the Taylor-Johnson Temperament Analysis (although he only briefly reviewed them for the reader). Throughout the manual, he included a wide range of recommendations for books that pastors could read themselves or suggest to couples, such as *Intended for Pleasure* on issues of sex. As evidenced by the conservative moral sensibility throughout his book, he offered an evangelical perspective on premarital counseling, but the book was also grounded in a wide range of sources including references to writings by secular social scientists, other Christian counselors, evangelical pastors and authors, women's magazines, newspapers, and even materials published by the Cana Conference of Chicago.

Although a lay individual interested in improving their relationship could have read these counselor books, they were not intended for nonexpert usage. Around this time, evangelical presses such as Moody and Zondervan began to extensively publish books aimed directly at helping the relationship life of the average evangelical person. In many cases, Christian counselors used these publishers as a way to speak more directly to premarital couples. For example, in the 1980s and 1990s, a number of psychologists and therapists made a name for themselves publishing widely read books, including P. Roger Hillerstrom's *Intimate Deception: Escaping the Trap of Sexual Impurity*, Gary Chapman's *The Five Love Languages*, and Les and Leslie Parrott's *Saving Your Marriage before It Starts*.[100] Often, as with the first two examples, these texts served as resources in the premarital counseling process that could be referenced or recommended for couples in need of more in-depth help on a particular issue. In the final example, the book could operate as a curriculum with accompanying workbooks available for purchase (including separate ones for men and women).

From an early point, however, Christian counselors were joined by others within the evangelical community—medical doctors, pastors, married couples, and even parent-child teams—producing a vast array of self-help literature. In fact, during the 1970s and 1980s as Christian counselors began to develop their professional networks, the evangelical popular culture industry flourished.[101] Expanding on the earlier precedent set by Clyde Narramore, the late 1970s witnessed an explosion in evangelical sex manuals that also doubled as marriage guidebooks.[102] In 1976, Tim and Beverly LaHaye published *The Act of Marriage: A Christian Guide to Sexual Love*, which discussed sex by examining its religious significance, physiological conditions, and social impact in marriages.[103] Although this type of publication was generally intended for married audiences as a form of marital counseling and adjustment, the 1980s experienced a surge in materials broadly oriented to family life issues.[104]

Whereas much of this literature focused on improving the lives of already married couples, commentaries on the premarital stages, such as dating and engagement, began to be produced more frequently in the 1990s and 2000s. During this time, an extensive "purity culture" emerged among evangelicals to convince young adults to commit to abstinence, but the topic of marriage was predominately abstract references about the possible impact that their choices will have on their future.[105] The publication of Joshua Harris's *I Kissed Dating Goodbye*, however, has been credited with bringing the relationship needs of unmarried evangelicals to light.[106] Unlike many other authors, prior to writing this book, Harris was neither an established pastor nor a counselor; instead, he was a young man beginning his career in ministry. His advice to reject "dating" in favor of "courting" launched debates about what is the "healthiest" and most "biblical" way that young Christians can form relationships prior to, and in preparation of, marriage.[107] Regardless of whether books recommended the more familial and gendered practice of "courting" or allowed that if done carefully and with Jesus in mind, Christian "dating" was possible,[108] the advice overwhelmingly presented "the naturalness of heterosexual marriage and the significant role it plays in God's created order."[109]

By the start of the twenty-first century, evangelicals had accepted the validity of therapeutic knowledge to the point that it had become ubiquitous within the subculture. From the colleges and universities that offered advanced degrees, to the development of professional networks of "Christian counselors" that allowed people to see a therapist from their community, to the extensive self-help literature aimed at improving relationships, the impact of the therapeutic turn could be felt widely. Unlike formalized systems of science with which evangelicals continue to maintain a conflicted relationship, the more flexible category of "expert" and the narrative of an individual battling temptations in their relationships (and ultimately triumphing) fit well within evangelicalism.

Conclusion

Both Catholics and evangelical Protestants invested substantial time and resources over the past half century to develop strategies to intervene in couples' transition to marriage. At various points, both traditions have been motivated by fears of divorce, concerns over secularism, a desire to improve relationships, and a need to ensure that marriages faithfully follow community expectations. In the face of these concerns, they sacralized the idea that marriage requires work and anchored it in the sanctification process. Embracing the expert advice of the time, religious leaders initially encouraged couples to conform to a gendered companionate marriage and taught that a failure to do so would be disastrous for their souls and relationship. Embedded within their advice, however, were the seeds of new social ideas on marriage that left the institution, and the people within it, transformed by the end of the 1960s. As

Andrew Cherlin notes, "it's hard to determine the extent to which the spread of a spirituality of seeking *caused* the changes in family life or was the *result* of the changes in family life."[110] He prefers to think "both religion and the family were swept up in the larger, more fundamental cultural change, [and the] rise of expressive individualism."[111] I agree that we cannot clearly isolate cause and effect; however, I would also suggest that we must better attend to the interplay of religion and family in this process. In telling the history of a practice that is religious, therapeutic, and about the family, it becomes possible to illuminate the cultural and structural interchange of these social institutions.

The therapeutic lessons of self-development and communication meant that the meaning of not only a good marriage changed but also the idea of a good Christian. In constructing marriage as a project for individuals to work not just *in* but *on*, early experts had taught individuals to articulate their emotions, viewpoints, desires, and frustrations. Over time, these self-reflexive insights destabilized claims that happiness comes from conforming to an external model of marriage. The individualized marriage shifted the emphasis from a role to the self,[112] and the guidance for a good marriage likewise became less proscribed and even more about internal exploration. The advice on how to develop communication skills, maintain romance, or ensure friendship drew on therapeutic principles and tools from the burgeoning field of relationship science,[113] but the goal was consistently grounded in Christian understandings that marriage is a religious process as well. Although it has been common among scholars of therapeutic culture to see its rise over the twentieth century as occurring at the expense of religious authority,[114] the history of Christian premarital counseling reveals a deep compatibility between these spheres of ideas and practice.[115]

In particular, the individualization of marriage and prevalence of a therapeutic ethos among Christians cannot be separated from the democratization of religious authority that occurred during this time.[116] For Catholics, a worry about the spiritual vocation of marriage elevated lay concerns in the Church, whereas evangelical Protestants' embrace of psychology and elevation of the home enabled lay expertise to be religiously authoritative. For both faiths, the early years after World War II were characterized by a centralization of religious knowledge and authority. In each case, clergy dominated the discussions of what marriage should be and how to make it happy and holy. Yet, by embracing, even at this stage, the idea that married life should be personally fulfilling, they helped to create an opening for lay knowledge and standpoints. In the Catholic case, this involved the elevation of the Sacrament of Matrimony and the active participation of laity in the transmission of religious education. For evangelicals, this manifested in the application of nonclerical and secular insights from psychology and counseling, which transformed the ways pastors discussed marriages and expanded the makeup of religious authority among evangelicals. For both traditions, these shifts culminated in enabling lay expertise to be religiously authoritative. Over this period, both Catholics and evangelicals increasingly approached their churches as a place to make individual choices that they believed would lead to self-actualization. This shift, however, was also encouraged by religious leaders who sought to cultivate an active faith in the everyday lives of the laity. In turn, laity also brought their own experiences and expertise to bear on how the faith traditions should understand the significance of marriage as a means to sanctification and the possibility for how best to ensure therapeutic love in one's relationship.

In tracing these shifts over the latter half of the twentieth century, we have seen how religious communities embraced therapeutic principles, helped to transmit them widely, and ultimately found themselves changed by them, like the rest of American culture. Rather than see this as a sign of diminishing religious authority, it better illuminates a transformation and expansion of who can be religiously authoritative. In the next chapter, we will continue to explore these themes of religious authority, therapeutic culture, and visions of the good marriage by detailing the contemporary organizational forms of Christian premarital counseling. From the collective classes where couples gather to listen to educational-confessional lessons on how to have a successful marriage to individualized counseling sessions that strive to cultivate deep conversations, clergy and laity are both drawing from religious teachings and a religion-as-lived perspective to authoritatively craft lessons on how to have a Christian marriage.

2

What Is Christian Premarital Counseling?

For once, I was not the only person sitting alone and unattached in a class of couples contemplating marriage. Creating a small row of observers, I joined what turned out to be two graduate students at the back of the classroom. Whereas they were obtaining credit for a master's in counseling and would be available to conduct personalized sessions with couples who wanted more than the discussions offered in class, I was there to complete my study of marriage preparation. As I got comfortable in my seat and opened my book to take notes, Adam entered looking around the room and declared, "Terrible. I hate this classroom." Then practically without pause, perhaps because he realized that people were meeting their teacher for the first time, he continued with "Great first impression." Eventually, he shifted tactics to making small talk as couples slowly filed into the classroom and took their seats. His question about whether any of the women proposed was met with silence; undeterred, he continued talking by explaining that he had a coworker whose girlfriend proposed and now the man wears a "man-gagement ring." As he mused to himself that he's not sure how it all works and about whether the man will get a new ring when they finally get married, Pastor Joe poked his head into the room and observed, "Good party. House is full."

As the family ministry pastor, Pastor Joe organized the two classes for premarital couples at Cosmopolitan Church. Unlike the other Catholic and evangelical Protestant programs I observed, Cosmopolitan Church was larger and more popular with professional, young adults. As a result of the high number of weddings, a few years earlier Pastor Joe had felt the need to institute classes because it had been impossible to conduct the needed number of individualized sessions of premarital counseling without sacrificing content. Taking advantage of their congregants' expertise, Pastor Joe opted to create two classes—one for dating couples and one for engaged couples—and recruited Christian therapists from their church to lead each of them. Even though other evangelical programs I encountered also called on therapists to facilitate their curriculum, Cosmopolitan Church's size and proximity to an urban center allowed them to create a larger and more intricate system for marriage preparation. If desired, a dating couple could participate in the first class, proceed to the second one when engaged, have personalized sessions with graduate interns in counseling, and also have an individualized session with the pastor marrying them.

Far larger than the half-dozen couples who attended the Catholic programs or the evangelical retreat that I observed, classes at Cosmopolitan Church maxed out the two small classrooms. In fact, the room initially had been arranged with sixty-two chairs in rows facing a whiteboard, but it still ended up being too few. As Pastor Joe left to locate more chairs, Adam decided to start the class by announcing, "Welcome. You are getting married." Perhaps because his wife still hadn't shown up yet, the class started off slowly with him explaining, "We won't tell you how to master marriage. Rather, we'll help you see where you are, where you want to go, and draw the line between these two points." Dryly, he continued, "After ten or so years, you won't remember what we say. But you will remember what occurs to you. Therefore, you should bring a notebook to take down what occurs to you or strikes you during our talk." Since not everyone had brought a notebook for the first day, he passed out sheets of paper.

While Adam handed out the paper for notes and Pastor Joe continued to fit more chairs into the classroom, Sarah finally arrived. After apologizing for being late, she introduced herself and Adam, who had never bothered to do so. After quickly taking care of some housekeeping issues, such as what to do if couples miss a week of class, Adam explained that they have some core beliefs and one of them is that it's important to have a community because "it's hard to get married in a vacuum." Energetically, Sarah interjected to explain how lifelong friendships emerge from this class, noting, "One of the best things we, and not even we, offer is the community." Jumping back in, however, Adam countered, "That being said, I think we have something to offer." Perhaps to establish their authority or expertise, he explained, "We have been doing this class three times a year for a long time and we love it. It's a place where we come together." Again, Sarah interrupted to dryly comment, "Especially after we've been fighting all day."

Pastor Joe had forewarned me that Adam and Sarah had an authentic and honest approach, which was one of the reasons that he had selected them, but still I found myself a little surprised that they began their class on marriage preparation with this type of confession. As I was still processing this announcement, Sarah continued without pause to explain how they had been separated for most of the day and she spent the afternoon fuming at a Starbucks. Meanwhile, Adam was laughing, which elicited a sharp look from Sarah before she turned to the class to explain, "That laugh means she's crazy." The room felt still for a moment as the awkward silence punctuated the air and I couldn't help but wonder what the engaged couples who were meeting these two for the first time must think about their ability to guide them to marital bliss. In what felt longer, but was probably only a second or so, Adam turned to face the class and calmly commented, "The first important thing to learn about marriage is when you're wrong, say you're sorry. When you're right, stop talking." Without missing a beat, he shifted to state the three goals for the day: "First, we want to help you understand us, to know our story. Second, we'll explain what the next eight weeks will be like. And third, we'll have a conversation and explain your homework." Before they started any of these tasks, though, he noticed Pastor Joe leaning in the doorframe and observing the class, prompting Adam to ask him to introduce himself.

After his introduction, which included explaining his many responsibilities at Cosmopolitan Church, Pastor Joe commented, "I'll pop in and out, when I'm not busy schlepping chairs." Smiling at his joke, he continued, "I'm excited for all of you. You have a great guide. After all, how many couples would admit they were fighting today?" Pastor Joe was correct because by the time I attended this class for engaged couples at Cosmopolitan Church, I had already spent years observing Catholic and evangelical Protestant premarital counseling programs and had never witnessed any leaders bicker in front of the couples they were supposed to be guiding. Despite the unusual performance, their introduction encapsulated key themes in how marriage preparation is constructed as a religio-therapeutic intervention to stabilize marriage and commitment to the community of faith. As a therapist, Adam's discussion of what to expect from the class showcased the "omnipresence of therapeutic narratives of self-realization"[1] and the centrality of the marital work ethic.[2]

Yet, the self-work, as Sarah reminded the engaged couples, is expected to occur within a community and represents a way to forge connections to one's community.

Whereas some have positioned the authoritative and communal commitments in religious traditions as oppositional to therapeutic culture,[3] Christian premarital counseling programs represent a case where religious groups have "embraced and enhanced [its] essential elements."[4] Therapeutic culture's beliefs and practices include individualism, working and cultivating the self, pursuit of self-betterment, expression of inner feelings, emotion management, and reliance on expert knowledge or intervention.[5] Rather than challenging religious authority, all these elements can and have been fitted within Christian beliefs, such as sanctification and battles against sin. Whether speaking authoritatively as therapists, religious leaders, or married couples, premarital counselors become "experts" who develop and facilitate curricula to socialize couples into a set of beliefs and practices that they believe will lead to happy, healthy, and holy lives.

This chapter describes the organizational forms and styles of contemporary premarital counseling. Whereas the next couple of chapters interrogate the content of the lessons, this one first situates premarital counseling within the broader field of relationship education and contrasts the two dominant modes: individualized sessions that facilitate couples' intimate conversations and collective classes that normalize marital experiences. As a form of therapeutic intervention, both collective and individualized counseling sessions similarly structured their limited time with couples to teach them relationship skills and emotional frameworks they associate with a "good marriage." In each case, premarital counselors have only four to eight sessions to guide people in identifying personal feelings and couple dynamics on topics ranging from families, money, communication, sex, and more. The transmission of religio-therapeutic views on marriage and opportunities to develop the competencies required by therapeutic love differed by the two organizational modes, however. As the opening vignette illustrates, in the collective classes the leaders blended a personal-confessional style where they shared intimate details to model how to work on one's marriage with an educational style that melded social-scientific and religious teachings on how the good marriage should look. In contrast, a more tailored and personalized mode of facilitation emerged in individualized programs where leaders were not expected to share or model but instead guide couples more explicitly and impartially to review their relationship. Regardless of the format, however, as a type of relationship *education*, both produce an organizational culture that privileges learning in the form of listening, articulation, and assessment.

Relationship Education in Premarital Counseling

As we saw earlier, the past half century left congregations and couples with a veritable cottage industry of relationship experts—both from within and outside the church—to help teach, counsel, and guide people from engagement to their goal of marital bliss.[6] Compared to the postwar era when Patty Crowley and her friends scoured parishes for enough volunteers to have the first Pre-Cana, today millions of engaged couples participate in some form of premarital counseling with estimates as high as 40 percent of Americans.[7] Churches help to drive up this number since clergy continue to officiate between 75 and 85 percent of American weddings and most of them require some form of premarital counseling.[8]

Despite occurring prior to marital vows, the relationship education in premarital counseling represents a type of "marriage education." Even in the program for dating couples, classes are structured to help people explore if a relationship is "marriage worthy" and develop strategies for how to address potential marital conflicts. As sociologists Orit Avishai, Melanie Heath, and Jennifer Randles define it, "marriage education is founded on the belief that relationship success is rooted in individual skills and couple dynamics, and that couples can learn specific skills to help them stay together."[9] Echoing this perspective, one pastor explained, "Premarital [counseling] is all about tools." Describing it as "investigative," he elaborated by noting that it "aims to help a couple discover their relationship blind spots [that] they need to talk about or [have] never thought about." The clergy, therapists, and laypeople who meet with premarital couples develop programming they believe teaches couples relevant relationship skills and prepares them for the most common examples of marital conflict. Topics across the programs included communication, sex, finances, conflict resolution, personality types, relationship roles, expectations of marriage, views on children, plans for the future (including career aspirations), family of origin dynamics, and faith. For all these issues, premarital counselors cultivated the therapeutic practices of self-work that they hoped would reveal unspoken assumptions and expectations to individuals and their partner. An important goal underlying this work is to help people recognize their own expectations about marriage and to see how those do or do not fit with their partner's worldview.

Unlike preexisting scholarship that has considered premarital counseling within the context of the "marriage movement" that has spent millions of federal dollars because they believe that poverty can be reduced by promoting and strengthening marriage,[10] the Christian premarital counselors I met were cautious advocates of marriage.[11] All of them dedicated considerable professional and personal energy to guiding couples toward the altar but not because they believed marriage itself offered a solution to social problems. Unlike the evangelicals (and presumably Catholics) who formed coalitions targeting marriage as a solution to youth violence, poverty, and any number of social ills in broader society,[12] the Christian premarital counselors I studied were more narrowly concerned with the relationships of people within their own communities. Although they believed premarital counseling has considerable value and could ideally even change the state of American marriage, they did not imagine this impact occurring through promotion but rather deterrence. As Adam explained at Cosmopolitan Church, "It's important to disabuse you of the idea that marriage is a solution to your problems. Rather, it's the birthplace of most of your questions."

To truly *prepare* for marriage, premarital counselors stressed that couples had to be willing to consider whether the present relationship should make it to the altar. To introduce the purpose of the Exploring Your Relationship Retreat, Joseph, a member of the leadership team, told the couples, "You are all present because you are focused on your relationship. The goal in these dialogue sessions should be to look for red flags." Challenging everyone to take this search seriously, he explained there are three potential outcomes to the process: "full-steam ahead," "a sense that you should slow down," or "a realization that perhaps you should end the relationship entirely." Reassuring them about these possibilities, he elaborated,

All three outcomes are acceptable as long as they emerge out of the deep dialogue and reflection of the weekend. We hope that people will take this period of reflection and examination seriously to help consider any strong warnings you've had without a fear about the invitations already having been ordered or what your families would think.

At some juncture in nearly every program I observed and in most of the interviews, premarital counselors made the point to clarify that "success" in this work includes couples postponing their wedding or breaking up entirely. In some cases, they told me that they celebrated these instances the most because they believed it meant they had saved a couple from what would have inevitably been divorce. Unlike the low-income couples who are not immediately pursuing marriage targeted by the marriage movement, Christian premarital counseling attracts couples actively considering and planning a wedding. As one evangelical therapist who worked in both a clinical and pastoral setting commented, "the *reality* [is] we do such a great job of promoting this idea of coupling, mating, and getting married. And a very lousy job of informing people and equipping them about what it means to stay married." Premarital counselors operated under the assumption that people already find marriage appealing—or at least the idea of marriage as encapsulated in the wedding—but that *staying* married and avoiding divorce represented the greater battle. To prepare couples, the various religious communities I spoke with used two organizational forms of premarital counseling to try to guide people through this discernment process and challenge them to critically evaluate themselves, their partner, and their relationship.

Organizational Forms of Marriage Preparation

Engaged Christian couples in the Pacific Northwest can (and do) choose from a variety of different forms of marriage preparation, from weekend retreats, to Sunday school–type classes, to personalized consultations with pastors, private sessions with therapists, or meetings with marriage mentors from their church. The particular offerings of any church varied in part by resources and personnel as well as the perceived demand of their congregants. For instance, a number of the Catholic parishes I contacted informed me that so few couples marry in their church in any year that they outsource the requests by encouraging people to participate in a weekend retreat offered by the diocese. In contrast, most of the collective premarital counseling ministries I observed operated within middle-to-larger-sized congregations that had a sizable population of young adults and/or more professionalized congregants from which to draw volunteers to lead the programs. To offset the sampling bias that this created, I also contacted other churches, including smaller and less urban ones, to interview whoever conducted marriage preparation. There were two general organizational formats that congregations consistently used: (1) collective classes where premarital couples attend structured sessions led by married couples with a small group of other couples like themselves and (2) individualized sessions where a pastor, therapist, or marriage mentor used assessment tools to guide couples to have conversations about the most vulnerable spots in their relationships. Both types of programming shared the above views of relationship education and emphasis on critical discernment of whether a relationship was "good" or "prepared" enough for marriage, but the divergent structures resulted in distinctive organizational styles.

Preparing for Marriage with Others

Individually, people may feel that their decision to get married is deeply personal and idiosyncratic, but the faith communities they approach to help them plan their weddings believe that enough couples share similar needs that they can be educated alongside others in their position. Although variation occurred in the size of the classes and number of people who actively led the programming, the collective courses shared several organizational traits. Across the two Catholic and two evangelical Protestant programs I observed, married couples worked to varying degrees with professional religious staff to develop a predetermined curriculum. In advance of meeting the specific couples, a set of relationship education topics and concerns was identified and lessons planned that would become individual sessions. Each of the sessions shared a broadly similar format where the leadership allotted time to presenting on the topic in a manner that blended therapeutic, personal, and religious insights, with time for couples to complete exercises and/or have discussions. Since the leadership teams who presented were generally comprised of married couples, they typically grounded their authority to guide couples in their own personal experiences. Some of the couples contained a spouse who was a pastor or therapist, but since it was unusual for one person to lead a session, their collective marital status and not individual professional positions tended to be the main locus of "expertise." As such, a presentational style of *educational* and *personal-confessional* emerged as the primary ways that leadership organized their specific lessons toward the broader goal of normalizing the challenges of daily life, relationship skills, and trials in marriage.

Working with a limited amount of time—six to eight evenings of approximately ninety-minute sessions or one weekend—the leadership teams had to both identify which insights were the most important for a successful marriage and consistently present them to a rotating group. Although one leader once balked when I offhandedly referred to the talks as "lectures" because he felt it sounded too dry and impersonal, the collective marriage preparation programs had an *educational style* that felt deeply familiar. For example, all the programs occurred in religious buildings but never in the spaces where worship would happen. Instead of meeting in a sanctuary or chapel, marriage preparation was always held in some type of multipurpose room that could be arranged to mimic classroom spaces. At both evangelical sites, they positioned chairs in rows that faced the leadership at the front of the room, who had access to a whiteboard or an overhead projector. Rather than the feel of a lecture hall, the two Catholic programs, which tended to have fewer couples, opted to sit in a circle and resembled a seminar. In addition to how the spaces were laid out like college classes, the programs had many analogous features to being in school: attendance (sometimes mandatory), homework, handouts and worksheets, assigned readings (and suggested reading recommendations), whiteboards where leaders wrote lists based on class discussion, PowerPoints of relevant quotes and information, breakout sessions for small-group conversations, and topical content that built on itself. Given these similarities, it's possible that college-educated individuals may have found it easier to navigate and draw out insights. Even though there was no formal assessment or grading as in a traditional school setting, the educational structure likewise served a comparable purpose of trying to ensure comprehension, engagement, and completion of the assigned materials.[13] As a therapeutic practice, however, the pedagogical elements emphasized self-reflexive discussion questions and activities aimed at cultivating awareness and, hopefully, the articulation of one's own assumptions.

For example, to prepare everyone for an upcoming unit, "From an 'I' to a 'We,'" Adam had the engaged class at Cosmopolitan Church do an exercise to practice for their homework assignment. The overall goal of the homework was to help each person learn about their own views on faith and reveal assumptions about what a "Christian marriage" means to them, but before detailing the actual assignment, he instructed the class to close their eyes. Seeming to take note of the commanding tone of his voice, he cautiously added, "You don't *have to* close your eyes, but just try to see God in your mind." After pausing a moment as the class sat in silence, he told them, "Take a snapshot of what you see and remember it." Next, he repeated the activity by telling them to see Jesus and to take another snapshot. With everyone's eyes wide open again and turned to pay attention to him, he explained, "You have these pictures and they mean something." Rhetorically, he asked what they saw for God and offered some possible answers, ranging from Aslan, to an ocean, to Alanis Morrisette. He instructed each person to remember what they saw and reminded them about the paper that he passed out at the start of class. He encouraged them to write down the images to help them return to these ideas later.

> Your [homework] assignment is to explore what God and Jesus means to you as a couple and how you can knit the two views together. Everyone should do this for themselves first, then sit down and compare notes. Get really curious about what your partner saw and about what you even saw. Because if you think that the person you're marrying sees God the same way and that's the basis of your hope for a Christian marriage, then that will be really painful.

Before letting everyone go for the day, he warned them that he *will* ask them about the assignment next week. He followed up on that threat and each week he began by inquiring about the type of conversations the homework had produced. Although not all leaders regularly checked in with couples about their homework, there was a consistent expectation that the time between sessions be used to talk more in depth about the materials, and leadership often provided them with these types of assignments to structure their conversations.

In speaking with the leadership, however, I often found that they viewed the strength of their talks as their ability to offer personal and relatable stories. The specific ones they shared were determined in large part by the themes of the sessions, which were structured around relationship education topics and often infused with social-scientific and/or self-help insights. A night on "Communication" at St. Bernadette, for example, included a presentation on John Gottman's research on conflict styles. After reviewing the "Fighting Fair" page in their workbook, Marcy and Darryl provided all the couples with a handout on Gottman's "Seven Principles of a Strong Marriage." Before discussing it, they noted that even though Gottman is not Catholic, he still offers some useful insights, "Based on his research in his Love Labs at the UW [University of Washington], he has been fairly successful at estimating when couples will get divorced. And he has come up with some key factors that healthy relationships, where couples fight fairly, tend to share." They highlighted two key points from this work: (1) "Be willing to edit yourself. You don't need to tell ALL. It is okay to let stuff go and not to say every thought that has bubbled into your head. Don't dump every thought on the other person." (2) "If you seek to first understand, then a lot of issues won't be there." In programs where the leadership team was dominated by lay married couples with no professional religious or counseling training, such as those that alternated leading the Catholic programs, there was a tendency to rely on popular therapeutic sources published for general audiences. Often describing their search to learn more as "research," they assured premarital couples that they had sought external and professional insights into how best to establish healthy marriages. Most often, this involved reading self-help books, such as John Gray's *Men Are from Mars, Women Are from Venus*, Gary Chapman's *The Five Love Languages*, or John Gottman and Nan Silver's *The Seven Principles for Making Marriage Work*.[14]

At Cosmopolitan Church in particular, some of the leaders' careers as therapists meant that they were able to draw on more professionalized training and examples of relationship science. For instance, before the dating class even began, everyone was forwarded a Myers-Briggs personality test to complete individually and told not to discuss it with their partner beforehand. After introductions and reviewing expectations, Michael provided a brief overview of personality tests to help people interpret their results. Drawing on what he learned in graduate school, he explained to everyone that personality "types" are better conceptualized as "spectrums" and that there's some flexibility in whether one feels "extroverted" or "introverted." Illustrating the contextual and situational dimensions to these concepts, he offered, "At work, I tend to lean more towards 'Thinking' because my job is administrative, but at home, I am more 'Feeling' because Rebecca leans towards 'Thinking.'" After giving the couples some brief time to discuss these personality types for themselves and asking for volunteers to share what they learned about the possible strengths and challenges of their personalities, he revealed a drawing of a "Johari window" on the whiteboard. Standing next to the whiteboard, Rebecca began to introduce the concept, but her offhanded comment "I'm not sure where it came from," resulted in Michael interjecting to offer a brief history that it had "emerged from a doctoral dissertation in psychology that sought to understand how people operate with other people." Proceeding with a somewhat technical explanation, he explicated how their journey over the next few weeks would be to do the work captured in this figure.

As indicated in the diagram, the goal in this process is to establish intimacy and trust. This also represents the process that the class will ideally follow—engaging in a process of discovery that starts first with the

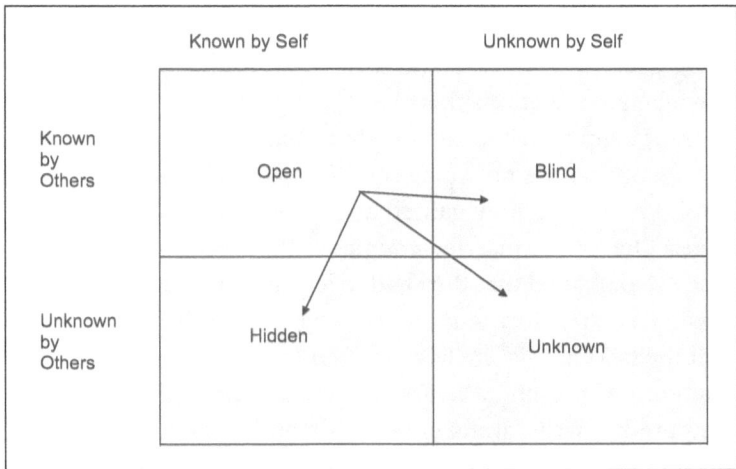

Figure 2.1. Johari Window

self, then one's family, and finally, the couple. We will start first with the "open" category, move towards the "blind" areas, and then move onward towards the "hidden" with the goal of hoping to smooth out and shrink the "unknown" areas. However, this is not a process that can occur instantaneously but takes time. Over the course of the class, there may be many topics that you have already talked about in the past, but the goal is that at least one of these conversations will be deeper and push the intimacy further. This illustrates the broader process of figuring out what you need to learn about yourselves and what you need to tell your partner. Importantly, however, it is a process and not meant to be done in one session of ripping off the Band-Aid.[15]

In comparing the discussion of the social-scientific research presented across the classes, there are differences in the academic depth between the Gottman and the Johari window examples. On the one hand, leadership teams that included people with professional therapeutic expertise benefited from their training and day-to-day job experience that allowed them to speak empirically on what's best for relationships. Yet, on the other hand, these professional backgrounds sometimes impacted the clarity and perceived applicability of what couples should do to improve their relationships. As a scholar of families myself, I found Michael's contextual discussion illuminating and well documented. However, based on interviews with some of the couples, they found his insights for personal growth sometimes to be too abstract and offered less guidance regarding what to do or where to turn when someone wanted to locate their own help on relationships.

The leadership teams, thus, sought to balance the educational tasks of their lessons with a personal-confessional style that focused on experiential knowledge they gained about relationships from their own marriages. One of the married couples at the Exploring Your Relationship Retreat explained that they had to learn the importance of this type of knowledge early during their training to join the leadership team. Since all the talks at this site were written in advance to help ensure that information was presented clearly and consistently, new team members were required to write drafts of their talk and workshop them with the other members. After writing one of their first drafts, Joseph and Bonnie recalled Paul and Kelly suggesting, "Focus more on your story, your experience, what you did and what you learned and what happened. The teaching will flow out of that by itself. Don't feel like you have to be a professor teaching the content of it." As with other therapeutic and religious settings, there is an emphasis on a "narrative concept of self" where "the events of people's lives are reshaped according to the storytelling norms of given situations."[16] Scholars of therapeutic culture have described how "the rise of the confessional"[17] has blurred the line between the private and the public by encouraging people to name and discuss their suffering.[18] For premarital counselors, the confessional narrative that showcases the type of self-reflexivity and open communication they're asking people to cultivate allows them to model sharing stories of relational growth.

To complement the relationship education topics, lessons regularly included leadership teams sharing mundane stories to showcase how to be the type of person who works on one's marriage. For example, during the session on "Communication" at St. Sebastian, the couple shared a simple story about a misunderstanding about antique tongs. Sue explained, "To me, they were special because they were a wedding gift and so I didn't want to use them often. I wanted them to last." Eventually, she told Graham how much it bothered her that he would regularly use them. His explanation that he was using them because they were "special" helped them both realize that a similar motivation can result in different actions. As Sue clarified, "I didn't use them because of love and he used them because of love." Likewise, multiple locations referenced Gary Chapman's *The Five Love Languages* to illustrate how couples need to learn about themselves and their partner and engage in small efforts to understand and translate their feelings in a way that makes sense to the other person. Knowing her husband's "love language" is "words of affirmation," one wife at the Exploring Your Relationship Retreat described how she left post-it notes with "sweet nothings" and encouraging thoughts around her husband's office. Personal examples such as these narratively highlighted the belief that, as one Catholic husband explained, "marriage takes vigilance, effort, and work all the time." Although leaders unlikely believed couples would face identical situations, the lessons served to normalize the idea that a healthy marriage is something that one can learn and practice.[19] These everyday examples of learning about differences in each other and how to best communicate a therapeutic understanding of love also normalized a marital work ethic and revealed possible points of tension in maintaining long-term relationships.

The personal stories also sometimes took on a more confessional dimension as leadership shared deeper points of conflict and struggle in their marriages. Adam and Sarah, who led the engagement class at Cosmopolitan Church, exemplified this approach in their teaching. The level of personal confessions only went deeper as the first evening's "introduction" continued with them taking turns to tell "their story." Included along with the obligatory details of how they met, how long they dated, their engagement, and their children were also two unexpected (and related) elements. First, Sarah expressed the pain of having a miscarriage. In addition to explaining how depressed she became, she described the wedge it created with Adam, "who in a deeply, profound way didn't get it." The wedge eventually grew into greater emotional distance, which included each of them trying to fill the void with separate activities to process their grief. Adam, next, informed everyone that during this period of disconnection, he had an affair with another woman. They concluded this revealing introduction by detailing the amount of work that followed and the arduous process of how they repaired their relationship. In closing, Sarah reflected, "It's sometimes worth the fight. It's always worth fighting for it."

Finally, collective marriage preparation broke with some of the individualistic tropes of therapeutic culture by also actively encouraging couples to seek out community. For most of the programs, community building operated as an explicit goal, and the leadership often made a point of discussing the significance of belonging to religious communities. At both Catholic parishes, for example, the leadership realized that many of the attending couples were not actively involved in church life. Marriage preparation, thus, represented an opportunity to connect with the next (potential) generation of Catholic families and welcome them into the parish. By rotating the leaders each week, they introduced engaged couples to more people and increased the odds they would see a friendly face if they attended Sunday Mass. St. Bernadette more purposefully embraced this community-building potential by arranging the time of the class to occur directly after the evening Mass on Sunday and encouraging everyone to attend it beforehand. For the first introductory session, they even moved class to immediately prior to the service and ended in enough time for everyone to walk over together. On subsequent nights, couples could join the leadership team's pew. Likewise, Cosmopolitan Church also intentionally sought to connect people with their faith community. As a large congregation that had grown relatively quickly over the past few years, the church staff realized that they had lost some of the previous sense of intimacy and that increasingly, people could attend services without recognizing anyone. Each of their classes required couples to locate a "marriage mentor" couple to meet with over the course. Although they did not require that the mentors belong to the congregation, leaders strongly encouraged it and offered the services of the church administration to connect them with possible marriage mentors.

In sum, collective marriage preparation programs seek to strike a balance between "objective" insights from relationship science that can inform the educational dimensions of the class and the "subjective" mode of therapeutic practices that emphasize confessional narratives where private feelings are placed on display. Of course, the public presentation of the private feelings of the leaderships' marriages serves both these purposes by educating engaged couples on the normative way to feel and act in marriage and shoring up the personal authority of the counselors to offer therapeutic insights. In the process, however, an organizational style results in curricula that center the premarital counselors themselves, who notably tended to be white, college-educated, heterosexually partnered, implicitly limiting the embodiment of a good marriage and whose stories are shared. Perhaps the individualistic emphasis within therapeutic culture[20] along with the assumption that couples need to work on their own relationship relegated concerns about representation. In some cases, leadership did indicate a desire to have more diverse premarital counselors but noted the challenges of recruiting married couples who were willing to be transparent, had the available time, and felt knowledgeable enough to teach others.[21] Another consequence of centering the leaderships' narratives was programs encountered a range of depth and engagement on the part of the attending couples, which led many congregations to expect they also participate in some element of individualized programming to address this limitation.

Individualized Premarital Counseling

In a collective class setting, much of the relational work was incumbent on couples to complete on their own. Although couples were always provided with breakout sessions to talk to each other, these were often brief ten- to fifteen-minute segments within the 1½–2-hour class. An exception to this was the Exploring Your Relationship Retreat, which always included time for self-reflection and for couples to dialogue on personal insights that emerged. Yet, in all the programs, couple time was unsupervised. As a result, people could participate in these programs without engaging the goals or tools that the leadership sought to provide either because they didn't take the activities seriously or because they weren't equipped to do the self-work required in the tasks. Based on the interviews with couples, I know that people ranged in how much they completed the assigned workbook activities, answered the discussion questions posed, or finished the required readings. Even though all educational settings contain people of varying levels of commitment and interest to the subject matter, the individualized structure shifts the engagement away from a passive classroom model to a more active *facilitation* framework that seeks to ensure that couples actually have the type of self-reflective conversations examining their pasts to prepare for their futures.

Premarital counselors in this format faced the challenge of how to best, and most efficiently, offer personal and insightful feedback to each couple. Occasionally, pastoral staff could rely on preexisting knowledge of the couple (or at least one of the people) to help guide this process. Increased geographic mobility, however, means that young people are less likely to marry someone from the community they grew up in,[22] and the age group most likely to marry for the first time is also the population least likely to be actively involved in church life.[23] Thus, most premarital counselors I spoke with explained that they could not rely on preexisting information, and even in the limited cases when possible, it often turned out to be skewed to be only a partial understanding of one person. Two strategies consistently emerged as useful in helping to learn enough about a couple to offer tailored feedback to their specific needs, strengths, and situations: conducting multiple sessions and using assessment tools.

As one therapist explained, "I don't do premarital [in] any less than eight sessions." While others reported being more flexible in working with a couple to determine how many meetings they would require, I often heard people discuss a four-to-eight-session model. Unlike the collective classes that replicated the curriculum each time the program was offered, in individualized counseling the particular content varied by counselor and by couple. Some described dedicating a session or two simply to learning about the couple to "get their story," allowing important issues to inductively emerge in this process. Realistically, however, most had topics that they always sought to address and used initial meetings to determine the significance or relevance for a couple. Even with a general checklist of topics and casual conversations, most relied on an assessment tool to guide and streamline their approach. As one pastor described, "At best, I have twenty hours with people [and] that's not covering a lot." In the face of these time constraints, almost all the premarital counselors appreciated the structure that assessment tools could provide them in identifying areas to encourage "growth" and potential points of tension to warn couples about. Citing social desirability, especially with clergy, some premarital counselors believed the information they obtained from the assessment tool was more reliable than what could be gained from exclusively speaking with a couple.

Every evangelical premarital counselor I spoke with discussed using the Prepare/Enrich program, whereas Catholics were more likely to employ FOCCUS (Facilitate Open, Caring Communication, Understanding, and Study).[24] Both programs were created over thirty years ago by relationship science experts, such as sociologists and marriage and family therapists.[25] Each curriculum offers certification for any interested individual to become an approved "facilitator" and to have access to the materials. The FOCCUS website carefully denotes the difference between a "facilitator" and a (licensed) therapist.

> Unlike a therapist, a facilitator is not expected to fix problems nor offer advice; he or she is a resource to support the relationship and promote healthy communication. Pre-marriage sessions offer a unique opportunity to celebrate a couple's strengths, practice positive communication skills, and explore important areas that may present problems later.[26]

Likewise, the website for Prepare/Enrich notes that "the inventory has been utilized by over 100,000 trained clergy members, professional counselors, mentors, and marriage educators throughout the U.S."[27] Despite, or perhaps because, both software packages market themselves as accessible tools for anyone to use, they framed their instruments in scientific authority. Relying on "inventories" and "scales," FOCCUS and Prepare/Enrich stress the quantifiable research behind their measures. For instance, FOCCUS notes, "The 156-item, research-based inventory assesses couples' agreement, disagreement, or indecision about statements related to important issues."[28] Likewise, Prepare/Enrich offers a facilitator access to fifty-five scales including those that target key dimensions of relationships—"communication, conflict resolution, roles, sexuality, finances, and spiritual beliefs"—as well as including options to customize the scales.[29] Although historically some religious leaders expressed reservations about these forms of assessment,[30] most of the ones I spoke with enthusiastically discussed their usefulness in premarital counseling and indicated a significant reliance on them.

All the students and alumni of the evangelical graduate therapy program I interviewed had received an introductory training to Prepare/Enrich during their coursework and many of them had opted to pursue a more complete course to become certified. The assessment was equally as popular with evangelical premarital counselors working in a pastoral setting, however, with everyone reporting having used it. Especially for pastors, who may not have much background or experience in counseling, an assessment tool such as Prepare/Enrich helps organize their approach and focus in the individualized sessions with couples. For example, a few pastors I interviewed reported that they had limited experience with this work, which led them to fully rely on the assessment tool and its accompanying materials to guide their own role in the process. In addition to completing an online survey (that provides the facilitator more detailed feedback than it offers the couples themselves), there is also an accompanying workbook that facilitators can recommend to the couples to help them work through the key areas of the results. On topics such as communication, it includes descriptions and examples of active listening; for financial management, it includes a meaning of money quiz; and for leisure activities, it includes an exercise on dating.

Additionally, throughout it recommends a variety of relationship books for future reference on these topics.

Only one time did I hear someone express significant ambivalence about relying on an assessment tool. An evangelical man who worked both as a therapist and a pastor admitted that the tools are convenient but argued that there were likely more useful activities. As he explained, "It can be a good talking point, [but] my experience is that most of the time, the couples sort of know that stuff already." Whereas everyone else I spoke with appreciated being able to hand couples a visual representation of their (in)compatibility, he estimated that he had used this assessment nearly a hundred times and it seemed that the information provided few novel insights for couples. Instead, he preferred to encourage couples to work through a book together, such as Les and Leslie Parrott's *Saving Your Marriage before It Starts*.

> If you can actually sit down on the loveseat, or a couch, and read it out loud together maybe every night till you're done—or maybe three nights a week or even one night a week or whatever—knock off half a chapter, read it out loud [and] sort of reflect, listen to each other, sit close enough [that] you can feel the vibrations of you, know, the process. To do that together is really good, and I think I see that [as] being a greater asset and a great[er] resource than scoring Prepare/Enrich.

Whereas others found the "scoring" indicative of the assessment's objectivity, this therapist-pastor saw it as too impersonal and less capable of producing deep, reflective dialogue. In general, he was also less optimistic about the prospects of premarital counseling than most of the people I spoke with. He admitted that in his more cynical moments, he often thinks to himself, "This is a waste of time . . . because they're just not ready to listen." But by all accounts, he continues to conduct sessions and noted that it can be "fun" because "you're meeting with usually some very nice people who are excited to be together." This diminished sense of efficacy, however, had led him to decrease the number of sessions he required with couples (down to four from eight). Highlighting the overall tension within premarital counseling, he explained, one can point out likely places of future conflict and remind people that these will only become more intense in marriage but that in the end, "I don't expect them to hear that and then make the choice not to get married." As a result, he has adjusted his goal: "I just want to put it out there for them to think more deeply and ask questions that otherwise they may not have asked."

In another case, a layperson who oversaw the marriage preparation at his suburban Catholic parish more narrowly critiqued FOCCUS. Despite witnessing some minor revisions to the instrument over the years, he felt that neither it nor the resource guide for the facilitator had aged well or were easy to use. His critique points to the tension in popular therapeutic practices that are designed by professional experts but not always administered by them. Unlike the collective classes where leaders blend personal experience and marital advice based on their reading of social-scientific research into a therapeutic narrative, the absence of the personal dimensions in the facilitation of individualized counseling removes the elements most clearly marked as subjective, which may exaggerate the impartiality and objectivity of the therapeutic principles in practice. As we saw earlier, the history of relationship science in the United States has long privileged gendered and classed recommendations for how "best" to be married that have tended to normalize the family structure of the white middle class. Furthermore, the scientific process of producing and understanding data, such as that resulting from assessment tools, is never self-interpreting. Rather, analysis is a learned skill that requires someone trained in the appropriate methodological approaches and theoretical frameworks to determine how best to make sense of the data. Even though the premarital counselors were certified in using the assessment tools and interpreting the generated reports, that didn't necessarily mean they were always trained in or educated on the empirical scholarship these programs draw on to construct their scales and make recommendations for "functional" relationships. With the intellectual debates within and about relationship science "blackboxed,"[31] it becomes easier to simplify insights into the medicalized and discrete categories of "healthy" versus "unhealthy" or "functional" versus "dysfunctional."

The final critique of the assessment tool I heard actually came from an evangelical pastor who saw the culpability as on the participant and not the tool or training. Since his job as a pastor of a fairly rural congregation had not afforded him much experience in premarital counseling, he explained that the Prepare/Enrich assessment tool was critical to his ability to structure his approach. However, after reviewing the results of a local, Latino couple that didn't belong to his church but planned to get married at a nearby park, he found that their scores were "totally opposite." Unsure about what to do or how to proceed, he even sought out the advice of his trainer in the curriculum who agreed that the results had a "high prediction of dysfunction." However, after sitting down with them, he realized that the man who predominately spoke Spanish couldn't really read English. Despite the assessment tool not providing him with reliable data, the pastor still recalled that he debated whether he should marry them. He found them a "challenging" case because the couple already had a child, were living together, and the father of the bride had refused to walk her down the aisle. However, he finally concluded that the best he could do was offer "life skills," such as "don't call each other names," and marry them anyway because "they were the most positive influences in each other's lives." This experience did not diminish his own support for assessment, but it reveals how the ability of a couple to demonstrate "preparedness" is predicated in part on classed social competencies, such as how to take a test, write coherently, or the ability to articulately express one's point of view. Although similarly reflecting the white middle-class assumptions found in the marriage movements' lessons on skilled love,[32] we see promoting marriage isn't the goal. Rather, the pastor was ambivalent about whether this couple should marry and felt conflicted about his role in sanctioning the union. Instead, it points to the ways that Christian premarital counselors' belief in a covenant marriage makes them hesitant to encourage the institution for those whom they worry may not be a good fit and ways "fit" is assessed.

For nearly all people offering individualized marriage preparation within the context of a church—lay staff, parish priests, evangelical pastors, and marriage mentors—premarital counseling is an unpaid service to their community. Even for clergy and religious directors for whom it may be part of their job description, it always represented a small component. At four to eight sessions per couple (plus the associated preparation), dedicating considerable time or energy may come at a cost to other duties. It is this time-resource management issue that resulted in many of the larger congregations developing programs that outsourced this labor to volunteers, such as the collective programs noted in the previous section or the use of marriage mentors.

The division of labor approach appeared most consistently in the Catholic parishes. In the end, I interviewed only two priests during this research because when I contacted parishes asking to speak with whoever was in charge of marriage preparation, I was always forwarded to laity (either a staff member or volunteer married couple). The limited role of Catholic priests makes sense given their overall shortage, which leads to significant demands on their time, not to mention their single status, which some engaged couples felt impacted their ability to speak on marriage. All the same, each indicated that they try to be involved in the process to some extent, but at their present parishes, it generally meant speaking at one session of the collective programming. Due to the size and demands of each parish, any individualized meeting was limited to a few consultations focusing on wedding details, such as selecting liturgy and discussing logistics of the service.

According to one priest, however, the meetings with couples offered a time for proselytization and redemption. He explained, "I enjoy wedding prep not because it is easy but because it is a chance to speak about the gospel." For people who are not active in their faith, he argued this as an important time to "reeducate" them about the actual teachings of the Church because "most people if they don't like the Catholic Church, it is not because they know what the Catholic Church teaches. It is because they know what they *think* the Catholic Church teaches. And there's often quite a gap." This belief was also shared by many of the other lay staff who facilitated marriage preparation. Compared to evangelicals, Catholics' view on marriage as a sacrament meant that they also more consistently featured religious education in their explanation of the purpose and need for marriage preparation. As one lay man described, "Certainly there's practical application, but there is also some other theology and catechesis to back up the application." The prevalence of convalidations (religious sanction to civil marriages) meant that Catholic premarital counselors were not always preparing couples for marriage itself but for a *Catholic* marriage.[33] In other words, questions about the expectations of marriage made less sense for civilly married couples. Catholic couples were also significantly more likely within my study to marry non-Catholics, which meant religious education could involve educating people who may never have been introduced to a sacramental marriage.

In a couple of cases, the time-resource demands of clergy led congregations to create marriage mentor programs that outsourced most of the premarital preparation to laity. Rather than create collective classes of engaged couples such as the ones I observed, one large evangelical church had a list of potential volunteers of married couples who could be matched to an engaged couple depending on background and need. Ideally, each mentor couple would work with one or two engaged couples who complemented their strengths or reflected their life situation in some manner. For example, in the case of remarriages, they selected an older couple from the church for whom their current marriage was both their second marriage and had required blending their families. To provide some structure to these mentorship relationships and ensure the general goals of premarital counseling were met, mentor couples worked through *Preparing for Marriage: Discover God's Plan for a Lifetime of Love* with each couple. Similar to the workbook supplied by Prepare/Enrich, it includes brief lessons and a variety of questionnaires and exercises for the couples to work through. Likewise, a Catholic deacon whom I spoke with felt, after reviewing research on different curricula, that the marriage mentorship model in *Together in God's Love: A Catholic Preparation for Marriage* offered facilitators and couples with the most accessible resources and was "just enough" without being "labor intensive." Yet, similar to those that recruited leaders for the collective programs in Catholic parishes, he noted that these types of peer-to-peer mentorship models require willing and relationally articulate couples in the parish to volunteer. He lamented, as did other parish authorities, that the superiority of using marriage mentors was circumscribed by the challenges in identifying and recruiting them. Notably, this also reveals how congregational leadership act as arbiters of who represents a "good marriage."

In sum, the individualized approach sought to be couple-centric and to ensure any exploration of the subjective dimensions of a relationship were focused on the engaged couple. Of course, this did not mean that subjective evaluations of how a couple ought to be or what a good level of preparedness were absent from the process. The ability of the couple to showcase learning appears to matter more in the individualized setting where premarital counselors are directly assessing the viability of their relationship. In particular, the positionality of the premarital counselor—therapist versus clergy versus married mentor—played a stronger role in whether they saw their role as instructing or sanctioning the relationship. Despite the use of similar tools and structure to the meetings, clergy were more likely to not only try to prepare the couple but to consider whether they as an authority within the religious community should sanction the union by agreeing to marry them.

Conclusion

Premarital counseling exists as a flexible organizational practice that a wide range of groups and individuals can mobilize to fulfill different pragmatic goals: religious education, community building, and cultivation of relationship skills. This ministry helps many religious communities to fulfill one of the "core" activities of a congregation—the expression and transmission of meaning through religious education.[34] Depending on the needs and available resources, congregations offered collective programming and/or individualized counseling options to engaged couples. Premarital counseling as a religious practice, however, is not bound within congregations. Christian universities, religious retreat centers, therapists of faith, and paraministry organizations also all engage in preparing couples for marriage. The combination of educational and confessional approach in the collective form provided an opportunity to learn about the intimate and private dimensions of marriage. In contrast, the tailored model of facilitation in the individualized form offers couples the potential to acquire personalized insights about themselves—their relationship, their background, and potential dynamics in their future. The divergent organizational styles of the two types of programs allow both congregations and individuals to make choices about how to religiously and therapeutically prepare for marriage.

Despite their significant effort to maintain these programs and their belief that this religio-therapeutic practice can help couples learn about a good marriage, the leadership did not envision these programs as a way to promote marriage itself. Although leaders would often note that they were "passionate" or "enthusiastic" about marriage, their discussions cautioned couples about the stressful and emotional drain that the institution could cause in people's lives. Premarital counselors were generally more motivated by concerns about divorce in the construction and development of their programs. They envisioned their efforts as an attempt to deter the poorly matched and provide relationship skills and a marital work ethic to the rest. In fact, many of the people I spoke with seemed unaware that across the country, others engage in similar relationship education practices to promote marriage as a solution to poverty. As a result, the Christian premarital counseling programs I encountered were removed organizationally from the broader marriage movement in the United States.[35] Of course, this gap makes sense when considering that the couples who attend Christian marriage preparation are there because they want to get married and are often planning their wedding. Thus, the motivations of the couples and organizational needs of the congregations result in a similar therapeutic practice as those sponsored by the state but without the politicization of whether marriage is a successful tool for poverty reduction. Instead, it operated as a localized practice that served religious communities and emotionally socialized couples into how to think about marriage.

Christian premarital counseling efforts to prepare people for marriage may not have promoted marriage as an economic benefit or a means of class mobility, but as a type of relationship *education*, it bears some of the classed markers of what constitutes "successful" learning. Sociologists have long noted that American educational inequalities reflect beliefs that there are "correct" ways to talk and demonstrate understanding.[36] In other words, the ability to be articulate in one's discussion of their relationship narrative privileges eloquence, past experience with exams enables someone to knowingly navigate assessment tools, and even familiarity with college classrooms that expect students to come to class having learned from assigned readings and homework may allow some people to take more from the programs. Likewise, many of these same traits also are helpful to premarital counselors who must construct clear and cogent lessons or interpret and apply the assessment data for each individual couple. Regardless of whether the "premarital counselor" was recruited because of professional expertise in therapy, their congregational position, or the sense that as a married couple they had made it work, most of them received limited specific training in how to do this work and had to rely on their existing knowledge and competencies. In the highly educated Pacific Northwest, most of the religious groups were able to draw on professional elites within their communities and expect them to independently craft these programs. For example, an overwhelming number of the premarital counselors I spoke with had some form of graduate training (even if it wasn't always directly applicable). Thus, both the learning of and teaching about a "good marriage" tended to privilege the dispositions and competencies associated with the white middle class.

By situating the divergent organizational approaches to Christian premarital counseling within the broader field of relationship education, it becomes clear that the goals of religious education and community building coupled with engaged couples already seriously considering their weddings shifts the logic of the therapeutic practice. Religious communities ultimately are trying to balance their aspiration to use these programs as a way to connect with young couples and their desire to ensure that only those prepared for a *Christian* marriage make it to the altar. The next chapter explores this theme in more depth by interrogating the lessons on what makes a relationship healthy and holy. Despite the Catholics' greater emphasis on marriage preparation as a form of religious education that prepares parishioners for the sacrament of marriage, both Christian traditions employed a covenant rhetoric to distinguish God's vision for the institution from the secular practice, which they saw as encouraging self-interested actors.

3

Constructing a Good and Godly Marriage

Since the Catholic programs always varied leaders from week to week, I never knew what to expect walking in. Unlike most other sessions I observed, however, this time when I entered the small meeting room at St. Sebastian, I discovered that the evening would not be led by a married couple. Instead, Karen, who worked as a lay religious director at the parish, waited by herself to greet the four couples as they arrived and passed out handouts. As we settled into the overstuffed furniture that had been positioned in a circle around a low coffee table, Karen explained that we would be starting without Father Lucas, who was running late because of an "emergency" funeral. To introduce her role and provide a sense of the scope of her work, she explained, "If you look in the bulletin, you'll see my name associated with a lot of the religious education programs." Before turning to learn more about everyone, she commented, "I like meeting couples now at the beginning of their relationships because if you stick around the parish, then I will get to see you baptize your children."

As an icebreaker to learn about those in attendance, Karen asked everyone to go around in a circle and volunteer two things that they do to keep themselves healthy. "By 'healthy,'" she clarified, "I mean it broadly and it can include anything physical, emotional, spiritual, etc." To start the process, she began by offering that to stay physically healthy, she regularly swims, and to stay spiritually healthy, she likes to read Catechism. Once others shared their own healthy practices, Karen formally opened the evening by reading a prayer from one of the worksheets she had passed out. When the prayer was finished, she turned to the large whiteboard that had been rolled into the room to write "Marriage as a . . ." at the top and then underneath it on their own lines, she listed out "Vocation," "Covenant," and "Sacrament." Explaining that this would serve as an outline for our evening, she informed us that we would be spending the next couple of hours considering how marriage fulfills each of these dimensions in our lives.

Before providing any commentary on marriage as a vocation, she first asked the couples, "How do you understand vocation?" Some of the words volunteered included job, purpose, and career, and one person even noted that it means "calling" in Latin. Building off the last comment, Karen elaborated, "If marriage is a type of calling, it begs the question 'Who is doing the calling?'" After a few moments of silence, she dryly joked, "Come on, it's not a hard one." Perhaps realizing that it wasn't a rhetorical question, one couple responded in unison "God." Excited by now having the answer she was looking for, Karen continued, "It's how God gets your attention. God loves to ambush us. He puts someone in our life that we eventually begin to realize we can't spend any more time without. And this is God's way of calling to us. In a way, we're placed in a moment of crisis where we realize that we must get married or break up."

Once Father Lucas arrived, he briefly introduced himself and then immediately began to discuss marriage by asking, "Does the word 'covenant' have any significance to you?" Before anyone could answer, Karen interjected, "It's not a word that we use every day." Nodding in agreement, Father Lucas followed with the observation, "We tend to use the word contract and not covenant." Launching into a longer definition, he explained, "Covenant is the word used for God's relationship with the chosen people. Something more characterizes a covenant in comparison to a contract because a covenant is built on relationships. It's built on love and trust. It is characterized by the giving of gifts as opposed to an attitude of 'I do this for you so that you do this for me.' It's a gift of self to the other person and asking for a gift of self in return. At its core, a covenant is an exercise in our humanity." As his explanation continued and began to drift off topic to discuss how God fulfilled the law as a sign of His love, Karen gave him a hard look. Turning to face the quiet group, he explained that she sometimes gets frustrated with him when he goes off on a tangent and concluded by noting, "As opposed to a contract which is for a limited time, a covenant is not temporary. It has no end date. It is based on love and on what you give it. There's no penalties because it's based on trust. It's a form of love and trust in that we express ourselves in the giving of gifts. We want to enter into a covenant because it's what makes us human."

Although lessons on marriage as a "vocation" and "sacrament" occurred nearly exclusively among Catholics, a similar covenant rhetoric emerged universally across all the programs to distinguish what makes a Christian marriage good and godly.[1] Faced with the challenge of guiding premarital couples toward their goal of marital bliss, religious communities struggle to explain why some marriages succeed and others fail, especially within the church, and seek to console them that God's vision for marriage is the best recipe for relational success. In response, premarital counselors constructed a clear boundary between a *covenant marriage* as a union fulfilling God's intentions and better positioned for success and a *contract marriage* as a less committed relationship where individuals focus on their own needs, which they argued is dominant in secular culture.[2] In the process, they reinterpreted the historical understanding of a covenant from a call for God's chosen people[3] to a more universal invitation to anyone interested and willing to commit themselves to following God's path to happiness. The discursive shift highlights how religious traditions create an "emotional subculture"[4] where members are not only taught what to believe but also what to feel.[5] As Father Lucas's opening remarks begin to indicate, the insights into how to have a successful marriage were conceptualized as divining God's truth about the relational needs and challenges posed by people's humanity. Thus, the question "What makes a marriage Christian?" reveals how the symbolic boundaries that religious communities construct with secular culture contains lessons on what one ought to think, how one should act, and what one is expected to feel.

This chapter describes how covenant rhetoric operates as an interpretative frame within Christian communities to make sense of how marital expectations have become more individualized and the institution more unstable.[6] On an ideological level, the blending of therapeutic and religious logics discursively constructs God's vision as more relational and healthier than secular society because it calls for people to be less focused on themselves and more other-centered in the relationship. Occurring against the backdrop of a "divorce culture,"[7] the covenant rhetoric provides a tangible explanation for why some marriages may fail and also a clear motivation for why one must learn the lessons in marriage preparation. Specifically, religious leaders teach people that to work at their marriage and engage in deep personal reflection are key to marital success. Thus, despite their attempts to challenge the self-focused tendencies of secular culture, they embrace the therapeutic tools and lessons that privilege the self as something to explore and manage.[8]

Making a Covenant among Contracts

Despite both being Christian traditions, there are some pronounced theological differences between Catholic and evangelical Protestants regarding marriage. Since marriage is one of the seven sacraments for Catholics, doctrinally it is something people *receive* from the Church, and to be "true," both partners must be baptized and married in the Church.[9] Although evangelicals also believe "God intends [marriage] to be a blessing, a way of carrying out the divine mandates of the Bible, and a means of self-understanding,"[10] they do not share a systematic theology that distinguishes this gift, nor do they believe that a civil wedding of two Christians would negate the religiousness of the marriage. Yet, despite their formal theological differences, in discussing the religious significance and how to meaningfully construct a Christian marriage, both traditions shared a covenant rhetoric as a way to convince people that God's vision of marriage differs from the self-interested contract marriage they believed permeated secular culture. The programs, and the leaders I spoke with, regularly used the language of "covenant" to describe some element of the relational qualities of how one should love their partner and the shared promise to continue to work on the marriage with each other under God's authority.

In fact, despite these theological differences, the final session of the dating class at Cosmopolitan Church mirrored much of the lessons presented above from St. Sebastian. To celebrate reaching the end of the program, there was a potluck where couples were encouraged to bring "church approved" food and drinks. The evening started later than usual as people helped themselves to the treats and occasional Pacific Northwest health food, like quinoa salad. Michael eventually began the class by announcing, "Tonight will be focused on marriage—both as a general concept and what it means for Christians." Quickly, he followed up with the caveat, "This isn't to say that everyone here has to get married or that this is the time to get married but that it is an important conversation to have and where relationships at this stage are generally oriented." By volunteering to write, Caleb drew everyone's attention to the whiteboard at the front of class with "Covenant" written on the top left and "Contract" on the top right. Over the next little bit, men and women from the class first volunteered what "comes to mind" when they hear the word "contract." Immediately, someone yelled out, "cell phones," which Michael offhandedly commented is always mentioned. Caleb's list grew longer as people volunteered more ideas, including "legally binding," "obligation," "not easy to break," "short term," "not about the spirit but the letter," "conditional upon each party holding up their end," and "do something to get something." Eventually, after the list filled most of its dedicated half of the whiteboard, Michael and Caleb switched to ask what comes to mind when people hear the word "covenant." Again, people easily volunteered ideas, including "Jesus," "commitment," "community focused because it involves more than two parties," "more permanent," "mutuality," "based on what you put into it, as opposed to what you get out of it," and "selfless."

As the speed of suggestions began to slow, Michael looked at the board and then turned back to everyone to offer a synthesis of some of the themes.

> Contract doesn't seem very relational. In fact, it's legally void of emotion and not a relational endeavor at all. In society, we make contracts a lot but not with personal thoughts or feelings tied into it because these represent legally binding agreements that we make due to a lack of trust and a concern about consequences. Fundamentally, we operate contractually in our culture with a quid pro quo approach. Yet, relationships don't function well in the long term with this model. If I had this approach in my marriage, then I wouldn't still be married and here today talking about my marriage because it wouldn't have lasted. Rather, in a marriage from a covenant perspective, the focus is on the promise of mutuality between partners.

Echoing much of Father Lucas's lesson from the opening vignette, both leaders shared the language of "relationship" and "trust" to describe the idea of a covenant and make the case that it offers a more fertile foundation for marriage than the secular model of a "contract." In particular, the power of emotions emerges as central to their argument that the union is superior because it allows for the greater fulfillment of humanity and possibility of authenticity. In contrast to the tendency to see emotions as irrational in other spheres of life,[11] the covenant rhetoric conceptualizes the ability to feel as core to being human, which subsequently constructs these marriages as truer to oneself. In contrast, a contract is characterized as constricting because it doesn't allow for the emotionality present in human relationships but requires peoples to act purely rationally and on the basis of self-interest. Without denying the legal foundation of marriage as a secular contract, the language of covenant emphasizes the promises made in marriage to commit to a relationship. In the process, it implies an intimacy in its construction of "relational" that presumes only positive emotions and ignores more negative ones such as guilt, shame, or even obligation.

The covenant, however, was not only between the spouses but more broadly seen as a tripartite commitment with God. As Arnie, the Catholic husband who co-led the class on sacramental marriages at St. Bernadette, explained, "It's about the three-person relationship that exists between you, your spouse, and God. Like a table, it provides more stability so that if you lose one leg you won't get into the same trouble." At the Exploring Your Relationship Retreat, they also used a number of analogies to explain the three-party covenant, including God acting as the pin that binds a door hinge together and ultimately makes it work. During a session titled "Covenant," they also projected the below image on a PowerPoint slide to illustrate what they called "new math." As encapsulated in the image, marriage unites three separate entities into one whole. In the final session of the weekend, they presented this triangle again with the new title "God's Plan for Marriage." Over time, they explicated how the triangle should become smaller because the distance between the partners shrinks as they move closer to God and to each other.

Both Catholics and evangelicals presented faith as a bedrock that provided couples with not only a shared worldview but also a protective quality for inevitable challenges and conflicts that emerge in sustaining a long-term committed relationship. Sometimes, as in the above Catholic example, this idea was predicated on the idea that a Christian marriage had another party working to support it. In other cases, this manifested in a presumption that the relational dimension of a covenant marriage provides Christians with an easier pathway to forming a deep emotional connection because it's founded on trust unlike a contract, which is conditional. As Kelly, from the Exploring Your Relationship

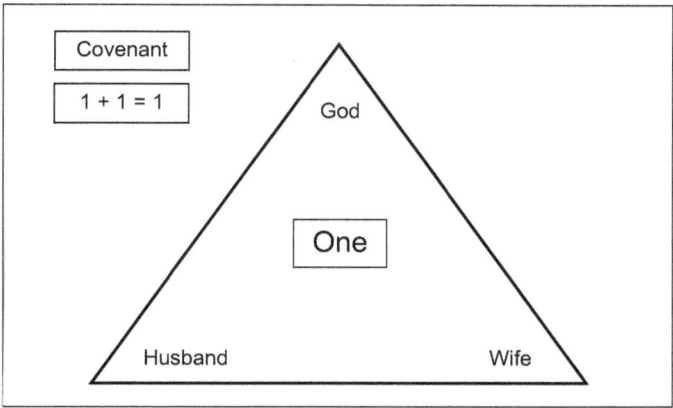

Figure 3.1. Covenant Image from Exploring Your Relationship Retreat

Retreat, explained in an interview, "[Oneness] changes the focus from myself to this is a team and this is a partnership." The covenant rhetoric positioned religion both as a relational resource in the form of faith that unites couples but also religious truth as containing therapeutic insights to make people happier.

For the most part, as these examples indicate, defining what makes a marriage *Christian* was accomplished by defining it in opposition to secular society. Advice on how to have a happy and healthy marriage, therefore, centered religious imagery, establishing an implicit, if not always subtle, hierarchy of marriage types in society. The "secular other"[12] and their selfish, contingent, and hedonistic approach to marriage was always present to explain how God's view was better because it divined the deeper needs of people, which meant His teachings would ensure a more satisfying and functional marriage. In fact, the concepts of "covenant" and "contract" were deeply interwoven, with one almost never appearing without the other. The qualities of the covenant marriage as a safe, permanent relationship where people can feel free to fully experience their emotional potential as humans were only clear when contrasted with the uncertain and contingent relationship that secular people supposedly find themselves in because they cannot trust in the longevity of the other person's affections.

The clarity and rigidity of the boundary between covenant and contract mostly tended to occur at a macro level where people constructed abstract presentations that positioned the religious community in opposition to secular culture. When conversations drifted away from "culture," however, to real people's actual marriages, there was greater hesitation. For example, when I probed further in the interview with Kelly, she stumbled as she considered whether Christian marriage actually does uniquely position couples to a teamwork ethos.

> I don't know if it's there as much, I mean, I suppose faith isn't the only way to have that teamwork concept. But just that deeper understanding of God's doing something in our relationship, more than just what makes me happy, or just that we have a good time, or we're compatible. You know, there's a lot more depth to the things that we're going after as a couple, as a family.

In contrast to the more confident answers presented to people in the collective classes, I found that when I asked in interviews about what distinguishes a Christian marriage from a non-Christian one or asked how people would explain the concept to a new believer, then participants were more likely to waffle. Although many admitted that non-Christians could have a good marriage and not all Christians actually do, this ambiguity rarely impinged on the conceptual discussions of what defines a Christian marriage and the relational-faith goals that God calls people to when they marry.

A covenant marriage, thus, primarily operates as a religious symbol that premarital counselors, as spokespeople for their faith communities, can marshal to justify and reinforce boundaries with secular culture. Overlaying the dimension of a healthier and happier relationship onto a covenant marriage also constructs the authority of the religious community as a pathway to marital success. The abstraction from people's lives actually better serves this end. Compared to more concrete cultural resources, sociologist Fred Kniss notes that the ambiguity within abstract cultural resources makes them more easily manipulated and available for mobilization.[13] A more tangible prescription for Christian marriage likely would have met with greater resistance from couples as they struggled to apply it to their own situations and would have been less likely to transcend the different denominational contexts. As a symbolic boundary, covenant marriages becomes a tool used by the community to make claims about the definitions of reality, but as is most often the case, this process is not without contestation or struggle.[14]

Is a Covenant Marriage Too Good to Be True?

The covenant rhetoric was ubiquitous, with clergy, therapists, and laity (both married and unmarried) all espousing it. Regardless of organizational or theological differences across the programs, the covenant rhetoric consistently emerged to frame God's vision of marriage as an unbreakable bond between Himself and the spouses. By creating a fine line between Christian and secular marriages, it articulated the characteristics that Christians ought to have, the ways they should feel, what they should believe, and how they should see themselves as living distinctively in their relationships. In other words, the covenant rhetoric operated as a boundary that marked group membership that was visible and meaningful to Christians. Sociologist Eviatar Zerubavel argues that social membership entails learning the particular distinctive classification schemas of the group and that part of belonging subsequently involves "seeing" the world through the lens they produce.[15] All the Christians I encountered could "see" the boundary encapsulated in the covenant rhetoric, but only a few questioned what they were looking at. Although all the program leaders engaged in this rhetoric, for some of the therapists, their professional training and experience counseling Christians navigating the transition to marriage led them to interrogate the reality of this distinction on the ground and to wonder if it was too idealistic. In particular, they expressed hesitation about idealizing a Christian marriage as inherently healthier and worried about creating unrealistic expectations for couples.

For example, after Michael, from the above example, asserted that "if I had this [contract] approach in my marriage, then I wouldn't still be married," Caleb quickly interjected. "Often when we haven't done well in our relationship, it is because it's become too contractual. At these times, conversations often turn to focus on what each of us did and whether the other person did enough to match." Continuing, he cautioned, "It will not always be possible to have a covenant relationship but it is a goal to strive for. Realistically, there will be times where it operates in a more contractual manner because it's unrealistic to expect that it never will be this way." Without challenging the reality of the covenant-contract division, he thus attempted to relocate it from the broader spheres of "culture" to a mindset that people can move in and out of occupying. As opposed to presenting *the* Christian approach as a covenant, he admits that it is an ideal from which to view one's partner and not a constant state to occupy.

Adam, the therapist who co-led the engaged class at Cosmopolitan Church, more explicitly challenged the tendency to define *Christian* marriages through rhetorical practices. In the first of a two-part series on "Biblical Marriage," Adam began by noting, "We're going to discuss biblical marriage. And going to see what it is. I don't think I know." Before he delved into his actually extensive view on the topic, he asked the class for their thoughts on the subject: "What do you think it is? In reality? Or as a cliché?" Writing the answers people easily and quickly volunteered on the board, he constructed an extensive list that included ideas such as "prayer," "two flesh become one," "service," "open to growth," and of course, "covenant." During this process, I was reminded that Adam spends his day counseling people, as he would probe for more information by asking, "Can you talk more about that?" or "What do you mean by that?" The young woman who offered "covenant" struggled to respond to these requests and eventually told him, "Don't ask me to explain this." After significant effort and more direct and leading questions—such as "Anything cheesy?" "How about stereotypes?" "Anything you were told in church?"—Adam and Sarah succeeded in filling the whiteboard with a list of ideas, some thoughtful and others critical.

As the sample of provided phrases indicates, much of the discussion of a "biblical marriage" was not explicitly religious, with couples instead volunteering ideas such as "enjoying one another" and "fewer problems." Returning to his original question, he asked the couples, "What makes the list a *biblical* relationship and not just a good marriage?" Closely examining the assembled list, he circled a few examples that made this distinction and asked the couples if he missed any. One woman encouraged him to circle "covenant" because, as she explained, "it is different. It is a Christian term and not one that my secular friends are into because in mainstream culture, marriage is more of a deal that people take part in until one of the people messes up."

Taking this as an opportunity to end the intellectual exercise and directly challenge the class, Adam turned away from the board and said, "I'm put off by a lot of stereotypes in the Church that haven't been put under a microscope. The Bible is profoundly quiet on the topic of marriage. It says a lot on loving your neighbor and that type of stuff but not a lot on what a marriage should look like." To illustrate this point, he turned to a passage that he confessed "likely doesn't make an appearance at many weddings" and "doesn't inform many people's understanding of a biblical marriage." He read aloud from Deuteronomy 24:5,

> "If a man has recently married, he must not be sent to war or have any other duty laid on him. For one year he is to be free to stay at home and bring happiness to the wife he has married."[16]

After finishing the passage, he looked up at the couples and asked, "Anyone doing this?" Not surprisingly, people didn't affirmatively respond. Filling the silence, he informed the couples, "Actually, in the Bible, there are few places where it talks about lifestyles for the home." Without rejecting the idea that Christians are called to live according to God's guidelines, he questioned what people "see" as biblical marriage. Even though he wouldn't disagree with the belief that a marriage is a lifelong commitment to not only one's spouse but to working on the relationship with God, he challenges the assertion that faith is inherently unitive and not also a site of work.

Similar types of critiques and ambivalence over the use of "Christian" as a descriptor for marriages appeared among some of the interviews with students and alumni of an evangelical counseling program. For example, one woman negatively reacted to my inquiry about how she would define a Christian marriage, telling me that "I think [a] Christian marriage is just a marriage with two people that are Christians. Honestly, I don't think a Christian marriage is really that different than any other marriage. Yeah, that's a hard question because I don't like that label." Elaborating, she explained, "I think people assume it's supposed to be better or have this value attached to it as like 'We're going to be fine because we've got God!'" As these examples reveal, for some, the experience of counseling couples seems to facilitate identifying potential drawbacks in constructing a Christian marriage as too ideal, such that it may be unrealistic. Aware that faith alone does not provide an easier path to marital bliss, they worried about the expectations that this type of rhetoric could create for people. By challenging idealized binaries, they sought to manage expectations and warn couples that God also calls Christians to work on their marriages. The professional training of therapists appears to help to remove what Zerubavel calls the "glasses"[17] that make the cultural distinction of a covenant versus contract marriage not only meaningful but also visible. Importantly, however, this type of critical position cannot be reduced to a therapeutic background. I exclusively heard this criticism from those with experience counseling distressed Christian marriages, but not all the therapists I spoke with held this perspective. Many of the counselors confidently drew on the covenant rhetoric to define Christian marriage as sharing a common foundation of faith, which is important for a successful marriage.

The critical perspective that sought to deconstruct the rhetorical power of a Christian marriage, however, also appeared to be circumscribed by local dimensions of authority. Many therapists, regardless of whether they supported or critiqued concepts such as covenant marriage, reported not offering their own religious worldview during individualized premarital counseling. Viewing it as inappropriate to tender personal religious commentary in counseling, they instead described refraining from disputing this sort of teaching in sessions with clients. Therefore, couples' primary access to these types of critical views that deconstruct Christian marriage may occur only within congregational contexts, such as the collective premarriage courses, where therapists who hold this view are selected to lead the curriculum. As lay volunteers, however, the therapists occupied a smaller institutional space from which to speak authoritatively on the religious dimensions of relationships. For example, at Cosmopolitan Church, a family ministry pastor oversaw both the dating and engaged class. He selected the leaders, would attend portions of the class, and supply some materials to the participating couples. One such document explained the church's views on relationships and expectations for conduct that framed these as covenants, including couples committing to abstinence while attending the program. Although the leaders of the dating and engaged class at Cosmopolitan Church often presented more nuanced views on sexuality that emphasized the importance of reducing stigma and shame, the church's staff formally held a different position, which included not marrying any couple living together.[18] Thus, any efforts by lay volunteers to deconstruct or challenge what they saw as "typical" and/or problematic Christian views could be undercut by a person with greater religious and organizational authority.

Ultimately, despite efforts by some to at least nuance, if not challenge, covenant rhetoric, it dominated understandings of a Christian marriage in premarital counseling programs. As an abstract concept, the metaphors and language used to define this idea varied to some extent across programs. Some notions appeared consistently, however, such as the belief that pursuing a covenant marriage should inculcate in each spouse an outward orientation, which helped provide a rationale for why these Christian relationships *can* be healthier. As opposed to the "contract" perspective that supposedly focuses on meeting one's own needs, the covenant rhetoric argues that each partner first must try to meet the needs of the other person. If each spouse approaches marriage from this perspective, it arguably would result in their own needs being met (by the spouse). For one to effectively do this, however, each partner must be willing and able to effectively communicate their point of view—fears, expectations, desires—to their partner. A covenant marriage, thus, sacralizes relationship skills, such as communication, conflict management, and self-reflexivity, and rhetorically intertwines a Christian relationship with more therapeutic principles of healthy and functional.

Christian Marriage in a Culture of Divorce

The distinction between the other-focused covenant marriage inspired by God and the self-focused contract marriage offered in secular culture allows premarital counselors to provide an explanation for the divorce trend in the United States. From this perspective, the ubiquity of divorce is not surprising because people are more willing to "call it quits" when they are no longer feeling fulfilled. While presenting arguably too simplistic a view of the broader American cultural approach to marriage, Christian premarital counselors do implicitly identify what sociologist Karla Hackstaff calls a "divorce culture"—"a set of symbols, beliefs, and practices that anticipate and reinforce divorce and, in the process, redefine marriage."[19] As discussed earlier, she argues that the "marital watershed" of the 1970s—when divorce surpassed death as the most likely reason for a life partnership to end—resulted in the emergence of alternative meanings around relationships and destabilized the previously dominant "marriage culture." As a result, today's married couples "are increasingly talking and reproducing the terms of divorce culture,"[20] which she notes includes the idea that marrying is now an option, contingent, and divorce is viewed as a possible gateway to greater personal satisfaction.

Amid this cultural backdrop, an implicit question emerged: How do you have a Christian marriage in a culture of divorce? In part, as we have seen, this concern helped motivate religious communities to offer premarital counseling. A general belief exists, as one therapist explained, that marriage preparation is an "intentional step to try and minimize, or at least push back against, the climbing divorce rate in our country."[21] This context also provides a new vantage point on the covenant rhetoric as not only a means to establish symbolic boundaries against secular culture but also as an explanation for why Christian couples are not immune to divorce.

The leaders at Cosmopolitan Church, for example, directly addressed this tension, with teachers in both the dating and engaged classes explaining to couples (and sometimes correcting couples' misunderstanding) that Christians divorce at rates equal to secular society.[22] In fact, one week, the two classes met together to hear a speaker present psychological research on marital conflict. Before reviewing the type of characteristics that scholars have found correlate with a successful marriage, the speaker opened by considering the divorce rate among Christians.

> Strong faith isn't enough to ensure marital success. If we were to have a reunion of this class forty years from now, it would be likely that half of all of you wouldn't still be together. Part of the issue is that no one really gets married expecting to be the statistic, which means that couples find themselves there.

As opposed to this direct engagement with the divorce rate among Christians, the nontherapist laity that led the programs in the Catholic parishes and the Exploring Your Relationship Retreat tended to present this threat more indirectly. In addition to claims that research finds that couples who pray together are less likely to get divorced (an assertion that no one was able to support with any reference), leaders would mention the divorces they had witnessed in their own lives (some of which were Christian couples). Thus, even these religious figures who all oppose divorce cannot teach on the topic of marriage without addressing its prevalence. Of course, couples attending these programs usually did not need the reminder that their relationships would not be divorce-proof. For some (especially evangelicals), this anxiety motivated their participation, and they hoped to gain tangible skills and techniques that would better ensure future marital success.

On the one hand, the culture of divorce provides the covenant marriage with greater rhetorical power. The claims by premarital counselors about the permanence of this union only hold significance within a cultural context where marriages are contingent. On the other hand, this also contributes to its abstraction because a faith in God will not ensure the permanence or happiness of any particular marriage. Thus, religious communities link teachings on how to have a *Christian* marriage with a discussion of how to have a *successful* marriage. The question, however, becomes, how does one go about successfully creating a covenant marriage? And how does one avoid divorce when they stumble in this process?

Making Marriage Work

Sociologists and historians alike have noted that the conception of "marriage as work" became increasingly popular and pervasive as the prevalence of divorce made marriage more contingent.[23] As noted earlier, Kristin Celello argues that Americans' desire to both avoid divorce and ensure a happy marriage led them to seek out experts' advice, which stressed the idea that "hard work could save their relationships."[24] Likewise, sociologist Karla Hackstaff notes that a "marital work ethic"—"the belief that one must *work* on a marriage if it is to survive"[25]—can at least partially be attributed to how it provides a seemingly universal and accessible way to address the uncertainty of contemporary relationships. Pointing to an important assumption within the covenant rhetoric, a marital work ethic implies that anyone can have a successful marriage if they work hard enough. For example, in the "Covenant" lesson at the Exploring Your Relationship Retreat, Monique, the youngest wife on the leadership team, shared, "I have a friend that when she got married, her father told her, 'You're always welcome in this house, as long as you bring your husband.'" As she explained, "I think this is a powerful message to remind my friend to work on your marriage with God and not run home to daddy if things get hard." Of course, this begs the question, *how* does one work on a marriage? This dilemma undergirded premarital counseling programs as the leaders sought to educate couples about relationship skills that they could enact as well as provide them a position from which to motivate and evaluate this work.

Since the covenant rhetoric frequently emphasized Christian marriage as less contingent, it motivated premarital counselors to teach couples that they can *learn* a marital work ethic and *choose* to stay in love. Rather than present marriage as a choice that occurs once at the moment of the proposal, they stressed the idea that people must constantly and consistently make this choice again and again throughout their relationship. For example, Father Lucas presented love as rational and agentic as well as something that individuals are responsible for maintaining.

> Love is a choice, a daily choice. While it's rooted in emotion, it is ultimately a choice. Furthermore, if you want to excel and thrive at it, then you must choose to say "I love you" every day. When you wake up next to your partner and they are lying on the pillow drooling, that is a great time to look at them and say to yourself, "I choose to love this person." Vows are a daily choice.

As with broader marriage education programs, a "skilled love"[26] permeated lessons, which treated the emotion as something that people can cognitively choose, practice, and even control. From this perspective, the quality of a relationship is a result of internal decisions within the couple and capable of offsetting any external stressors such as economic pressures or work conflicts. The emphasis on choice, thus, implies that marital quality and the condition of a relationship are a matter selected by those within it. Likewise, if people have fallen out of love from this perspective, it indicates that they either chose to do so or, at the very least, have not chosen to remain in love. The language of "choice," therefore, normalizes and sacralizes the emotion management of "trying to feel the 'right' feeling."[27]

Making a choice, even a daily one, however, is not sufficient for the success of a marriage. The marital work ethic, therefore, must be accompanied by actual marriage work, which consists of real ongoing practices aimed at meeting relational needs in the relationship.[28] As sociologist Kathleen Jenkins explains, "Marriage work thus involves emotional management of the relationship through development of communication skills, creative management of romance and friendship and the sharing of religious/spiritual orientation."[29] Much of the programs focused on teaching couples a variety of relationship skills they could practice to improve communication, to better avoid unnecessary fights, and to manage the more serious forms of inevitable conflict.

For instance, the entire Exploring Your Relationship Retreat involved socializing couples into a particular relationship skill: writing letters to express one's view on sensitive issues in an uninterrupted manner. After all the talks, people were provided with a series of topical questions from which to choose to write a letter to their partner. In addition to meeting an immediate goal of premarital counseling—helping each person to articulate their point of view and allow the couple to locate potential relational flags—the leadership presented this activity as a type of relationship skill that couples could take with them into their marriage and use when verbal communication broke down.

Although admittedly, writing letters would not be a daily relationship skill, all the leadership team at some point during the retreat mentioned using this tactic to help move past emotional impasses in their marriages. For example, Kelly and Paul explained that after five years of being (for the most part) happily married, they encountered several stressors. Pregnant after years of trying and a miscarriage, they found themselves in a financially tenuous position because Paul had lost his job. When he finally found a job, it came with a number of new hardships. Meanwhile, Kelly at home faced her own challenge of postpartum depression. As each of them individually struggled with their specific stressor, they found it more difficult to communicate with each other about what they were feeling or how they were dealing with these transitions. Eventually remembering how useful the letter writing had been when they had participated in the weekend retreat as an engaged couple, they began to write to each other. As they explained, "these letters began to overcome the emotional distance and build up our relationship to be even stronger." In ending this story, they reiterated the marital work ethic through the covenant rhetoric, saying, "This dark period allowed us to see how people get led to divorce. But because of our initial commitment to lifetime commitment, that was not an option." While acknowledging the ability of external conditions to impact a relationship, their narrative focuses on the ability of couples to choose to stay married and the emotion work that this choice requires.

Sue and Graham, the married couple who led the class on communication at St. Sebastian, presented another tool to monitor the relationship and avoid the type of situation presented above. Describing a similar process of relational separation that developed early in their marriage when they still had young children, Sue and Graham discussed how they established a process of checking in with each other every day. At this point in their marriage, Sue stayed home with very young children and had no one to talk to while Graham worked all day in an office setting. Explaining how she found this really difficult, they established the practice of Graham calling on his way home to have a quick conversation in which they told each other the status of their "emotional bank." As Graham described, "It can be at a high when you're feeling well or low when you need to borrow from the other person." Sue noted that they simply used "a scale of one to ten" to quickly identify their emotional state and inform the other person about what to expect. For instance, if one person was feeling substantially lower, then the other person would know to put their own stuff aside and be sure to make time (and to emotionally prepare) to listen. This practice, according to Graham, "helped me learn that I need to be a listener when I get home." Being sure to indicate the two-way street of this, Sue countered with, "Or, if his number was lower, then sometimes I would let him know to go play a couple rounds of golf to relieve some stress and help him unwind. Since he always had his golf clubs with him, that was an easy option." In concluding their description, Graham clarified the importance of this type of intentional and reflexive practices in one's marriage.

> At this stage in your relationship, a lot of what you do together builds up your emotional bank together. But you will need to learn how to build your own emotional bank because you will become frustrated with your spouse. Also, you will need to find ways to let the other person build up

their own emotional bank. It's important to not forget your own needs, which may require waiting to have some conversations.

As opposed to the previous example of a relationship skill that was meant to address high-stakes turmoil and recommit a couple to their marriage, this tool addressed more mundane stressors and emphasizes the importance of regular and consistent marriage work.

On the issues of communication and conflict management, premarital counselors tended to offer elaborate discussions of highly intentional practices. Stressing the learned dimension to the skills, leaders would occasionally admit that these strategies may seem silly or feel insincere at first, but over time, they should become habitual parts of the way couples interact with each other. Stressing the importance of this work, Darryl told the class at St. Bernadette, "Fighting is hard, and it takes both of you learning how to listen and how to heal afterwards." Likewise, Adam from Cosmopolitan Church warned the engagement class, "Conflicts tend to operate as 'Flare up! Snap! Snap!' You must have the skills to break the momentum of escalation. Escalation is your enemy." In both cases, the ability and necessity of *learning* how to act in a relationship was stressed as a key dimension of the program's potential. As with most types of skills, premarital counselors emphasized practice as a means to help couples make the strategies feel more natural and to become an interactional habit. Toward this end, wedding planning tended to be presented as an ideal time to begin practicing relationship skills because, as leaders would explain, ultimately the stakes are lower and emotions are less intense over decisions about flowers.

Although much of the discussion of relationship skills emphasized these more somber conditions, premarital counselors also encouraged couples to approach their friendship and the romantic dimensions of their relationship as work. Since all the married couples who led the programs had children (many school-age or younger), "quality time" had become a subject of work for them. As mentioned above with the concept of "emotional bank," premarital counselors tried to teach people that eventually, the ease of friendship in the dating stage would wane and companionship would begin to require more careful cultivation. The intentional work of developing good and regular relationship skills, therefore, wasn't only about avoiding conflict but ensuring intimacy by guaranteeing shared time and interests. Reflectively, Darryl told the class at St. Bernadette,

> From what I've seen, the people who do better in their marriages are those that carve out time as a couple. For some, this has meant setting some time in stone. Our neighbors, for instance, go to breakfast together alone on a regular basis and have done it through all four of their children. However, even if you don't set something in stone, you can have other things that take its place. We used to go on walks together.

Laughing, he follows up his point by admitting, "It might have been better if we set things in stone, though." Unlike the relationship skills associated with communication and conflict management, which more clearly delineated states of learned and unlearned, monitoring and maintaining romance and friendship in relationships was less structured by specific strategies. Instead, leaders across the different programs often commented on the type of activities that they enjoy as a couple and the ways they try to carve out space for each other. Recognizing that each couple will have to find the type of activities that actually work to help them feel connected, this topic produced less concrete advice.

Professionalizing the presentation of this approach, Adam, the therapist who co-led the engagement class at Cosmopolitan Church, presented a concept he acknowledged heavily using in his private practice. Describing what he called a "sound relationship house," he explained, successful marriages are characterized by a foundation of a solid friendship that includes, among other things, establishing a shared sense of meaning. To help couples cultivate a shared sense of meaning, one homework assignment required that they think about "their thing" by brainstorming relationship rituals they could develop. Drawing from his own marriage, he informed them that these rituals may need to change over time but that this practice of searching for ways to define themselves as a couple should not.

Marriage work, therefore, represents a lifelong project that one will never perfect. As with the broader neoliberal economy where those who work are seen as more morally deserving,[30] the covenant rhetoric similarly constructs a worthwhile relationship as one where couples work on all parts of it. From Monique's example that people shouldn't "run home to daddy" to Darryl's subtler observation that those who "do better in marriage" work at it, the moralizing of work results in love being earned through hard work. Furthermore, the rationalization of love[31] has meant that all dimensions of a successful relationship from conflict to intimacy require that couples must work on their marriage the same way that people engage in all work, by developing, practicing, and mastering skills. Within a divorce culture where marriage is contingent, to be, and stay, in love requires that people not only have the right tools but make the right choices.

Cultivating a Therapeutic Self

A central tenet within the covenant rhetoric is that it is less self-centered than a contract marriage because it requires couples to work on their marriages by being other-focused. To successfully accomplish this work, however, requires each partner to engage in a deep, self-reflexive process to be able to identify and communicate their needs. Thus, regardless of their call to move from an "I" to a "We," premarital counselors predicate this process on an interrogation of the "Me." Despite positioning itself against secular culture, marriage preparation actually embraces broader cultural trends that understand the self as a "reflexive project . . . a more or less continuous interrogation of past, present and future"[32] and as "something we can work to cultivate and improve."[33] In nurturing this "therapeutic self," premarital counseling teaches people "to identify pathological thoughts and behaviors, to locate the hidden source of these pathologies within one's family past . . . and to triumph over one's past by reconstructing an emancipated and independent self."[34]

At a basic level, all the exercises assigned in marriage preparation programs that are designed to get to know one's partner first require learning to understand oneself more deeply and fully. For example, St. Bernadette's program began by having couples complete a worksheet titled "Discovering Each Other." Next to a series of prompts, such as "My strongest quality," "My usual means of dealing with conflict," and "The biggest adjustment I'll have to make in our first year of marriage," there were two columns that instructed each individual to first identify their own feelings (column A) and then to imagine what the other person wrote down (column B).[35] Likewise, in a session titled "Encounter with Self" at the Exploring Your Relationship Retreat, everyone was provided a list of questions to prompt their personal journaling session that included "How do I see myself?" "How does my description of myself make me feel about myself?" "What masks do I need to remove to reveal more of the real me to you?" All these questions direct the internal reflection process toward articulating the more intangible elements of oneself, especially focusing on the domain of feelings and emotions.

Whereas the exercises often posit this process as merely exploratory about one's inner world, the context of the marriage preparation classes provide people with a sense of what type of self is acceptable, healthy, and moral. For instance, amid these types of activities, Father Lucas at St. Sebastian observed, "It's important to avoid withdrawing and keeping secrets. When you don't want to communicate, then you should ask why?" Likewise, a guest speaker spoke to the classes at Cosmopolitan Church about Gottman's research on the "Four Horsemen": criticism, contempt, defensiveness, and stonewalling.[36] Thus, any self-realizations that occurred within these classes were not without a context or explanatory frame. If, for example, someone realized that they preferred to deal with conflict by going to work out at the gym and never sharing their feeling with their partner, they (or their fiancé[e]) might learn to interpret this as an example of withdrawal or stonewalling.

To fully understand one's innermost self—reactions, emotions, preferences—according to the programs required an interrogation of one's family of origin. As Karen, the religious director at St. Sebastian, explained, "When you form a family, you draw on your own family of origin and their views." The dating class at Cosmopolitan Church dedicated an entire session to exploring the influence of one's family, complete with an assigned reading from *Family Ties That Bind* that explains how one's particular personality develops in relation and response to the other personalities in their family, as well as how families create a series of both spoken and unspoken norms about how to approach all aspects of life.[37] Using the insights hopefully gained from this reading, couples were directed to reflect individually and then talk about "what is it about my family of origin that helps or challenges me in my pursuit of intimacy with my partner?" Sharing their insights from this homework assignment in a small group, a man volunteered that his girlfriend's family "wasn't super close and she's really not used to open communication." To explain, she offered, "I really resonated with the part of the reading where it discussed what was off-limits in our families. In general, I felt like emotions were off-limits, especially excitement and anger." Exercises such as these taught individuals to identify, as well as sometimes pathologize, differences produced by family backgrounds.

Indicating the necessity of completing this type of self-work, especially in the engagement stage, premarital counselors implied that differences in family backgrounds may operate as a "ticking time bomb." As Mary, one of the wives at St. Sebastian, warned,

> The better you know the other person's family of origin the easier it is to be more proactive and less reactive in your relationship. The problem is sometimes people suppress or deny qualities that emerge from their backgrounds because they don't realize what they're doing. It can sometimes take forever for people to recognize this as problematic.

To illustrate this point, she told a story of a friend who married a man who failed to acknowledge or address issues from his family background. Starting off innocently enough, she noted, "Our friend and her husband ended up developing a close relationship with another couple in their church." As time went on, however, the husband apparently became closer to this other wife and even "gave her emotional intimacy." When their unhappy friend objected to the situation, the husband accused her of being "controlling" like his mother. She eventually found out that the husband's father had also cheated on his wife. Locating the problem in a lack of self-work, Mary explained, "Because of these family of origin issues, he had trouble with intimacy, but he didn't see it." From this perspective, a failure to interrogate one's past runs the risk of threatening one's future. By framing this self-work as a necessity, it also positions it as a sign of maturity.[38] In this case, Mary presented the husband's unwillingness to engage as a personal flaw that led to a moral failing.

While sharing a call for all individuals to engage in this process of self-discovery, the nature of selfhood in this "therapeutic self" tended to differ between the evangelical and Catholic programs. Evangelicals more often characterized this process as an attempt to discover one's true and immutable self. For example, in presenting Gary Chapman's *The Five Love Languages*, the leadership team at the Exploring Your Relationship Retreat warned, "Love languages fall under an individual's personality type. You will face colossal failure if you try to change your spouse's personality." In both evangelical programs, premarital counselors privileged psychological concepts, such as personality, to frame the self as something bounded and discoverable. Or to use the language from Michael's lecture on the Johari window discussed earlier, the goal is to ask enough questions to discover the "blind" and "unknown" dimensions of one's self. In contrast, Catholic premarital counselors more often highlighted how people will change over time, offering a less settled conception of "self." As Marcy, one of the Catholic wives at St. Bernadette, told couples,

> It's possible you will continue to have the same conversation over and over again in your marriage, but that's okay because you change as people in the marriage and so you're never the same people. It's important to look at yourself and to describe your views to the other person to check in to see when a change has occurred.

Offering a more mutable conception of the self, Catholic programs focused less on exposing the depths of a person and more on reminding couples that views and feelings on issues may change over time. Although Catholic programs also discussed personality types and love languages, leaders tended to present them as fun and casual exercises to start conversations or to continue learning about one's partner. For both religious traditions, however, the self remained a project to constantly explore, learn to articulate, and share with their partner. Focusing on the self and working to get to know oneself, thus, represented the pathway to intimacy and commitment.

The therapeutic expectation of self-realization and self-improvement[39] becomes sacralized with the therapeutic principles of working on oneself converging with a Christian understanding of sanctification as a process. According to many of the premarital counselors, this work, if done with God in mind, has the potential to deepen one's spirituality. As the leadership team at the Exploring Your Relationship Retreat explained, "We are only as sick as our secrets . . . [but] God has a plan for everyone and this plan entails the construction of our unique personhood, even the trauma that we experience importantly shapes our heart." Likewise, one Catholic wife challenged couples to stop the next time they have an argument and reflect on what it looks like from God's perspective. Specifically, she instructed them to "think about whether you're using the tools He's provided" and to see this "fight as a type of test" and consider how "this helps connect you more to your self and to God." Human imperfection, as discovered through the therapeutic self, becomes a pathway to cultivate deeper intimacy with God and a reminder to trust Him over one's fallible self.

Conclusion

As representatives of their religious communities, Christian premarital counselors presented a covenant marriage rhetoric that blended theological and therapeutic insights to explain how to have a relationship that would be pleasing not only to couples but also to God. On an ideological level, the covenant rhetoric represents an explanatory tool that allows religious communities to repackage and explain macrolevel shifts in family formation, such as the increasing contingency around marriage that sociologist Karla Hackstaff has called divorce culture.[40] Furthermore, as a cultural resource, it became a way that individuals and faith communities justified, legitimated, and reinforced boundaries with secular society.[41] By locating the challenges to a happy marriage externally in the secular culture, the church emerged as authoritatively able to offer the necessary lessons for how to avoid divorce. Embracing and reenvisioning the insights of therapeutic culture, such as a marital work ethic and the self as a project, faith communities have transformed them into tools of religious belonging. The covenant rhetoric ties together happiness and sanctification through claims that living up to God's vision for marriage will combat the more selfish tendencies of human nature and produce a more rewarding experience. Thus, discussions about how to have a *Christian* marriage also represent teachings on emotion management that reflect and refract broader cultural changes in intimacy and relationships.

Despite any nostalgic claims that may have occasionally emerged about Christian marriages as traditional, the covenant rhetoric contains within it assumptions about the salience of love and happiness that reflect what Aziz Ansari and Eric Klinenberg have called a soulmate marriage.[42] Contrasting the "companionate marriage" that dominated older generations, they note that a shift has occurred from "finding someone decent to start a family with" to "finding the perfect person whom you truly, deeply love. Someone you want to share the rest of your life with."[43] As noted earlier, premarital counselors hold marriage to a high standard and believe that only relationships that can last for a lifetime should make it to the altar. Likewise, the covenant rhetoric presents a good marriage as one characterized by more love—for not only the other person but also for God.

Within this framework, "happiness" emerged as both a marital goal and a way to potentially recognize divine approval. Similar to the dynamics uncovered in sociologist Amy Wilkins's analysis of a young college-aged Christian ministry, happiness operates as a moralized emotion that denotes symbolic boundaries and became a way that Christians identified the work of God in their lives.[44] Yet, feelings such as love and happiness were also constructed as requiring careful cultivation on the part of individuals and their ability to recognize their own needs and desires. As evidence of a broader therapeutic ethos, this cultivation points to the expectation that people view themselves as unfinished projects in need of constant work. Couples, thus, found themselves paradoxically situated between trying to fight against a contract perspective on relationships that promoted the self over one's partner and the covenant rhetoric that called them to engage in self-work as a means to become a better partner.

The tension about the role of the self in the covenant rhetoric points to a broader neoliberal dilemma within contemporary American marriage and therapeutic culture. Since the mid-twentieth century, a narrative of personal risk and responsibility has come to dominate key American institutions and transformed our cultural understandings of obligation and dependency.[45] For marriage, this has meant that the new cultural ideals that privilege love and happiness in marriage have transformed the institution to be potentially more equitable but also more fragile.[46] Against this backdrop, the emphasis on a marital work ethic and cultivating a therapeutic self are strategies that individualize the broader challenge of "insecure intimacies."[47] After all, today's couples face "rising job uncertainty, increasingly fragile relationships, and mounting work-family conflicts,"⁴⁸ which can result in pressures and tensions on both the individual and couple. These challenges, however, are deeply gendered and reflect the legacy of gender complementarianism, which has been popular among Christians. The next chapter turns to explore when and how gender emerged as a form of difference that people must negotiate in their efforts to obtain a covenant marriage.

4

Teaching Gender (and) Differences in Marriage

On a gray Saturday morning typical for the Pacific Northwest, I joined six couples for what would be our first full day of the Exploring Your Relationship Retreat. Whereas the previous evening we had a few introductory sessions, this morning had started early at 7:00 a.m. with time to eat a continental breakfast before meeting promptly at 8:00 a.m. for our first session on the "Self." As I returned to my seat after our short break between sessions, I noticed a handout had been placed on my desk. The bright green page stood out against the light wood of the desk and emblazoned on it were the words "DO NOT TURN OVER UNTIL INSTRUCTED TO DO SO!" As I waited, curious about what could be on the other side, I looked around and noticed a PowerPoint slide on the overhead projector with the title "Chances of a Man Winning an Argument." Underneath was a chart that listed phases of a relationship on the x-axis—dating, engagement, and marriage—and the likelihood that a man will win an argument on the y-axis. In a series of descending steps, the graph illustrated that men's chances of winning decrease over time as the commitment of the relationship increases. Between the mysterious page and the faux-scientific chart, I began to wonder about what would be next on our agenda. Since I still had a little time as I waited for everyone to return from their couples conversations, I turned to the schedule to learn that our next lesson would be "Different by Design."

Once everyone had taken their seat and was quietly facing the leadership at the front of the room, Kelly, one of the wives who co-led the program, announced, "Turn over your handout and quickly answer the questions." It turned out that on the other side of the page was a short "Difference Questionnaire" that included eighteen questions. Before I answered them, I first read the written instructions, which reiterated the importance of not overthinking the exercise, stating, "Answer on the basis of your knowledge and feelings at this moment. Do not spend too much time on each question." As I looked up and down the page,

I noticed that the questions ranged. Some asked for my feelings about my "fiancé" as a person, such as "Does he/she notice new things?" or "Does he/she express respect and admiration to others?" Other questions inquired about feelings that they may elicit in me, such as "Does your fiancé's voice irritate you?" A number of questions required me to reflect on how we interact and communicate, such as "Are you usually the listener in conversations?" or "Does he/she interrupt and anticipate what you wish to say?" In less than two minutes, I had finished reading each question and selected either often, seldom, or never. As I came to the end of the questionnaire, I noticed the bottom of the page warned, "Realize DIFFERENCES. Become AWARE of how you feel about them. Share your feeling. *Do not create differences that do not, in fact, exist.*"[1] Perhaps because of the PowerPoint slide that emphasized gender differences, I had expected the worksheet to be similar. Yet, I was struck by how the "differences" on the questionnaire were less innate characteristics and instead focused on my feelings about interactions, communication styles, and perceptions of the other person. In fact, the worksheet felt cautionary, especially with its ending warning that differences are something to be aware of but not to cultivate in relationships.

My internal contemplation about the dissimilar approaches to "difference" was interrupted by Paul's announcement that "this could be a thing to go over during your discussion time." Without inquiring about how people responded to the questionnaire or commenting on the "Chances of a Man Winning an Argument" chart, Paul and Kelly changed the slide. With "Learning to COMPLEMENT and COMPLETE . . ." projected behind the leadership team, Paul explained, "It is common to find opposites in spouses. People can be opposite in a variety of ways from worldviews, sibling order, or personality. They can differ in how they do things, such as how they sleep, drive, prefer to vacation, or food choices." To illustrate their own differences, Paul and Kelly quickly took turns explaining how their favorite foods differ. Shifting to adopt a more serious tone, Paul continued, "The differences between partners are rooted in the creation story in Genesis, which describes the creation of men and women." With a quick aside that "feminism" and "secular culture" have made this message difficult to hear, they explained that "God intentionally made men and women different. Specifically, He has made them to complement one another. The differences were meant to be advantageous but due to the Fall became a source of constant struggle." The Exploring Your Relationship Retreat's introduction to the "Different by Design" session illustrates the prominent ways that difference emerged as an individualized but inevitable challenge in couples' journeys to a covenant marriage. Yet, it also showcases the complexity and variability contained within the rhetoric of "difference."

Marriage as a social institution has long been predicated on the assumption that individuals' social differences must be overcome as people transition to become one happy family. As historian Rebecca Davis observed in reflecting on changes in marriage counselors' advice, however, "marriage experts who once envisioned marriage as something two people *became* as they adjusted themselves to marital roles began to describe marital success as something a couple could *do* as it practiced the requisite skills and communicated the appropriate emotions to achieve mutual fulfillment."[2] Whereas in earlier eras, the model of a companionate marriage was founded on strict roles that made gender the primary axis of social difference, the shift to an individualized marriage that calls for partners to practice therapeutic skills has reenvisioned the types of differences that are seen as salient. In an individualized marriage characterized by both partners being "expected to develop a separate sense of self, to communicate more openly about their needs, and to have more flexible roles,"[3] difference has expanded to a number of factors, including personality, ambitions, neuroses, family of origin, and more, which all are seen as having the potential to be disruptive and put a relationship at risk. As a consequence, the explicit "gendered self" in marriage has largely been discursively supplanted by a "therapeutic self"[4] informed by a diffuse system of knowledge known as "psychology," which includes both the theories produced by more formalized systems of expertise and those more colloquially seen as "self-help."[5]

The shift away from marital advice that emphasizes "gender roles" mirrors the egalitarian ideals of younger generations contemplating what they want from marriage, whether to enter into the institution, and how they want to *do* marriage.[6] For example, sociologist Kathleen Gerson's interviews with young adults found that "most want to create flexible, egalitarian partnership with considerable room for personal autonomy."[7] This personal goal emerged in part from watching relationships in their parents' generation—their efforts to balance work and family, the unequal consequences of divorce, and what seemed to make people happy—and they realized that instead of "fixed, rigid behavioral strategies and mental categories demarcating separate spheres for women and men,"[8] gender flexibility characterized by fluid boundaries and obligations was more effective in negotiating the challenges in family life. Despite this realization and their own aspirations, people find themselves confronting how marriage operates as a gendered institution that delineates behaviors, feelings, and expectations.

This chapter interrogates the variation in the type of "differences" that marriage preparation programs presented as potential barriers to the covenant rhetoric's goal of oneness. Although all the programs emphasized that couples must identify and evaluate how differences shape their relationship, there was a split on whether gender or psychology operated as the primary axis of difference. Discursively, the two *gender difference programs* presented gender complementarian views that sacralize gender roles that contend God created "ontological differences between men and women" and that specifically conceptualize men as innately "predisposed to leadership, activity, and a strong work ethic, while women are naturally nurturing, passive, and receptive."[9] By situating the explicitly gendered discourses within the broader curriculum, however, we will see how this view did not dominate their overall advice and examine how lessons on what to do in marriage actually destabilize claims about gender difference. Next, the chapter illustrates how *gender-blind programs* constructed the challenge as a multidimensional task of exploring psychological differences and those emerging from social background. Gender was not only rarely openly used to account for behaviors or attitudes in relationships, but the same examples that would be coded as masculine or feminine in the other programs were explained with gender-neutral concepts, such as extrovert versus introvert or family of origin. Regardless of the degree to which programs were vocal or silent on gender differences, all four exclusively imagined gender as a property of individuals, which rendered invisible how marriage operates as a gendered institution. Thus, marital advice on how to manage differences to attain the covenant rhetoric's goal to have a good, godly, and happy marriage fail to prepare couples for how to negotiate dimensions of gendered power.

Recognizing and Embracing Difference in Marriage

The covenant rhetoric sacralizes secular marital advice to "create shared meaning"[10] by calling couples to join with God. It suggests that in addition to the external challenges posed by secular culture pushing an "I" orientation in relationships, couples face an internal challenge of negotiating and overcoming their differences to reach a state of oneness. As such, the work of premarital counseling challenges each person to ask themselves: Who am I? Who are you? How are we different? How do we become a "we" despite these differences? Since any marriage inevitably requires two individuals to craft a shared life together, premarital counselors work to guide couples in recognizing important points of difference in a manner that forges a unitive relationship. As a result, acknowledging, working with, and overcoming differences featured prominently in all the programs.

Much of the discussions and activities began from the assumption that couples must explore internal differences within their relationship. For example, at St. Sebastian, the leadership team provided everyone with a handout on forgiveness that asked them to evaluate how each partner handles feeling hurt, when they are wrong, and how they behave when they have hurt someone else. The associated writing activity for "Different by Design" at the Exploring Your Relationship Retreat, discussed earlier, asked couples to reflect on "What are some of our biggest differences? How might those differences help us complement and complete each other?" Exploring points of individual difference was predicated on the idea that it could help assess the viability of the relationship (whether they should get married) and mitigate assumptions each person had about the other (reducing the tendency to project one's own expectations onto their partner). After establishing this landscape of relational difference, premarital counselors sought to equip couples with a variety of relationship skills aimed at reducing interactional differences and replacing them with a common ground. The "emotional bank" practice discussed earlier, for example, requires that each individual identify how they feel, share it in the form of a number, and then compare the difference with their spouse. Many programs also tried to facilitate "active listening" skills by encouraging each person to try to restate the view of their partner before proceeding to explicate their own position.

Working to identify and soften differences, however, was framed by an explicit discussion that differences are natural and often God-given. For example, the leadership team at the Exploring Your Relationship Retreat told everyone on the first night, "The goal in marriage is oneness and unity with someone who is different than oneself. . . . Marriage is a place to learn about loving God because the oneness in marriage deepens our understanding of God." Likewise, Michael cautioned dating couples at Cosmopolitan Church,

> The goal isn't to be the same or to try and change the other person to suit one's needs. Rather, the goal is to celebrate the differences between oneself and one's partner. According to longitudinal studies, satisfaction is highest when couples celebrate differences and similarities. In this way, relationships make us better versions of ourselves. By not just accepting the "warts" but by celebrating them as the unique design of God, couples are happier and more satisfied.

Reflecting their tendency to operate from a more immutable sense of self than the Catholic programs, the discussions among evangelicals conceptualized difference as something that couples *must* accept about the other person. In each case, difference became part of a way to witness God's vision and to reflect on His intentional design. Trying to change one's partner, therefore, was not only presented as foolhardy but as working against God, who created this person to be a particular way.

Similar to their evangelical counterparts, the Catholic parishes also made sure to inform couples about the inevitability of difference, but they less often presented difference as a tool of sanctification. For example, Marcy, the wife who co-led the session on communication and conflict at St. Bernadette, explained,

> As part of getting to know each other before you get married, it's important to recognize the big differences because getting married is a big step. But it's also important to remember that even as well as you know your partner that you don't know everything and that they will not stay the same. It's important to respect that we all change over time and that there are multiple perceptions.

Even though difference remained a real and important part of a relationship, it was less severe from this perspective. As Father Lucas from St. Sebastian offered, "It's important to recognize that the qualities that you love about your spouse, those aren't going to go away, but they will deepen and change." Operating from a framework that viewed the self as variable, the Catholic parishes depicted difference as a constant dimension in marriage but not necessarily consistent in form. They stressed the idea that interests, opinions, hobbies, jobs, and even abilities may change over time. Difference, thus, operated less as an avenue into God's intentions but still required intentional monitoring and regular renewal of one's commitment to the relationship. Or as Father Lucas also noted, "We discover ourselves in the other. The importance is saying, 'I'll stay here.'"

The divergent conceptualization of the nature of the self likely helps explain the disparity in the attention to the topic of difference I observed between the Catholic and evangelical programs. Both operated from the assumption that marriage preparation must involve exploring individual-level differences among the couples, but evangelicals tended to focus almost exclusively on exploring these (presumably) discrete internal worlds. With their greater emphasis on marriage preparation also serving as a form of religious education, Catholic programs tended to veer from this topic to pontificate on the religious and personal significance of marriage. Regardless of variations in the intensity, every program operated from the perspective that differences must be recognized and addressed in marriage. To confront this issue, however, required the leadership to identify what they saw as the most salient examples of difference in couples' education. Despite the dominant trend in scholarship on gender regimes in conservative religions that have emphasized the salience of complementarianism, I found that gender difference rhetoric emerged inconsistently and infrequently across the programs.[11]

Explanations of (Gender) Difference

As historian Nancy Cott observes, "the whole system of attribution and meaning that we call *gender* relies on and to a great extent derives from the structuring provided by marriage."[12] For example, the constructions of men as active and predisposed to leadership and ideas that women are nurturing and passive both describe and prescribe how men and women are expected to act in marriage. These "gender roles" create social scripts for the division of labor in marriage but also extend earlier into relationships by patterning how men are expected to take the initiative to ask women out, pay for dates, and propose.[13] Broadly, sociologists conceptualize gender as a "social institution, not an inherent trait . . . that shapes organizations and opportunity structures as well as personal experience."[14] One of the key ways that gender shapes marriage is by organizing distinct social practices for men and women that in turn pattern the heteronormative expectations and feelings people encounter as wives and husbands. In other words, sociologists highlight that the differential ways that men and women experience and feel about marriage emerge not from internal characteristics but as a result of social expectations and accountability systems that establish different ways of "doing" gender[15] in marriage.

Compared with the earlier eras where men and women could have been more likely described as existing in separate spheres, contemporarily they are educated alongside each other, work together, and aspire to similar goals in work and family life.[16] Yet, despite these shared characteristics, "in the most common usage," gender continues to "mean the cultural differences of women from men, based on the biological division between male and female."[17] Next, we explore this tension by investigating when and how gender was conceptualized as different, as well as what impact this had on advice for how to obtain the good marriage encapsulated in the covenant rhetoric. In reviewing how premarital counseling constructed the challenge of difference, I found that two programs emphasized gender and two emphasized psychological explanations. Importantly, these patterns occurred within both religious traditions with one Catholic and one evangelical Protestant group belonging to each category.

TABLE 4.1. Explanations of Gender and Difference in Marriage Preparation

	Gender as One Source of Difference	Explaining Relational Difference through Psychology
View on Gender	Gender Essentialism	Gender-Blind
Perspective on Difference	Difference Is Necessary	Difference Must Be Managed
Scriptural Model for Marriage	Genesis Stories	Jesus's Love for His Disciples
Marriage Preparation Programs	Explore Your Relationship Retreat and St. Sebastian	Cosmopolitan Church and St. Bernadette

Gender as One Source of Difference
LEARNING THE DIFFERENCES BETWEEN MEN'S BRAINS AND WOMEN'S BRAINS AT THE EXPLORING YOUR RELATIONSHIP RETREAT

The Exploring Your Relationship Retreat emerged as the only marriage preparation program to espouse what many consider to be the standard rhetoric by conservative religious groups on gender and relationships.[18] As sociologist John Bartkowski found in his review of evangelical advice manuals, many of the bestsellers posit that "men and women are different in a range of psychological and social capacities," a view authors believe emerges from God's divine plan.[19] The session discussed earlier, "Different by Design," operated from this perspective.

As already described, the leadership conceptualized gender differences as part of God's original design in the creation stories in Genesis but argued that the contemporary relational challenges they present are a consequence of the Fall. The session continued by using the self-help book *Men Are like Waffles, Women Are like Spaghetti* by Bill and Pam Farrel to explain how gender differences must be understood before couples can mitigate them.[20] Describing the central argument of the book to a room full of people like myself who may not have had any experience with it, Paul and Kelly explained,

> Men think in terms of boxes. When they are in one box, they focus on that but don't think about any other boxes. Some boxes are even men's space to not think at all but to escape and recharge. In contrast, women are like spaghetti because they approach life in an intricate and interconnected way that involves seeing the connections between things, as opposed to viewing them separately. Due to women's spaghetti brain, they are better at multitasking and processing the connections between things. Men's box thinking, however, makes them better [and] natural problem solvers.

These differences, they clarified, "can lead to difficulties in men and women's communication with each other." To illustrate the concept in action, they offered an example from their own marriage of when Kelly approached Paul to talk but had not realized that he was in "his empty box." Although she had interpreted his sitting on the couch as him "not doing anything," Kelly explained that she had failed to realize that he was actually "recharging." Despite the difficulties to marriage that gender differences may pose, they stressed the importance of learning these communication patterns as critical to marital happiness. Joking that "a happier woman means a happier man," Kelly offered insights into how men could help women work through the limitations of their communication style. Commenting on her own experience, she noted, "Sometimes I get so hung up in seeing all the intricate connections that I need someone to sort my spaghetti and put it in boxes. In these situations, his box thinking can sort my spaghetti."

From this perspective, men's and women's distinct ways of processing their social worlds need not necessarily produce conflict and it only will do so if people deny the reality of gendered modes of communication. Implicating the covenant rhetoric's "other-orientation," they urged couples to approach their partner from the communication style that fits the other person's needs and not their own. In practice, they counseled, couples should ask themselves, "Whose needs does this conversation satisfy?" If the man needs the conversation, then the focus should be "only on the one box." For women to help this will require that they "refrain from trying to jump between boxes and focusing on interconnections." In contrast, in conversations for the woman, they advised, "It may be helpful to begin processing your thoughts before the conversation by praying or journaling because this will help you think about what you want to talk about."

Although presented as a type of mutuality in marriage, these examples actually normalize an understanding of masculinity as taciturn and encourage more emotion work for wives, as well as imply her greater responsibility for managing the relationship.[21] In their personal example, Kelly presented herself as more responsible for monitoring Paul's moods. Likewise, their ending advice offered two examples of emotion work for women that operate against her supposed natural state: women must refrain from thinking about the interconnections in men's conversations *and* must think on their own before bringing their topic to their husbands. This type of discussion, of course, is not unique to evangelical Protestants. A significant number of secular self-help publications articulate a similar view, with John Gray's *Men Are from*

Mars, Women Are from Venus as a classic example.[22] More recently, sociologist Jennifer Randles found in her review of curricula used in the state-sponsored Healthy Marriage Initiative programs that many, including the most popular ones, "emphasized that men and women have distinct gendered communication styles that thwart interpersonal marital happiness."[23]

In an interview with Paul and Kelly, Paul explained that "the roles of marriage" could be found in the Ephesians 5 assertion that "wives submit to your husbands and husbands love your wives." Yet, he also wanted to complicate what he saw as the "general Christian understanding of the guy is supposed to somehow be the head and the wife is supposed to somehow submit." Returning to Genesis, Paul clarified that the origins of these roles come from the complications of the Fall:

> Going back to Genesis—with Adam and Eve, when God came in and said, "Okay, you're going to do this, and you're going to do this"—what was God trying to do there? A lot of church history ends up somehow saying because of what God did, the woman is somehow [in] a lesser role. Like, she sinned a greater sin than Adam. And you see that in church hierarchy, and in teaching, and in cultural kind of things. Our opinion would be that this couldn't be further from the truth. God created man and woman equally. He loves them equally. He just assigned [them]—because of the Fall and what happened in that Fall—different roles. Not as punishment, but he assigned them roles that made them more dependent on God to be able to fulfill that role. Roles that were almost opposite of what their personality and their abilities were, so it made them function in a way that makes them rely on God more.

This presentation of Genesis differs from both camps of formal discourse that Bartkowski identified in his review of the scriptural interpretation in popular conservative Protestant advice manuals on gender and family.[24] In stressing the importance of different roles for men and women, their view aligns with the essentialist perspective. Yet, as opposed to men and women having been created differently by God, Paul casts the scripturally sanctioned gender roles as only emerging *after* the Fall and, specifically, stressed the original equality of God's design. To clarify the intentions of these assigned roles, he went on to say,

There's a deeper thing going on there in God assigning roles. In God saying, wives submit to your husbands, and husbands love your wives and be a leader. Those weren't like punishing her and rewarding him; they're putting us in positions that are difficult to walk out [on]. And, therefore, we need to rely on God in order to work on them. Adam and Eve didn't rely on God; Eve led without relying on God [and] Adam followed without relying on God. So God said, "Okay, Adam, you're going to have to lead. Eve you're going to have to follow." And to do that, it's really going to take God for you to work [it] out.

Elaborating on this explanation, Kelly noted, "He gave us different types of personalities because that's another place that we can do this deeper transformational thing in our hearts and learn to depend on God for something that isn't natural."

Their understanding blends the different views of gender as natural and as a social construct, as well as essentialist and sameness rhetoric. Men and women are presented as naturally different—distinct communication styles and personality traits—but this is not presented as the foundation of gender roles. Gender differences instead represent a barrier to unity with God, calling couples to resolve it through the covenant rhetoric by being other-centric (adopting traits that are not easy or natural but focus on their partner). Paul and Kelly believe this rationale may help people to understand and be challenged by the call in Ephesians 5 and replace the notion that it devalues women. As Kelly expounded, "There's something He's wanting to do in women that's deeper than 'Eve screwed up, so I'm going to punish all women for the rest of eternity.'" Because, as Paul summed up, "God didn't create women to be doormats."

The essentialist and complementarian view on gender, however, largely operated as a background framework to the retreat. As noted earlier, explicit examples such as the above discussion on gendered communication actually occurred infrequently. Most lessons and exercises involved the leadership team unpacking the types of issues couples would confront in marriage. In fact, the rest of the "Different by Design" session also focused on other topics that could produce dissimilar expectations for the home, such as finances and family of origin. Based on previous research that highlighted the primacy of gender complementarity and essentialism among evangelicals, I had anticipated that marriage preparation would spend considerable time articulating visions of a "good wife" in opposition to a "good husband." Instead, most of the content aimed at educating *both* men and women toward the nongendered goal of how to be a "good spouse." Offering more universal advice, for example, the ending discussion in the difference session used language of "spouse," indicating the importance of the message for both men and women.

> To not fall victim to man's view, it's important to learn to not be dissatisfied with differences. Too often, we try to change our partner to be more like us; we think that our way is the best way to deal with a problem or solve a dilemma. But trying to change a person doesn't allow them to be the person God created them to be. God knows that a person needs their spouse's differences to be a whole person. God created these differences with the goal of the spouses completing each other and to process parts of their self.

With the exception of the still fairly popular convention of describing "humans" as "men," gender did not emerge explicitly as part of the discussion. On the one hand, as it was part of a session that presented distinct patterns of communication for men and women, it is possible to interpret this advice as implicitly gendered. On the other hand, the quote more immediately followed an explanation on how one's family of origin can produce different ideas of "normal." Rather than return to highlight gender, the emphasis is more broadly on the challenges of recognizing myriad of differences between oneself and one's partner.

Furthermore, despite explicit claims that men and women communicate differently, the retreat structured communication between the partners in the same manner. Men and women were provided the same list of questions on which to journal individually. During couples time, both were instructed to read the information twice to fully process the material. To help "deepen and enhance dialogue," the leaders also provided them with a list of suggested prompts to elicit greater detail from their partner about how they feel. In fact, the welcome session that introduced couples to the structure of the retreat never mentioned the idea that men and women do or must communicate differently. The session described above on difference did not occur until the following day. Thus, the Exploring Your Relationship Retreat did clearly and explicitly construct gender along lines of difference to engaged couples, but it was not a central or consistent part of the weekend.

In sum, the retreat's position on gender complementarianism, submission, and essentialism reveals the instability and flexibility of salient and sacred beliefs within conservative religious groups. Consistent with other research on evangelicals, the leadership drew on social and scriptural logics to assert the validity and importance of gender as a system of difference that can produce a multitude of problems in relationships. Yet, over twenty-five years have passed since the polarized debates on mutual submission and male headship, which occurred in the 1960s to mid-1990s.[25] The evangelical views presented at the Exploring Your Relationship Retreat provide insights into how this intellectual and theological legacy has been renegotiated and reinterpreted over time. The inconsistent use of gender difference rhetoric points to concerns about alienating today's young adults and a sense that it is not the primary purpose of premarital counseling. As much as they believed in the transformative value of this teaching on God's vision of gender, leadership worried about it getting in the way of the overall experience, which they envisioned as helping couples assess and prepare their relationship for marriage. Most of the other sites did not even emphasize gender as much in their programming.

LEARNING THE CULTURAL DIFFERENCES OF GENDER AT ST. SEBASTIAN

St. Sebastian also explicitly included gender as an axis of difference but was less articulate or, apparently, committed to this view than the Exploring Your Relationship Retreat. With the weekly rotation of leadership, the Catholic marriage preparation programs spent more class time on "get-to-know-you activities," which created less opportunity for new content. Additionally, as a form of religious education, the Catholic programs dedicated time to explaining a sacramental marriage, which also contributed to shifting the attention away from explanations and pursuits of individual-level differences. St. Sebastian, however, did briefly address "gender differences."

The first class at this parish entailed a middle-aged couple covering a wide array of topics, each with limited depth, to explore the theme of "expectations on marriage." In addition to an introduction and icebreaker where everyone listed characteristics of their "ideal marriage," Linda and Dennis provided brief description of four types of love (*storge, eros, philia,* and divine), family of origin, cultural differences, their experiences with natural family planning, gender differences, personality differences, love languages, and what marriage will be like. As with the Exploring Your Relationship Retreat, there was an explicit section on "gender differences," as they called it, but proportionally, it accounted for less of their time on relational differences. Since this one evening covered several topics that the retreat divided across multiple sessions, the examples and descriptions were less detailed.

To start off the discussion on "gender differences," Linda and Dennis provided a little personal background on gender roles in their homes growing up. Dennis explained that his dad worked full time and his mom had only worked part time. Before he could get any further, Linda interjected, "She had the hardest job of all—raising four kids." Acquiescing, he continued by mentioning that since his dad worked the graveyard shift, it was difficult for him to rest in the house with all four kids running around. Without too much detail on Linda's family background (her father had died young), Dennis shifted to comment opaquely that "the drive for equality has created new stereotypes and even created reactionary stereotypes." Warningly, he advised everyone, "Do not equate equality with sameness. The differences in male and female are part of the intent of creation."

Stepping in to provide a personal example, Linda clarified that she really needs a "compassionate listener," and he tends to offer advice, which is "okay about half of the time." Turning to look at her husband as she said this next part, Linda reassuringly reminded him that he does not really do this anymore, "but in the past, Dennis tended to say things like 'It's no big deal,' which was bad. This is a classic gender difference. In general, women want to talk out issues and men want to act on them. Of course, this is just a generality." Reaching out to the coffee table in the center of the circle of chairs, she picked up a copy of John Gray's *Men Are from Mars, Women Are from Venus*. As she did this, Linda explained how they read this book as part of a couples' group they belonged to in the parish and found it "really helpful." Again, undercutting their gendered assertions, she added the caveat, "But we don't fit into the gender differences in places. He isn't very into sports. He *may* know what they are." Dennis jokingly responded that since he had recently taken to wearing a jacket with a sports team logo, he has had to learn a little bit because people always ask him how the team is doing. Linda continued elaborating on their non-normative interests by announcing how she enjoys classic cars. Looking intently at his wife, Dennis affectionately commented, "It's pretty cool when she throws out stuff like info on cubic inch displacement when we go to car fairs." Linda merely shrugged nonchalantly in response as Dennis repeated, "Pretty cool."

With that brief and personal introduction to the idea that men and women differ because of gender, the discussion ended. Next, the couples had a ten-minute breakout session in which they completed a worksheet titled "Family of Origin Roles and Styles of Relating." As opposed to picking up on the theme of gender, it asked couples to reflect on their families: "What do you find attractive about your family?" "How has your family dealt with pain and crisis?" "In what ways has your family been generous?" Once they finished quickly answering these questions and talking through their responses, Linda regained the couples' attention by explaining, "Let's keep moving forward."

Similar to the Exploring Your Relationship Retreat, the leadership presented gender as a source of difference that manifests in a distinct set of communication styles, needs, and interests. To support these assertions, both programs turned to an example of a popular self-help book to bolster anecdotes about how the couples differ as men and women in their own marriages. Linda and Dennis, however, appeared less committed to or invested in the idea of gender difference. Unlike the detailed discussion of *how* men and women process their social worlds and communicate differently, they simply asserted that differences exist without providing a clear or detailed account of the ways that they manifest or their scope. In contrast to the retreat, Linda and Dennis offered no universal explanation for or consistent presentation of gender differences. Furthermore, the claims were undercut by a series of caveats that cast suspicion on the universal declaration that they began with.

A story Linda shared in our interview indicated that she and Dennis view gender differences as mostly a cultural product and not a result of innate qualities. In explaining their goal for the class that they led, Dennis commented, "You have to examine the stuff you've been used to doing all your life that you take for granted as being accepted and normal." Providing an example of how people can have knee-jerk reactions to what appears different from their normal, Linda described her brother, who married a Middle Eastern woman and lived abroad at the time of the interview:

> [My brother and sister-in-law] have some huge cultural differences, especially in terms of gender roles. Like, a quick example is my brother is, you know, he had four sisters. He was saying that he just does not relate to most of the men in that culture. It's so much more . . . the social structure is more male dominated. And he just makes friends more easily with women. Well, his wife got all upset. Her dad never had female friends, you know? Didn't talk with them. I think he was maybe just texting one of his coworkers, or, you know, it was all very innocent. I know my brother. But she took it as this threat. I mean, it was kind of a big crisis in their marriage. And it was just this huge cultural difference.

While ostensibly discussing gender roles in this example, she mostly uses it as an entry point into the significance of how cultural backgrounds and family of origin shape individual expectations of what is normal or appropriate ways to interact with other people. In fact, it's possible to read this as less an example of "gender differences" but a coded discussion on race, Islam, or non-Western countries. Altogether, however, Linda and Dennis's lessons tended to deemphasize gender complementarianism to instead construct gender as one form of difference that couples will have to negotiate in marriage. At best, gender difference appeared to be broad generalities that could always have outliers.

The notion that gender complementarianism is divinely inspired was only put forward during St. Sebastian's class on sacramental marriage. After drawing a yin-yang symbol on the whiteboard, Karen, the religious director, described,

> I'm going to use a non-Christian symbol to think about fruitfulness and completeness with God. We, as humans, aren't complete and we only represent part of the species. If you were to gather all the women together,

that'd be great, but it wouldn't be a representation of the fullness of humanity. Father Tony one time explained in a homily how all the systems of the body are essentially the same in men and women. The one system where they are unique is a great sign of the need for men and women to be together—it's a sign of physical complementarity, a sign of unity, and how we are made in this world. It shows us how we are to experience ourselves as oriented towards another: man to woman and woman to man.

As a religious professional, Karen stressed the official teachings of the Catholic Church, which view gender as divinely designed to be different. Specifically, her perspective reflected insights from Pope John Paul II's *Theology of the Body*, which asserted, "The body, which expresses femininity 'for' masculinity and, vice versa, masculinity 'for' femininity, manifests the reciprocity and the communion of persons."[26] Likewise, Pope Francis reaffirmed this view:

> Valuing one's own body in its femininity or masculinity is necessary if I am going to be able to recognize myself in an encounter with someone who is different. In this way we can joyfully accept the specific gifts of another man or woman, the work of God the Creator, and find mutual enrichment. It is not a healthy attitude which would seek to cancel out sexual difference because it no longer knows how to confront it.[27]

As with the formal Catholic teachings on gender complementarianism, however, Karen reduced gender to sex.[28] In other words, this is not an explanation about how gender produces different styles of communication or needs between men and women but, instead, focuses on the physiology of bodies. This emphasis on embodiment may explain why gender did not emerge significantly in considerations about how to negotiate differences in marriage.

As with the Exploring Your Relationship Retreat, gender difference rhetoric represented a minimal amount of the overall content. Most of the programming focused on instructing both men and women on how to become good spouses and to create a meaningful partnership. For example, in a discussion on "Moral Decisions in Marriage," Karen and Father Lucas explained how the Ten Commandments can be applied to thinking about marital life. For the seventh commandment (Thou shall not steal), they noted that this obviously indicates that you should not steal another person's spouse but that a more positive interpretation would be to think about stewardship. As Karen clarified, "We are called to be good stewards of our home." Encouraging the participants to be intentional about their home life, she cautioned against allowing other things to "steal time away from them as a couple." Without singling out either men or women, she informed everyone that "how much time one commits to their job is a moral decision." Overall, gender differences emerged occasionally within this program, but the leaders did not dwell on them in their exploration of dimensions of difference.

Explaining Relational Differences through Psychology
LEARNING ABOUT THE SPIRITUAL SIGNIFICANCE OF THERAPEUTIC ADVICE AT ST. BERNADETTE

While following a similar organizational format with married couples rotating each week to talk on different topics—including communication, conflict, wedding liturgy, and a sacramental marriage—gender complementarianism was absent at St. Bernadette. This program dedicated little time to exploring matters of interpersonal differences, such as personality, love languages, family of origin, or gender. Each evening, the married couples (and the priest who spoke on wedding liturgy) instead wove in relevant insights about personal differences that they believed emerge in response to people's family backgrounds. At times, this approach resulted in a subtle critique of the perception that Catholic marriages involve gendered hierarchies.

The first evening of class served as an introductory session with everyone, leadership and participants, going around in a circle to share reflections about adults in their lives whom they have looked up to as role models for marriage. Going after the two other married couples on the leadership team, Marcy and Darryl shared how they had to learn "what the church and a community of faith can provide" by looking at relationships other than their parents' marriages. As Darryl explained, "Both of our parents are still married, but their marriages weren't necessarily the model that we hoped for in our own relationship." To elaborate, Marcy described how she had to relearn the concept of a Catholic marriage because of the way that her parents had modeled one.

My parents were loving but more traditional with my mom serving my dad. Growing up, I associated a Catholic marriage with this more hierarchical model and had to learn to see a Catholic marriage in a more egalitarian manner. I had to grow to understand that mutual serving is the basis of a Catholic marriage and it's not about a subservient expectation where one person gives up themselves for the other person and is in a state of inequality. It took me a while to see this other model and I found it in watching how the marriages around me functioned in a way that the couples served each other in a lot of ways.

Setting the tone for the class, she offered a soft criticism of the headship rhetoric that has dominated many Christian ideals of marriage.[29] Marcy's personalized discussion helped ensure it was not a critique of the Catholic Church and, instead, cast hierarchical marriages as personal choices, rather than religiously sanctioned.

The remainder of their introduction continued with this redemptive story by detailing how returning to the Church as adults helped them to find role models for happy and spiritual marriages. Following this night, subsequent classes operated from a similar subtle and implicit gender egalitarian framework that remained silent on the existence of innate and complementarian gender differences as espoused by the broader Catholic Church. Since silence can be more difficult to empirically locate than vocal rhetoric, I focus the analysis here on the topics that produced gendered discourse in the other programs.

Both Catholic parishes dedicated an evening to refreshing (or more often, teaching) couples about the significance and value of a sacramental marriage. Following writings from the Vatican, Karen at St. Sebastian had made a point of discussing God's vision of gender complementarianism during the creation of humankind. In contrast, the married couple who led the sacramental class at St. Bernadette, Arnie and Leslie, never explicitly mentioned gender differences as part of God's vision. In fact, the creation stories of Genesis did not appear in their talk. Instead, they elevated the relationship between Jesus and his disciples as a model for marriage. After an awkward silence produced by Arnie asking all the couples to define a sacrament, they spent some time elucidating sacraments and detailing all seven of them. Putting it plainly, Arnie offered, "A sacrament, then, is about asking Jesus Christ to walk with you and become present in your life. So what does this mean in marriage?" After breakout sessions where the couples had five minutes to discuss the type of things that they can "do to bring Jesus into their relationship," everyone regrouped and provided answers such as "coming to church together," "a family altar," and "prayer." Turning their attention to actual actions of Jesus in the New Testament, Arnie reminded them, "There are some basic things that Jesus did to bring himself into this world, such as washing feet and cooking for his disciples. These are good reminders. Doing the dishes and laundry are ways to express your love for your partner. Because doing everyday things brings Christ's love into the world." "Selflessly," interjected Leslie, "Marriage is supposed to be similar in how it's a selfless act. Everyone wins when we do it selflessly. But when you keep score about what you do for each other, then you will lose."

Using covenant rhetoric to distinguish a sacramental marriage as other-focused, the leadership emphasized small acts of service in marriage as both healthy and spiritual. Importantly, however, this sacralization of household chores did not implicate a model of household labor where the husband "helps" the wife. The gender difference programs rarely explicitly instructed women to do more of the housework or childcare, but their stories often indicated an inequity in these areas. From Paul, the evangelical husband who needed to be allowed to sit on the couch to do nothing as he recharged in an empty box, or Sue, who encouraged her husband to go and play a round of golf when his emotional bank was low instead of coming home to help her out, examples of household labor at the other sites subtly demonstrated beliefs in gender roles. In contrast, by sacralizing household chores as a way to embody Jesus Christ, Arnie offered an almost imperceptible challenge to modes of masculinity in the home. The shift away from Genesis toward Jesus also importantly established a different foundation from which to craft a Christian view on relationships. Rather than an abstract presentation of an "other-orientation" that relied on a gendered metaphor of sexed bodies, Arnie and Leslie emphasized an active model based on serving others through tangible actions. Without circumscribing a Christian marriage into a defined set of tasks, however, they constructed a more attainable model of marriage.

Likewise, the topic of communication also provided another example of an alternative model to gender difference. During the night on communication and conflict, Marcy and Darryl predominately focused on therapeutic principles that they argued could improve the ways people can express themselves and provide healthier ways to fight. As with other marriage preparation programs, the leadership referenced a popular book that had helped them in their own marriage. Unlike the two gender difference programs, however, St. Bernadette did not rely on a self-help book about gender dynamics (such as *Men Are like Waffles, Women Are like Spaghetti* or *Men Are from Mars, Women Are from Venus*). Instead, they provided the engaged couples a handout summarizing key insights from John Gottman and Nan Silver's *The Seven Principles for Making a Marriage Work*, which emphasized tasks and approaches for each person to become a good "partner" in marriage. All the advice—nurturing fondness, turning toward each other, or creating shared meaning—represented nongendered suggestions for how to think and act, which don't presuppose men and women communicate or behave differently.

Darryl also implicitly challenged some beliefs about men's style of communication in the one example from fieldwork at this parish that involved directly calling attention to generalizations associated with gender. Before ending for the night, he read a list of his observations after twenty years of marriage, which included the advice to "turn the TV off." He followed up this general statement by specifically holding men accountable: "This is an important one for the men to listen to. And now, I actually need to extend this advice to turn *things* off, such as smartphones." Although this advice in some ways follows the other programs' commentaries about how men tend to be poorer communicators, it differs from the evangelical discussion, which naturalized this tendency. Darryl challenged men (along with their future wives) to work together to create a shared communication style that benefits both partners, without mentioning complementarity. Providing an example from their own marriage, he elaborated that they eventually learned that serious conversations needed to occur in the mornings because Marcy would lose focus at night and the argument would often drift to other topics. In turn, this would exacerbate conflicts because Darryl wasn't good at letting an issue go once it had been brought up. Thus, one of the next items on his list was to encourage couples to "find the best time to talk." The advice on communication notably differed from that at the

Exploring Your Relationship Retreat, which argued that conversations can either meet the needs of the woman or the needs of the man but suggested strategies that ultimately placed greater relational work on the wife. In contrast, this recommendation doesn't attempt to generalize from their experience or presume that there are universal patterns to men's and women's modes of communication. Rather, the example privileges therapeutic insights that emphasize how couples must strive to develop their own approaches that work within the challenges of personality differences. By identifying individual ways that each person can focus or become distracted in conflict, their advice illustrates the central tenets of the covenant rhetoric, which call people to be both self-reflexive and oriented toward working to meet their partner's needs.

As opposed to a gender complementarian framework, the leadership team who led this program tended to operate from a spiritualized-therapeutic perspective. Insights from the Gottman Institute even permeated the class on sacramental marriages, with Arnie referencing research from their "Love Labs" to support the construction of an egalitarian, sacramental marriage. After restating the institute's claim to be able to tell within fifteen minutes whether a marriage will last, he explained that "the number one thing they know that doesn't work is contempt." A brief discussion ensued about the definition of "contempt" since there were several Latino couples, including at least two people for whom English was a second language and did not recognize the word. "To define 'contempt,'" he clarified, "it's a lack of respect and not real equality. It isn't the same thing as a sacramental marriage. Basically, if you think of your partner as unworthy, then the relationship is not going to work." Infusing a therapeutic discourse with religious meaning, the leadership at St. Bernadette articulated a vision of faithful marriages as an egalitarian partnership in which both spouses strive to meet the needs of the other. Yet, they made a point of cautioning couples to be self-reflexive and aware in their attempts to live and love their partner selflessly. Before ending this evening, they stopped to clarify "selfless sacrifice doesn't include letting people abuse you."

LEARNING TO USE PSYCHOLOGICAL CONCEPTS TO EXPLAIN DIFFERENT VIEWPOINTS AT COSMOPOLITAN CHURCH

The two premarital classes at Cosmopolitan Church professionalized a similar spiritualized-therapeutic framework that focused predominately on the psychological differences within a couple. As opposed to a lay interpretation of therapeutic principles, however, this program relied on the expertise of trained and practicing therapists to offer their academic and clinical insights from working with couples, many of whom are in the type of crises that premarital couples hope to avoid. As with their evangelical counterpart at the Exploring Your Relationship Retreat, the curriculum explicitly explored differences between partners, but gender did not emerge as a pertinent dimension to dissect. Instead, counselors guided couples through exercises that taught them to see their differences as a result of their personality, background, and goals.

For much of the dating class, the leadership presented and explored a variety of factors that clinically emerge as significant types of difference within a relationship. The first evening explored "personality types" by offering a brief lecture to help people understand the results of the personality test they had completed before class and a set of discussion questions to explore how these traits may become salient in their relationship. The second week involved couples identifying and exploring differences produced by family of origin since, as Michael explained, "generally, there are more differences between families, than there are similarities." To help investigate these differences and provide a concrete tool in their conversations, couples were assigned a homework activity to create a "family genome" (a type of family tree). During the third week, people were provided a sheet of paper and instructed to fill in each of its four quadrants—Values, Goals, Dreams, and Assumptions—to identify different priorities. Exploring differences, thus, centered prominently, but at no point did these sessions include a section on "gender differences."

In addition to never labeling characteristics as masculine or feminine in this multifaceted deconstruction of difference, the leadership also avoided some of the key conditions associated with gender difference rhetoric in other programs. Following a broader cultural trend that posits gendered forms of communication, the gender difference programs each highlighted the topic of "communication." The classes at Cosmopolitan Church, however, opted to more narrowly focus on how people communicate during conflict. Both the dating and engagement classes, therefore, included an opportunity to listen to a guest lecture that presented Gottman's "Four Horsemen"—criticism, defensiveness, contempt, and stonewalling—that contribute to marital conflict.[30] The speaker briefly noted that research has found a gendered pattern, with the final one more common among men. Unlike the explanations of gendered communication strategies in the other programs that would present it as a trait *of* men, however, he offered an *interactional* explanation for this pattern within heterosexual relationships:

> Unlike some of the other tactics, there tends to be a common gendered pattern for stonewallers—they are more likely to be men. Of course, women are more likely to bring up issues to discuss, which means that stonewalling is part of a pattern of interaction within couples. Specifically, women are 80 percent more likely to bring up an issue. Therefore, women should work on gentle start-ups to discussions of issues, and men should work on not stonewalling when an issue is being discussed.

Using psychological principles that framed this tendency as emergent, the guest speaker reoriented the notion of gendered patterns of communication. Men do not "stonewall" because they are men with waffle brains, but instead, he explained that what appears as a trait of men often results from a culmination of how partners relate to each other. Likewise, his recommendations did not disproportionally place emotion work on women to relationally address these types of interactional dynamics. Rather, he further offered nongendered advice for both men and women to practice, such as being aware of an elevated heart rate during an argument since research correlates it with less active listening.

In the engagement class, they also included a follow-up session to further explore the topic of conflict. After briefly offering a "theoretical" discussion on how conflicts tend to occur, Adam conducted a public counseling session with a volunteer couple who recently had an argument. He walked them each through a five-step process—(1) I felt, (2) What happened, (3) Triggers, (4) Responsibility—I'm sorry, and (5) I will/I want. These phrases were intended to cultivate a "radical subjectivity" in each person where they talked exclusively about what they personally felt and thought during the recent conflict. The volunteer couple recounted a story that could have been interpreted through the gendered communication lens because it consisted of a reticent man and a woman wanting him to share his feelings. Instead, Adam relied on therapeutic concepts such as "stonewalling" (a partner not appearing to be checked in emotionally or mentally) and "flooding" (a heightened state of physiological stimulation that makes it difficult to process another person's point of view).

Both classes also differed in their presentations on a "Christian marriage." Neither used the creation stories in Genesis to provide a template for God's view on relationships but, rather, sought to deconstruct premarital couples' assumptions about biblical marriage. Offering a similar activity as St. Bernadette, Adam and Sarah encouraged couples to study Jesus's actions as an example for how to love. To justify this perspective on biblical marriages, Adam read the contentious passage from Ephesians that "everyone reads at weddings":

> "Wives, submit to your own husbands, as to the Lord. For the husband is the head of the wife even as Christ is the head of the church, his body, and is himself its Savior. Now as the church submits to Christ, so also wives should submit in everything to their husbands. Husbands, love your wives, as Christ loved the church and gave himself up for her, that he might sanctify her, having cleansed her by the washing of water with the word, so that he might present the church to himself in splendor, without spot or wrinkle or any such thing, that she might be holy and without blemish. In the same way husbands should love their wives as their own bodies. He who loves his wife loves himself. For no one ever hated his own flesh, but nourishes and cherishes it, just as Christ does the church, because we are members of his body."[31]

When he finished reading, he looked up at everyone and sarcastically asked, "Right. That's clear. Women, you should submit?" Meeting his tone, one guy jokingly responded, "Cool. She's not here. She's at work." Ignoring the comment, Adam suggested matter-of-factly, "I think that it's clear that it's mutual submission but tucked in love. We are called to love as Christ loved the church. How did he do that?" To begin this conversation, he erased the previous list on the whiteboard that consisted of clichés and abstractions that couples had offered to define a biblical marriage. With a fresh whiteboard, everyone began to volunteer examples of Jesus's actions, including "becoming one flesh," "washing feet," "he got mad," "prayed," and "fed them."

Rather than use this passage to support gender difference or distinct roles for men and women, Adam explicitly interpreted it for the couples as being a statement on mutual submission. Honing in on the discussion of *how* Jesus himself loved, Adam transformed the passage into an activity about tangible actions that can (and implicitly should) define a Christian marriage. As such, a biblical marriage was not defined as a gendered pursuit or occupying a gendered state but instead emphasized the covenant rhetoric call to be other-oriented. Overall, relying on psychological concepts to explain social life, these leaders deemphasized gender as a form of difference and instead explained away much of what the other programs identified as gendered. From the perspective that each person represents an amalgam of personality and family norms, differences were presented as too multifaceted to be reduced into a binary classification. In other words, women and men are different in relationships because they are different *people*.

Conclusion

Religious institutions serve as a key site for the production of gender ideologies.[32] For Catholic and evangelical Protestant communities, this has often resulted in normative calls that marriage is and ought to be an institution heterosexually predicated on distinct gender roles.[33] Yet, as I listened to religious leaders offer counsel to premarital couples, rhetoric of gender differences emerged infrequently and inconsistently. With limited time to prepare people for married life, premarital counselors must make decisions about the most significant and salient topics that will help improve their impending marital life. In two programs, gender made the list but was not accorded as much attention as other issues. In the other two programs, however, leaders appeared gender-blind, with a reliance on therapeutic principles. In all the cases, these lessons never amounted to distinct presentations about how to be a "good wife" versus a "good husband." Rather, these lessons reflect the principles of therapeutic love and follow recent shifts in marriage counseling that place greater emphasis on strategies of action that enable partnership.[34] It thus appears that even among conservative religious communities that have long sacralized gender differences,[35] some of the ideological support for this framework may be destabilizing. Yet, the question remains, to what extent has the undermining of gender roles ideology challenged the inequitable ways that marriage operates as a gendered institution?

Although not all the programs reproduced gendered ideas of "roles" in marriage, and some even offered minimal critiques, the overarching therapeutic framework that encouraged couples to work on themselves still individualized gender. When gender was discussed, it tended to be conceptualized as cultural differences and personal characteristics, which means that it "excludes processes which lie beyond the individual person."[36] For example, discussions on how people have distinct desires and aspirations that emerge from their families of origin do not acknowledge the available power of any individual to enact these goals. As men and women form families and pursue careers, they will encounter structural expectations for how women/men, wives/husbands, and perhaps eventually, mothers/fathers should act. A focus on desires and choices does not engage or prepare couples for these systems of expectations or obligations. In other words, everything from announcing last names at the altar to who will pick up a sick child from school represent "choices" that will be interpreted differently for men and women in heterosexual marriages because of structural expectations. Therefore, these programs may prepare couples for how to reflect on and talk about some issues of gender, but they do so by flattening social institutions to a level playing field of differences in personality and interests only.

The individualization of gender further masked how gender is structured hierarchically in a manner that continues to disadvantage women in heterosexual marriages. Although marriage work can be broadly defined as the "chronic intentional emotion work meant to build competence in life partnership skills,"[37] both the labor of emotion work and responsibility of marital quality continue to fall on women.[38] For example, at the Exploring Your Relationship Retreat, Paul and Kelly's personal example of how they employ the suggestions of *Men Are like Waffles,*

Women Are like Spaghetti support ideas about gendered emotions and that it's a wife's responsibility to monitor both her own and her husband's emotional states. Research regularly finds that women become responsible for the real work of maintaining, monitoring, and cultivating emotional conditions in families.[39] Even though the gender-blind programs did not disproportionately place emotion work on women, the psychological emphasis that individualized differences are about families of origin or personality also didn't challenge the gender socialization about family life. Likewise, the therapeutic ethos that called people to learn these insights by engaging in self-work failed to acknowledge the ways that individual autonomy is gendered.[40] Even as the historic conception that women support the "self-invention" of their sons, husbands, and brothers[41] may have largely subsided, women continue to feel pressures to explain their own decisions about work as "for the family"[42] and the ideology of romantic love reinforces a division of labor where women subordinate their needs to men's desires.[43] The circumscribed ability women have to identify and articulate their own desires and needs thus constrains their ability to negotiate for an arrangement that they prefer in their relationships.[44]

Ultimately, the programs fail to prepare couples for the ways that work, both paid and unpaid, positions men and women with different access to marital power. For example, sociologists Paula England and Barbara Kilbourne found that the combination of women's lower earnings and greater domestic work historically has provided men with more bargaining power in heterosexual marriages.[45] Although they argued paid employment granted women some greater access to power, it appeared mostly in terms of the ability to leave a relationship, which is an option that the covenant rhetoric ostensibly forecloses. Building on their theory, sociologist Jaclyn Wong more recently found that when faced with "competing desires" about how to negotiate the tensions of work-family life, "many women eventually compromise their own desires to make the couple's life livable."[46] Thus, even as programs sought to create a setting where men and women could cultivate relationship skills and collectively identify their career and family aspirations, the efforts remain partial at best. By continuing to conceptualize gender "as a set of individual inclinations to be discussed and negotiated,"[47] couples are left unequipped to identify, evaluate, and communicate about the socioeconomic factors impacting both their decisions and ability to bargain within marriage. The next chapter further considers the subtle ways that seemingly individual expectations reify systems of power by exploring the process of emotional socialization. As it turns out, lessons on sex and money also operated from a gender-blind framework across the programs and instead transformed both topics into an exercise in identifying, monitoring, and disciplining what people view as their internal desires.

5

How Do You Feel about Sex and Money?

As other people streamed into the sanctuary for the Sunday evening service, I broke from the crowd to head to Cosmopolitan Church's small classrooms. As I passed the first room, I noticed engaged couples were already beginning to find their seats for their class; instead of joining them, I proceeded to the second room, where dating couples interested in reflecting on the possibility of marriage met. Unlike the Exploring Your Relationship Retreat that had dating and engaged couples participate in the same curriculum, the size of Cosmopolitan Church and the high number of mostly professional young adults meant that their premarital classes had become popular enough to necessitate creating separate programs. To begin, Michael, one of the four leaders who comprised the two married couples, asked for everyone's attention to open in prayer. As he concluded by asking God to "bless this intentional time together," I looked around the class and noticed that the slow decline of couples had continued. Compared to the other programs that I observed that were designed for engaged couples, the attendance in the dating class tended to fluctuate more and dwindle somewhat over time. As this was one of the last sessions, there were more chairs than people by the time we began with a dozen or so couples scattered among them.

Michael opened by checking in with everyone about their thoughts on last week's guest lecture on marital conflict. After a brief pause, someone volunteered, "Good, overall." Continuing, the man explained, "Some of the numbers that they threw out were interesting—the idea that only 70 percent of people's problems are 'unsolvable' stuck with me." In response, Michael, demonstrating his training as a therapist, probed, "Was this encouraging or discouraging?" After pausing as if unsure how to respond, the man finally replied, "It seems encouraging because we so often go about our lives trying to problem solve and come up with the final solution. But it was good to know that some problems may never truly have a solution."

In contrast to this optimistic view of marital conflict, the other couple on the leadership team briefly recalled their own opposing reactions on learning the statistic. Whereas Lauren-May had found it encouraging to know "that this is normal," Caleb, her husband, jokingly exclaimed that he had thought, "What the crud? This isn't going away!" After Caleb quickly turned to his wife to explain that he was "just joking" and let her know "I love you," Michael shifted to offer social-scientific context for the figure. "Depending on how you measure it, the numbers can vary a little bit between 68 percent, 71 percent, etc.," he explained. "Yet, generally there is agreement that the number of unsolvable issues to solvable issues is about 3:1. This requires that we recognize that sometimes there may not be a solution and learn to be okay with that." "However," he stressed, "that doesn't mean that you can't move forward in the relationship or on any topic. But it does mean that you may not solve it. Some of these issues are less about coming up with a definite solution or agreement but trying to seek compromise because having issues, especially unsolvable ones, is not a sign that a couple shouldn't be together, but it does require that you're creative in coming up with workable solutions."

"The idea that there is always a deeper issue to the fights was impactful to me," volunteered one woman once Michael and the rest of the leadership team had quieted and looked expectedly out at the dating couples again for their impressions. "Even in smaller fights, there are deeper issues that need to be figured out," she offered. "I really walked away with the idea that it is important to get to know one's self better because then you can be a better partner." Encouragingly, Michael initially exclaimed, "Great!" but quickly followed up by warning everyone that "this task is hard" and "it's easier to point a finger" in arguments. "However," he continued, "it is important to acknowledge how deeper issues can impact the reactions we have. Often, we have a tendency to focus on the window covering as opposed to the structure of the window itself." In addition to illustrating the predominance of a therapeutic ethos that privileges the expression of inner feelings as a form of growth,[1] the examination of unresolvable issues during this liminal moment serves two purposes: (1) as part of the raison d'être of premarital counseling, it asks couples to assess whether this relationship has "marriage potential" by considering if they want to perpetually address the same issues forever, and (2) it emotionally socializes couples into understanding that conflict is unavoidable but can be managed through relationship skills and emotion work.

In her discussion of feeling rules, Arlie Hochschild, a pioneer in the sociology of emotions, argued that "a role establishes a baseline for what feelings seem appropriate to a certain series of events."[2] Most of the time, the presence of these emotion norms—or cultural expectations that shape the appropriateness of emotions—are pervasive but imperceptible because they are so normalized.[3] Hochschild argues, however, that change, such as adopting a new social role and/or periods of cultural transition, can render feeling rules visible.[4] Engaged couples occupy a liminal space that positions them on the precipice of adopting a new social role, which requires that they make sense of the broader cultural changes to the meaning of marriage. In part, this reflects an insight offered decades ago by sociologists Peter Berger and Hansgried Kellner that people have each been socialized into general definitions and expectations of marriage but that when they marry, "these empty projections now have to be actualized, lived through, and filled with experiential content."[5] In fact, research finds that even for couples who have lived as if they were married—such as cohabitating or gay couples upon receiving the right to marry—marriage holds the cultural power to reshape the meaning of their relationships by providing them with a new social role that transforms their internal evaluation and the accountability of others.[6] This highlights how individuals' emotions are not their own to make sense of but how the available discourses amount to a regime that sensitizes people to their emotional state and orients them in how to interpret others they interact with.

This chapter examines what the lessons on specific relationship issues reveal about emotional socialization. Religious leaders employing the covenant rhetoric draw on therapeutic tools to reframe conflict for couples from a source of disruption to a site to work on marriage and learn more about the self. Whereas the past chapters documented the integral role that the marital work ethic played in constructing moralized boundaries within the covenant rhetoric, the locus of this work wasn't specified or analyzed. Although leaders often sought to make their advice general enough to fit as many people as possible, they also created curricula that involved identifying the type of issues they believed most relevant and necessary to educate couples about. Recognizing how often couples argue over sex and money, these topics consistently emerge across curricula. In my fieldwork, evangelicals tended to prioritize sexual preparation, whereas Catholics privileged financial preparation.[7] Lessons on both topics, however, offered less informational insights than instruction on identifying, disciplining, and managing emotions.

Learning to Regulate Money and Sexual Feelings: Emotional Socialization and Emotion Management

In their book, *Modern Romance*, comedian Aziz Ansari and sociologist Eric Klinenberg argue that Americans have intensified the love-based marriage culture and now desire a "soulmate marriage" to someone who is their best friend, a true partner, and whom they sexually desire.[8] Yet, at the same time that people hold high emotional expectations of the intimacy and companionship of marriage, the institution is still an economic unit that must be financially successful in earning money and paying bills. To be married, therefore, requires couples to negotiate and regularly make emotional, financial, and embodied decisions. In the language of the opening vignette, these decisions will sometimes represent a type of "unsolvable issue," or at least never-ending work, because financial and intimate scenarios will change over the course of marriage and each partner may bring with them different understandings.

In the past, the social scripts for who made decisions were more profoundly shaped by the gender roles of the companionate marriage—men were charged with financial concerns and women with caregiving duties. Even a few decades ago, Christians, especially evangelicals, overwhelmingly reported that men are "ultimately responsible for the family,"[9] which included their role as financial provider and spiritual leader.[10] As we have seen, however, the distinctive gendered roles for spouses have been destabilized and people increasingly strive for a therapeutic love that calls both partners to work on and commit to the relationship. Yet, despite young people's overwhelming desire to have egalitarian marriages that allow both partners to balance careers and caregiving,[11] getting married transforms men into husbands and women into wives, which means each takes on a new social role that contains cultural guidelines for how to act and feel.

Broadly speaking, as sociologist Rebecca Plante notes, "the primary goal of socialization is to structure and guide people into socioculturally defined, acceptable, and expected roles."[12] The term most often invokes images of small children learning, such as sociologist Heidi Gansen's study of preschool teachers' use of romantic language, like "crush," to describe cross-gender friendship, which implicitly teaches normative understandings of gender and sexuality.[13] However, socialization is a lifelong process that occurs with each new transition and acquisition of a social role, necessitating that people learn anew how they're supposed to act and feel.[14] Specifically, emotional socialization involves learning three dimensions: (1) to *identify* one's own and other's emotions, (2) to *manage* one's expression of emotions, and (3) to be able to *know* when and what emotions are appropriate to display.[15] This learning can happen both directly, such as the explicit lessons on how to love as part of the covenant rhetoric, or indirectly, such as observing the leaderships' actions as married couples. To examine the emotional socialization embedded in the lessons on how to be married, this chapter explores two important issues in marriage—sex and money—that can often produce relational tension, if not marital conflict. Both topics could have been approached from an informational frame that emphasized how-to lessons, such as creating a family budget or educating on family planning, such as contraceptives or natural family planning. Or the leaders could have encouraged gendered decision making by delineating money questions to men and sexual negotiations to women. Instead, the curricula offered little direct lessons about what to do or who should be responsible but rather encouraged people to turn inward to identify and manage how they feel about each issue.

Sex: Preparing for the Pleasure of God's Gift

Sociologist Amin Ghaziani notes that "acts of sex are meaningful only because of the communities in which we experience them, because of the institutions that try to regulate them, and because of the traditions that celebrate them."[16] In the United States, the state and Christianity have long operated as all three and promoted marriage as the only permissible context for (heterosexual) sex.[17] Over the past few decades, efforts by Christians to contest the decoupling of marriage and sex in both laws and popular opinion have earned them an "anti-sex" reputation.[18] For example, both Catholics and evangelicals promote abstinence messages that contend that people should wait until they are married to have sex, and have been active in efforts to restrict marriage to heterosexual couples. Whereas outsiders may view these endeavors as a form of social control emerging from a negative view toward sex(uality), Christians contend that their stance emerges from a deep reverence that values sexual intimacy and sees it as a gift from God.[19] In fact, scholars examining (mostly evangelical) Christian sex manuals regularly find that they contend that frequent and pleasurable sex is not only part of a strong marriage but also tied to salvation and a way God reveals His love.[20] In the marriage preparation programs, both Catholics and evangelicals sought, to varying degrees, to redeem Christian views on sex through the application of the covenant rhetoric. In contrast to what they saw as contractual and selfish beliefs about sex in secular culture, they argued that God desires sex to be a source of pleasure, enjoyment, and emotional connection. The (heterosexual) institution of marriage was not merely seen as fulfilling God's vision but rationalized as the only space where sex can truly be relational and feel secure. Sex, from this vantage point, serves as an embodied and emotional representation of the marriage covenant between husband, wife, and God. From the leadership's perspective, couples in premarital counseling are on the cusp of a turning point that not only would allow them to begin to engage in regular (permitted) sex but that should holistically transform how they feel about sex, their view of themselves as sexual beings, and even their understanding of how God feels about their sexual activity.

Aware of their general reputation of being sexually restrictive and possibly condemnatory, all the programs I observed sought to correct some of the ways they felt that Christian views on sexuality have been misrepresented. The evangelical groups, however, emerged as more vocal and committed to ensuring that premarital couples be (re)educated about God's vision of sex. On the one hand, this is to be expected given their vociferous discourse on sex, which includes everything from dating guides extolling young Christians to be sexually pure to extensive manuals encouraging married Christians to feel free to explore sexual possibilities. Yet, as the personal narratives and questions from premarital couples reveal, the evangelical programs were not only reacting to what they viewed as an overly sexualized secular culture but were also a direct response to the challenges, confusion, and frustration emerging from young Christians trying to make sense of this cacophony of advice. The dedication to emotional socialization thus emerged at least partially from the task of undoing or at least mitigating the consequences of existing evangelical discourses on sexuality. Both evangelical sites dedicated sessions to the topic of "sexuality," which they defined broadly as matters of sexual intimacy and not as an identity. Both the dating and engaged classes at Cosmopolitan Church committed an entire evening to this topic, but since the "approved" threshold of sex was further away for dating couples, their lessons contained more pronounced discussions of the emotional challenge and need to manage one's feelings.

To open the evening's discussion, Michael asked, "How has the Church talked about sexuality?" One man volunteered, "There is a heightened emphasis on premarital sex as a sin that is different than other sins. It's like there's a hierarchy of sins and the Church says premarital sex is very high and dramatic." After explaining that she had grown up Catholic, another young woman shared, "In my experience, the Church didn't really talk about sexuality, because it is shameful. I'm not sure if this was particular to my upbringing, though." Michael, however, turned to everyone to commiserate. "Shame is something that keeps coming up with this topic. We hope tonight will be shame-free. All are welcome here in whatever way you are here." As he continued, he located the locus of shame culturally: "Whenever you have something so powerful and important that it becomes clouded in shame, it sends it underground. I hope that the Church will make sexuality less taboo in the future and celebrate it more. God is clearly good with sexuality because He gave it to us as a gift, which can be seen in both the Old Testament and the New Testament." Michael's first step in redeeming the Christian view on sex was to target the Church, specifically the emotional socialization that has taught young people to negatively identify sexual feelings. To be able to change their ability to know when and what emotions are acceptable, however, meant not only challenging the existing lessons young people had internalized but also replacing them with a new framework. Thus, after another person agreed that they had never experienced celebratory discussions of sex in church, Michael rhetorically asked the class, "How do we talk about this in a better way given that the focus on behavioral processes makes it difficult?" Before anyone could respond, he proceeded to suggest, "One of the issues is in how we define sexuality because it is more than arousal. Sexuality is a part of our self and we can't turn it off. However, we don't have a lot of sex-positive messages in the Church to help understand this."

A few minutes later, Lauren-May, one of the other leaders, returned to this expectation that young evangelicals are taught they must "turn off" their sexual feelings prior to marriage and then afterward are expected to easily "turn on" the switch again. After Michael invited her to share her experience, she began by asking, "How do you make the jump from a 'little' to 'now it's all on the table'?" To illustrate the difficulty of this transition in her relationship with Caleb, she recalled, "We had a lot of guilt and shame prior to marriage because of boundaries we had not successfully maintained. Somehow, we thought that being married would solve those feelings. It took time, however, to negotiate these previous feelings and to realize the impact of the expectations that I had brought into marriage." She believed her expectations had been partially skewed by living in a sorority house in college, which left her with a sense that couples have sex four to five times a day. After Caleb interjected to quip, "I'm not a machine," Lauren-May noted, "This is a perfect example of how even in marriage, the topic of sex may not be easier. Communication is key because marriage won't solve any preexisting issues or problems with sexuality. And while sexuality eventually is more of a source of joy and delight, as it is for us, it takes time and communication to accomplish this." In support of his wife's narrative, Caleb concluded by noting, "Marriage magnifies whatever you already experience or feel about sex prior to getting married." An important subtext, therefore, was that to have a good sex life is to learn to feel the right way about sex before marriage.

Rebecca, Michael's wife, followed up to provide a different vantage point about struggling with the Christian view that getting married suddenly provided freedom to explore sex. Although she experienced little guilt because their long-distance dating relationship meant they had crossed fewer personal boundaries, she observed, "It was just hard to go from 'No, no, no' to 'Okay' because I said, 'I do.' Sex took a long time for me to adjust to . . ." Pausing, she continued, ". . . especially because of the pain. Initially, it was so painful. I thought it would be instantaneously pleasurable. In fact, I even went to a doctor because the pain was so significant, and I didn't know what to do." In a frustrated voice, however, she noted, "But the doctor just told me, 'It will get better after you have a couple kids.' That wasn't very useful since we weren't planning on having kids right away." Offering a similar conclusion as Lauren-May, she recalled, "As a result of the pain, we really had to work on our communication about sexuality because Michael didn't want to cause me pain." Both women's stories undermine the dominant perception that marital sex will be instantaneously easy and enjoyable; instead, they reveal how their emotional (and embodied) management strategies involved a continual process of shaping and reshaping their emotions to align them with personal, couple, and cultural expectations for how to feel about sex in marriage. As with their advice in the covenant lesson on how to have a good marriage, pleasurable sex is presented as emerging only through a marital work ethic, which requires relationship skills, such as communication, and an other-centric approach.

Despite blushing a little after Rebecca's discussion of their sex life, Michael offered what he saw as the underlying theme in the women's stories: "Sex in marriage is not one thing. In fact, sex in marriage has to do with the level of trust between the partners." In contrast, he complained that "all of the stuff in the magazines about how to please your man or the new, hottest sexual acts isn't the point because none of that is really related to satisfaction. Research shows that people over seventy have the highest level of sexual satisfaction but the lowest level of physical ability. Therefore, it's clear that sexual satisfaction isn't about accomplishing the latest and greatest sexual position or using the latest or greatest toy but about trust." Positioning God's vision of sex as countercultural, he concluded, "In Western culture, we turned sex into a product. But it's less about sexual compatibility and more about spiritual compatibility. People can work it out when they are spiritually compatible." Approaching his original point that "sex in marriage is not one thing" from a different perspective, Lauren-May elaborated, "Even in marriage, there will be periods of abstinence because of pregnancy, children, or just life getting in the way. Also, sex in marriage means a lot more than intercourse. I initially thought that was all there was to it. But recently, I was at a bachelorette party and someone asked, 'What if it's not good?' I explained to them, 'It's not about that and that at times it may not be good.

But the foundation is what's important.'" Finishing up this discussion, Caleb concluded, "When we focus on the physical, it's all about what the self gets out of it. But when the focus is on the couple, it's more about being together and what together the couple gets out of it." From the perspective of the covenant rhetoric, the discussion here illustrates how sex represents an embodiment of therapeutic love. Contrasting the contractual view in secular culture as selfish, they argue that great sex reflects the relational work in marriage as well as the intimacy that comes from long-term commitment. In addition to what they saw as a shallow view of sex in secular culture, they also critiqued the existing emotional frameworks in Christianity that presuppose that unmarried individuals are nonsexual beings prior to marriage. While they maintained Cosmopolitan Church's commitment to abstinence, they encouraged people to reframe how they think about sex as part of a broader process of changing how they feel about it. Likewise, they challenged Christian views that marriage is a guaranteed pathway to sexual pleasure by instead showcasing that it requires work to accomplish a desired emotional state. From this vantage point, an enjoyable sex life is yet another facet of marriage that requires cultivation—self-reflexivity, communication, and a marital work ethic.

Although less critical of the consequences of Christian discourses for inculcating shame, the Exploring Your Relationship Retreat also dedicated an entire session to "sexuality" (which again they interpreted broadly as sexual intimacy). After the other two married couples shared their initial sexual experiences during their honeymoons, Joseph and Bonnie took over to reflect on the complexity of how sex changes over the course of a marriage. Similar to Cosmopolitan Church, Joseph started with a redemptive effort to carve out a space for Christians to have positive conversations about God's view of sexuality. "Sex used to be something that was never discussed, which resulted in room being left for hurt," Joseph began. "The media doesn't help with struggles around sexuality because it offers a one-dimensional presentation of it as self-seeking. Compared to these images, God designed sex, as noted in the first two chapters of Genesis, to provide unity and delight. Throughout scripture, it discusses the pleasures of sex—mutual pleasure which satisfies both partners." Joseph also situated the Christian view as countercultural to the supposedly selfish pursuit of sexual pleasures in secular culture, but the Exploring Your Relationship Retreat's gender essentialism briefly led to more heteronormative claims. Joseph proceeded by simply declaring, "Sexual intimacy reflects gender complementarianism." To illustrate this point, he noted that there are "factual" differences between men's and women's hormonal cycles, which must be valued. Without much more of an explanation of gendered sexuality, he shifted the embodied discussion to sexual urges by noting, "Sexual drives are similar to other bodily needs—take eating for an example. Sometimes meals are full course and sometimes they are a snack. The same is true for sex." Echoing a metaphor that I also heard in the engaged class at Cosmopolitan Church, Bonnie and Joseph explained that sometimes a spouse needs to offer the "gift of availability" to their spouse because their bodies belong to each other. While restricting sex to the context of marriage, the evangelical programs maintained the view that it is a natural part of life because God has willed it so.

To share their story about the ways sex goes through different periods and changes over the course of a marriage, the more loquacious Joseph quieted and allowed Bonnie to take the lead. She began by making the same point as both wives from the dating class at Cosmopolitan Church: "Good communication enables better sex." Without ever sharing details of their private moments, she recounted how she had "struggled" with sex in their relationship, which manifested in some times where they rarely had sex and other times when she felt compelled to satisfy *his* sexual drive by having a lot of sex. "Initially, I thought sex was only to meet his physical needs. I didn't realize it was an area for relational development. Over time, I began to understand sex was his way to demonstrate a relational commitment to me, and so we began to have sex more regularly." Yet, just as she felt that she finally had made sense of sex, "he explained that it wasn't all about sex" and she again "felt confused about sex in our marriage." Regardless of these periods, it was clear that the frequency of sexual activity wasn't emerging from a sense of her own needs but what she *thought* would please Joseph. It wasn't until she began to reframe her thinking about sex as something for them—their marriage—and not only her husband that everything really changed.

Her personal journey with sex led to the realization that "the levels of sex are less important than the communication and how sex serves as a way to bring married couples together in deeper unity. We have God's permission to enjoy sex within marriage because God intended sex to be exclusively within marriage. The sexual drive for another person is part of God's design for spouses to need each other. Sex is most enjoyable and rewarding when it further serves the relationship." Sexuality, from this perspective, is core to humanity as ordained by God. To experience the fullness of this gift, however, they argued that sex must happen within a covenant marriage where couples are committed to working on their relationships. Elaborating, she noted, "This is why angry sex isn't rewarding. For sex to be enjoyed, it requires that spouses resolve their problems and communicate. Marriage provides a context of security and freedom because you know sex will only be with this one person. This knowledge provides each person, and subsequently the couple, with safety, trust, and endless possibility." From this perspective, the indissoluble features of a covenant marriage create conditions that they argue best motivate and ensure sexual pleasure. Specifically, the view that these feelings cannot be recreated outside the institution becomes both the incentive to abstain prior to marriage and the rationale for why one would need to continue to work on the relationship instead of getting a divorce.

Bonnie finally concluded her reflection with the opaque observation, "These realizations allowed us to develop a better sex life." Although her tone may have been subdued and thoughtful as she finished speaking, Joseph enthusiastically nodded his agreement to her final statement, which elicited a round of laughter from everyone. Bonnie and Joseph's narrative unequivocally contends that God views sex as a positive gift for married couples to embody the covenant. Despite this potential, their account, along with those at Cosmopolitan Church, illustrates that although good sex may fulfill this covenant, it does not automatically emerge from the institution of marriage. Rather, enjoying sex was presented as knowing how to feel the right way about sex. In the end, these lessons predominately operated as a form of emotional socialization that transmitted an ideology for how to interpret events that people will experience.[21] Specifically, that God views sex as pleasurable and to receive this gift requires couples to augment their own embodied and emotional experiences in preparation of marriage.

Despite evangelicals' tendency to cast their own views as authentically Christian against what they saw as false teachings among Catholics who promote celibacy, overemphasize the procreative dimensions, and denigrate the body,[22] sociologist Mary Ellen Konieczny observed that Catholics also believe "sexual expression is given particular importance in marriage . . . as a primary site for human happiness in its capacity to unite couples."[23] Although the Catholic programs never dedicated a full session to exploring sex(uality), they shared evangelicals' perspective that God designed people to relationally be sexual beings. Furthermore, they employed the covenant rhetoric to argue that God gifted sex to be the embodied manifestation of His call to become one in marriage. The lessons on sex and intimacy, however, tended to be buried in the Catholic programs and subsumed in the weeks dedicated to religious instruction, such as moral decision making, sacramental marriage, and liturgy. For example, Karen and Father Lucas at St. Sebastian incorporated a brief discussion on sex as they reviewed how the Ten Commandments provide principles on how to make moral decisions within marriage. Sandwiched between the first commandment's call to have "no idols" and the seventh commandment's "no stealing," they briefly discussed the sixth commandment ("Thou Shall Not Commit Adultery") and the tenth commandment ("Thou Shall Not Covet") together because, as they noted, both are "broadly about issues of sexuality." "Marital sexual activity should be life giving," stated Karen. "Another way to think about it is that these commandments call for the healthy integration of minds and hearts with one's partner and their physical lives. This is called chastity." Unlike evangelicals' tendency to use the term interchangeably with "abstinence," she drew on Catholic speaker Christopher West who, as she explained, views chastity as something that frees people from selfishness and enables more "authentic love, specifically expressions of marital love."

The remainder of the short time was spent reviewing how the four elements of a sacramental marriage (discussed in an earlier week)—freedom, permanence, unity, and fruitfulness—provide insights into marital sexuality. Freedom translated to principles of consent or, as they clarified, "sexual relations shouldn't violate the freedom of the spouse—it's important that people have the ability to say 'no' and that one party isn't forcing themselves upon the other." Father Lucas also further expanded the principle of freedom to an emotional domain, explaining, "As a priest, I sometimes hear this come up where one party doesn't feel comfortable or safe saying they aren't in the mood. Sex shouldn't be used as a reward or punishment. This reduces sex to the point where it's an expression of the marriage contract, it's a tool. I've been told that sex is more enjoyable when it isn't used as a tool."

Sex, from this perspective, fits within the covenant rhetoric that calls for oneness in opposition to the purported secular model of a contract marriage where people focus on their own needs at the expense of others. Likewise, the next two elements—permanence and unity—further served to construct this distinction. After noting that "sexual expression is committed to being in a permanent unit," they bemoaned that too often, "society" and "media" celebrate examples where the union is violated. Emphasizing the emotional demands of these principles, they argued, "faithfulness is not just about action, but it can also be about the mental commitment" because "if a person spends their sexual life thinking about someone else, then that can create a wedge and become a source of hurt for the other person." With brief, almost dutiful, reminders that porn, artificial insemination, and sterilization "break the unity of the couple," they finished their discussion on sex.

Even less was said about sex at St. Bernadette, where it was not even elevated to a stand-alone topic. During the evening dedicated to the sacrament of marriage, the married couple leading the class briefly mentioned the Church's view on sex as part of a broader point about the problem with cohabitation. Emphasizing the theological element of freedom, Arnie clarified, "A sacramental marriage has to be of your own free will. If you've already been in a sexual relationship, then you may feel obligated." Shifting to two of the other theological elements, fruitfulness and permanence, he continued, "The Church doesn't say sex is bad. Actually, the Church is a fan of sex and having babies. But if you've already had sex, then you may not be as open to the idea of whether the marriage is a good idea or bad idea." In contrast to the associated lessons that emphasized teaching people how to think religiously about sex, the double-sided homework page listed twenty questions that predominately asked couples to reflect on how they feel about sex. Starting with "Do you think that sex is fun, frightening, threatening, satisfying, holy, expression of your relationship, other?" the questions continued to probe the participants for how they feel about sex, affection, and their bodies and even to consider how they will respond when their partner turns down an offer to have sex. Questions such as "Once married, who do you expect will be the one to initiate lovemaking?" and more specific ones about men's and women's roles in sex further challenged people to articulate their assumptions about sexual scripts. The Catholic programs' emphasis on educating couples about the theological significance of sex in marriage resulted in less direct socialization for how people should feel about sex or the ways that they may need to augment their current feelings. Yet, contained within these brief religious lessons on sex was also an underlying understanding of therapeutic love that established feeling rules for the appropriate conditions for when to be sexual and how to feel about it.

Regardless of the intensity or dedication to the topic, the lessons about sex remained focused on the domain of emotions and did not include information on sex education. Even among the Catholic programs, contraception was minimized to an occasional comment about the Church's teachings on natural family planning. Even though it wasn't formally part of the curriculum, St. Sebastian did notify everyone about a married couple in the parish whom people could consult with for more information. As opposed to the early decades of Pre-Cana, there were no doctors providing instruction on reproduction and physiology. Likewise, compared to the physical intimacy scales in Christian dating books or the diagram of sexual organs in early evangelical sex manuals, the programs contained none of the specific and embodied guidelines found in published advice. Instead of these informational frameworks that denote how bodies work and what they can(not) do, all the programs addressed the emotional questions of how sex makes people feel. Whether out of an assumption that couples were already engaging in sex, had learned these lessons in school, or simply that it wasn't worth their time, marriage preparation's instruction on sexuality exclusively focused on emotional socialization by providing metaphors and vocabularies to identify and make sense of embodied feelings.[24]

Premarital counselors drew on the covenant rhetoric to argue that God's vision of sex would best ensure mutual pleasure by contrasting it with what they viewed as the selfish tendencies and contingent approaches to sexual commitment promoted in secular culture. Any sex outside of the permanent bond of marriage was constructed as only fulfilling an individual's need and as not unitive or secure, which they argued meant that it was not a place to obtain real sexual satisfaction.

Christian calls against premarital sex, adultery, and pornography thus frame these as problematic because they represent individuals choosing self-gratification over acts that prioritize their partner and ensure mutual pleasure. In other words, sex signifies part of the project to become Christian and an opportunity to sublimate selfish desires to fulfill God's calling. Participants were taught not only when and why sex is permissible but also that engaging in sex is a natural part of life and a religious act that can connect them to the transcendent. Sex became a way to feel the love, security, and commitment espoused in the marriage covenant.

Money: Identifying Financial Desires and Moral Spending

Sociologist Jan Pahl opens *Money & Marriage* by noting that "the financial arrangements of married people must be one of the most private, yet also one of the most important topics. The secrecy with which couples protect their financial affairs is as great as the secrecy surrounding sexual relationships."[25] While rising rates of cohabitation and women's increased economic independence have decoupled both sex and money from marriage, Christians have typically contested only the former. For example, even in Christian debates over "gender roles" that have argued whether men are naturally or spiritually sanctioned to be a breadwinner,[26] household finances tend to only operate in the background. In other words, both within the academy and in congregations, the gendered questions about who works versus who cares for children or whose job should be prioritized have taken precedence over concerns about how couples ought to manage their money. Although the "privileged" nature of marriage to legally govern financial affairs may have destabilized,[27] money continues to play a significant role in people's decision to marry and their relationship scripts.[28]

The increasing preference to wait to get married until one is "financially ready" has produced a marriage gap in American society where those living in poverty and with fewer economic resources marry less often.[29] Furthermore, young people express hesitation to marry across class lines, in part out of concerns about the incompatibility of experiences and attitudes toward money.[30] Despite a general perception that money taints intimacy,[31] it thus continues to importantly shape how people determine "marriage potential" and becomes a core dimension of household management for married couples. After all, constructing and maintaining a married household is full of economic activities including ensuring production of money, its dissemination, patterns of consumption, and the transfer of assets.[32] Whereas money matters often appeared in the workbooks as basic budget guidelines and as a series of compatibility questions on the assessments in individualized premarital counseling, the topic emerged less consistently among the collective programming. In my study, only the Catholic programs formally dedicated class time to finances; among the evangelical programs, the topic tended to emerge as a site to discuss the importance of therapeutic, relationship skills, such as communication.

For example, St. Sebastian held a "Finances and Wine" evening, which notably differed from their other class sessions not only because alcohol was served but also because it was held at the nearby home of a parishioner. While the couple hosting the event floated around in the background, a "money guy" from the parish led the class. After everyone had received a small handout, Gordon began. Reading from page one, he explained that the evening would be divided into two parts—theory and practicalities—to allow everyone to consider "how do principles of God and the Scripture relate to our finances?" To start, he read a passage from Matthew, chapter 6 that deemphasized the pursuit of wealth: "Do not store up for yourselves on earth, where moth and decay will destroy them, and thieves can break in and steal them. But store up treasures in heaven, where neither moth nor decay can destroy them, nor thieves break in and steal them. Remember, where your treasure is there your heart is also." Continuing with the theme that Christians shouldn't be driven by financial concerns, he read another passage without pausing: "No one can serve two masters. . . . You cannot serve God and wealth." Rather than discuss the question listed on the handout—"How do these teachings of Jesus apply to our spending and our saving?"—Gordon continued with the "theory" section of the evening by explaining the importance of budgeting.

"Why have a budget?" posed Gordon. As the person sitting closest to him, he asked me to start and indicated we would proceed around the circle. Misunderstanding the request, I offered my thoughts on why a budget could be useful. "That's nice," he smiled before explaining he only wanted me to read the first line on the handout. Slightly embarrassed and still a little confused, I looked down at the paper and read, "Argue less—or argue more fruitfully—about money, since you'll have some concrete documentation that shows what your spending intentions are." One by one, our small group read the remaining listed reasons, which offered a religio-therapeutic framework for identifying and monitoring income and expenses. Some provided emotional rationales for a budget, such as "experience less stress about money and spending." Others identified value-driven reasons, such as "allocate money for the activities that are important to you" or "give support to the people who (and the causes that) are important to you." Finally, some were simply descriptive, such as "be better able to track how your money is spent," "get out of debt," or "live within your means and develop savings." Without any further discussion or contribution from the group, Gordon turned the page to begin reading the third topic under theory. "Budget basics," he explained, "means spend less than you make and live within your means." Drifting only slightly from the printed material, he elaborated, "It is important to first establish goals about where you will allocate expenses because that will help you realize where to be less frivolous in your spending, such as all the little trips stopping at Starbucks. By curbing certain spending habits, you will be better able to reach your financial goals of paying off student debt or your honeymoon or whatever." Returning to read the final bolded point on the handout, he suggested, "Track your purchases to determine where your money goes each month. Don't forget to track the little purchases that add up quickly to big amounts." By tracking spending, he suggested people can locate what he called "fritter finders" and give more thought to whether to go out for that beer with friends, order lunch at work, or treat oneself to coffee. Notably, many of these expenses could be seen as sources of pleasure and social connection, implying that the primary challenge in budgeting is actually emotion management. The specific examples of pleasure also reflect larger generational assertions that millennials' financial challenges result from, and can be remedied by, adjusting their spending on small items.

After briefly offering rough percentages for how much monthly income should be allotted to different categories such as housing and retirement, the emotional socialization became more explicit and guided. As he passed out an additional handout, Gordon explained, "When it comes to constructing a budget together, it's important to weigh expenditures in light of the mutual values, goals, and expected fulfillment." For example, "before making any purchases but especially major ones, you should ask yourselves, will the purchase reflect the values we believe in? Will it help meet our goals as a couple/family? And do we expect that it will provide fulfillment?" Drawing attention to the handout, he suggested that another way to think about what he was asking was the "fulfillment curve." In a dry joking voice, Gordon commented that he thinks of this as the "life cycle of a boat" or ski equipment because these items are expensive and often used for only a short period before they need to be maintained or upgraded. Instead, he suggested that people rent equipment for their occasional use, which has the added benefit of not only reducing expenses but also clutter. Before turning to an exercise where people could consider how their own values shape their attitudes toward material possessions, Gordon briefly brought the evening back to faith. "It seems like once people find faith, then they don't worry so much about the superficial stuff like clothing, etc.," he added. "It's a psychology thing that when people find value inside of themselves, they are less likely to require external things to validate them. People are more at peace because of their faith and so they spend less money." Obliquely referencing the earlier scriptural lesson, Gordon's claim that "psychology" positions people as motivated either by God or wealth individualizes economic position by eclipsing social class and instead reducing financial situations to a series of moral decisions.

Finally, breaking from reading the handouts, Gordon shifted the evening to allow people time for personal reflection to evaluate their own views on spending by completing a quick worksheet called NUDEL. As each person tried to find a way to comfortably write while sitting in couches and overstuffed chairs, I read over the page to discover that NUDEL stands for Necessary, Useful, Desirable, and Extra Luxury. Each person individually had to classify a list of twenty-nine items into these categories. The range was broad, including cable TV, kids, savings accounts, extra bedroom in house, two incomes, stocked liquor cabinet/wine clubs, stocks and bonds, continuing education, home ownership, tickets to the opera (as well as separately listed sports teams), seasonal decorations, cell phones with data plans, home phone, retirement savings, and trip to visit parents. By asking each

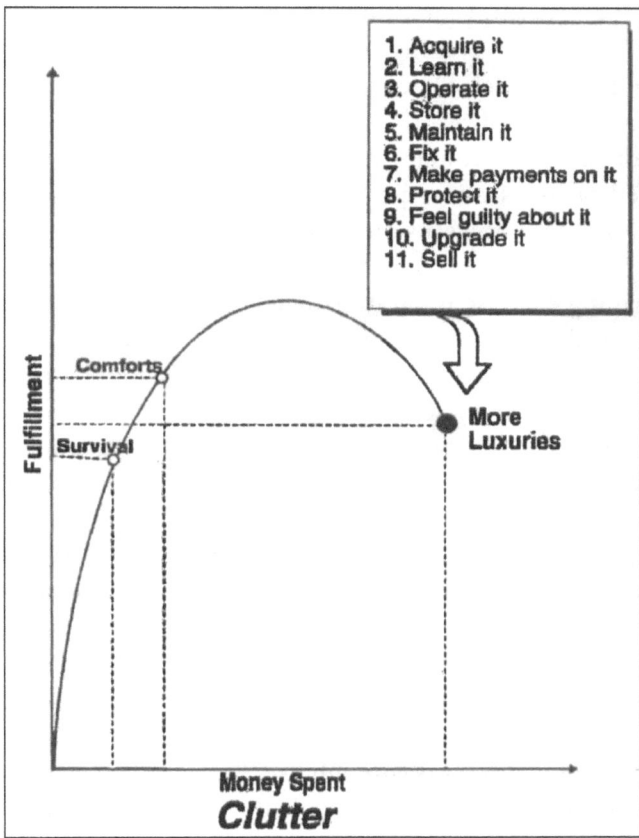

Figure 5.1. Fulfillment Curve from St. Sebastian

person to distinguish an expense as "desirable" or "necessary," the underlying question becomes how do people feel about an item and not how much does it cost. Notably, the exercise didn't ask couples to assess their finances to consider whether people can afford any of the items but created an opportunity for them to assess compatibility by determining whether they share similar values. In the process, this reduces couples' money management to a series of decisions, which can be evaluated for their moral and emotional motivations. Furthermore, the focus on spending on "luxuries" normalizes a privileged class position by assuming that people's underlying challenge in budgeting is noticing where their desires become expensive liabilities and conceals the structural conditions of financial management. Thus, the reflective work of the evening emphasized identifying, managing, and knowing how one feels about spending and ignored the other side of a budget: income and wealth.

In contrast to the Catholics, neither of the evangelical programs I observed dedicated a session specifically to money, budgets, or finances. Nonetheless, these concerns did emerge occasionally in the context of other topics. For example, all these terms were generated as part of a brainstorming exercise in an unnamed session that Adam, co-leader of the engaged class at Cosmopolitan Church, flippantly exclaimed, "if there were a title to today's class, it would be 'Defining Marriage.'" After a brief review of their homework assignment, Adam announced, "Today is one of my favorites because *we* stop talking and have *you* talk to each other." Sarah, his wife, proceeded to write down two questions on the whiteboard as Adam announced them to the class: (1) What are you excited about when you think about getting married? (2) Where do you have anxieties or resistance? A dull roar of conversation arose as the twenty-two gathered couples first privately discussed the questions and then again as they broke into small groups. Finally, Adam called their attention back to the front of the classroom, and Sarah wiped the questions off the board and wrote "Excited" on the left side and "Anxious" on the right. About halfway through listing marital anxieties, someone volunteered "finances" to which people then continued to call out new related words that Sarah wrote alongside it, such as "debt" and "spending habits." The exercise continued and ultimately resulted in a longer "Anxious" list than "Excited" list. Since the activity of writing on the board mostly consisted of people shouting ideas and some offhanded comments made by leadership and gathered couples, Sarah finally turned to directly face everyone and exclaimed, "Now that the board is a chaotic mess of circles and lines, it seems like this may be a good time to decompress and not just leave this all up here." Since the classroom remained silent when she asked whether "anyone has a topic that they want to go further on," she looked back at the board and observed "money is often on the positive side as well."

"One of the things that Adam always asks is, 'Who is getting richer? Who is getting poorer?'" explained Sarah. While some people laughed and others shrugged in response, she continued, "We don't go in as much detail about finances and spending habits in this class because we're not the best examples. To us, it comes down to good communication. But we just don't feel comfortable saying that you have to get your own checking account or that you have to have a joint checking account. If you are concerned about this topic, you should see a financial adviser sooner rather than later for advice." Whether a reflection of the marriage gap that finds class-advantaged people are more likely to get married or the professional membership that attends Cosmopolitan Church, the recommendation of a financial adviser provided a telling insight into the type of money challenges that they anticipate couples face (or don't face). Furthermore, it again eclipses any discussion of whether people have money to manage by focusing on finances as a series of individual preferences and choices. In other words, young people's concerns about money are presumed to be about what to do with it, rather than how to earn it or if they even can earn enough.

At this point, Adam interjected to explain the comment that his wife credited to him. "One is getting richer, and one is getting poorer but only mathematically. Rather, you are adding value to each other. There's a whole lot of economies in play. For example, one person may be better at balancing accounts, and one may be better at housework. In terms of money, you should ask yourself two questions: How do you spend your time? How do you spend your money? Think about how you expect that to change when you're married. Both basically come down to math. After all, there's only twenty-four hours in a day." Shifting from this abstract advice, he provided couples with "fun conversations" to help them explore their expectations. Similar to an earlier assignment where people imagined and verbalized their conceptions of God, he asked everyone to "think about an amount of money." Pausing a moment to allow some sum to come to mind, he followed up, "How much was it? Why did you pick that amount?" Suggesting that they can later compare their answers to learn more about their views on money, he moved on to provide "another fun exercise." "Imagine your answer to the following story. If a magic fairy came to you on your wedding day and said that your life would be exactly the same but with one difference that you would make 20 percent more than you make now. How would you change your life? Conversely, if a fairy came to you and said that you would earn 20 percent less. What would have to go? How much you work will not change in these scenarios, just how much you make." To emphasize the value of the exercise, he finished by explaining, "These conversations are to learn the difference between math and meaning." Unlike Gordon's efforts to teach couples about the principles of constructing a budget, Adam focused the lesson on considering what money *means* to couples, which indirectly included an evaluation of income but, again, only toward the end of identifying one's values and desires that motivate decisions. In practice, this exercise provides a different means but the same outcome as NUDEL—determining what people see as luxuries (e.g., what they may give up with less income) and what they view as necessities (e.g., a change in income will have no impact on having or doing something). Entirely absent from either exercise are questions about whether couples have sufficient income to pay their bills, how to plan for their future, or even the impact of how money management may become an "unresolvable issue" in marriage. Again, notably, the topic of finances was not part of the planned curriculum but only emerged as a brainstorming exercise on the topic of emotions. Money, ultimately, was seen as a site where couples can refine their therapeutic skills by cultivating open communication habits and seeking professional intervention.

Whereas the Catholic programs provided more concrete information about budgeting and some Christian framing for how to think about money and finances, all the leaders tended to construct money as a matter of "feelings." As a form of emotional socialization, the lessons were structured to help people identify, manage, and know about the underlying emotions that motivate their financial decisions. The emphasis was on engaging in self-reflection about how one personally feels about money, maybe including how that emerges from family of origin, and the extent to which this matches one's partner. Money thus tended to operate as a way to assess compatibility, practice communication skills, and engage in emotion management. The underlying framework presumed that controlling one's feelings will control spending. In other words, couples are called to engage in what sociologists call cognitive deep acting—the process of changing how people think about a situation in an effort to feel differently about it.[33]

Guiding questions, such as those in each vignette that asked couples to consider if a purchase reflects their values or helps meet goals as a couple, focus nearly exclusively on spending. From this perspective, poor money management is implicitly constructed as an issue of emotional control and disconnected from structural inequality. Beyond assuming a level of financial privilege of couples, the lessons shifted money from a material commodity to an emotional object. Couples were never directly instructed in how to spend their money or provided with concrete financial advice about investment, retirement, or savings. In fact, unlike emotions, which are always expected to be publicly and explicitly discussed in these classes, money was treated as a private matter. Leadership's advice was often evasive and not personally revealing about how much they earn, their wealth, or their debts. In classes where I learned about married couples' experiences with infidelity, histories of sexual abuse, and other deeply personal topics, the evasiveness on finances was pronounced.

Conclusion

In a society where unmarried couples can, and regularly do, have sex and share finances, it may begin to appear that marriage is less distinctive. Yet, in her conclusion of *Marriage, a History*, social historian Stephanie Coontz surmised, "I believe marriage itself adds something extra. . . . It remains the highest expression of commitment in our culture and comes packaged with exacting expectations about responsibility, fidelity, and intimacy."[34] A critical component of this "extra" is emotions—Americans feel that marriage is special, and subsequently, it holds the power to transform the feeling rules people use to evaluate and work on their relationships. After all, getting married represents a public demonstration of couples' private feelings of love and companionship and is expected to distinguish the union by making it more permanent and intimate. Among Christians, this view that marriage holds a distinctive emotional power is intensified with the covenant rhetoric. It teaches that God wants people to have a happy and successful marriage but that they must work with Him and on the relationship. As the examples of money and sex reveal, learning to have this covenant marriage requires an emotional socialization where people determine the appropriate feelings and motivations to cultivate that will ensure oneness and success.

The instructions for both sex and money focused on identifying, disciplining, and managing emotions. The logistics and concrete practices of how to manage a budget or have sex were largely absent and sometimes even avoided altogether. Whereas historian Amy DeRogatis notes that evangelical "sex manuals run the gamut from suggesting loving language to put your spouse in the mood to providing information about STDs" and that "sexual techniques, positions, and specific acts are discussed in detail to provide guidelines for the married faithful,"[35] these topics were opaquely referenced at best and generally eclipsed in favor of lessons on what feelings one ought to have and the therapeutic techniques to reach the desired emotional state. Likewise, financial guidance offered minimal insights into what to do with money but rather encouraged people to interrogate the motivations for spending and the meaning of money in their lives. Although most often, emotion management refers to "lone individuals modifying their own emotional experience and displays,"[36] there are also times when feelings can become a group project where one controls, induces, and sometimes changes one's feelings with the help of others. Or as sociologist Linda Francis describes, "people look outside themselves for clues about how to interpret emotional signals."[37] From the leadership of the marriage preparation programs to the guided exercises to the conversations with a fiancé(e), individuals in these programs did not explore or manage their feelings in isolation. In fact, the covenant rhetoric's call to be other-centric sacralizes the processes of interpersonal emotion management by establishing a religio-therapeutic expectation that monitoring and sharing one's internal emotional state is part of the unity of marriage. From this perspective, the topics of money and sex were mostly treated as significant because they served as sites for couples to cultivate relationship skills and not because they constitute an embodied or material dimensions of marriage.

While these lessons on emotion management help to develop the type of person that is successful in today's workplace and home,[38] they also individualize all marital issues and treat them as something that can be resolved by reframing how one feels. However, this doesn't address the gender inequality of sexual pleasure, including women learning to prioritize men's orgasms or a sense of discomfort with their own genitalia.[39] Likewise, for an issue such as money, this doesn't contend with structural inequalities that result from the wage gap between men's and women's earnings, intergenerational transmission of wealth, or workplaces determining the type and cost of one's benefits. Although advice on money and sex can often be gendered, there was little in the call to identify unresolvable issues, practice relationship skills, or to manage emotions that distinguished between the roles of men and women. The lack of gendered advice, however, doesn't negate the dimensions of gendered power on either subject. The historical conjugal contract that trades a husband's financial support for a wife's domestic work has declined with the breakdown of the idealized homemaker-breadwinner model family,[40] but its legacy maintains emotional power that permeates Americans' lives. For example, sociologist Cristen Dalessandro found that young, especially class-advantaged, men expressed anxiety about getting married because of a sense that they must financially provide.[41] The gender-neutral framing of emotional socialization doesn't create much space or structure for couples to identify or discuss how their feelings on money emerge from gendered pressures.

The emphasis on spending further fails to help couples identify how these intersecting structures of gender, class, and age factor into individuals' employment and subsequently the incomes that they're able to bring into the household. It doesn't address the poignant underlying anxieties about money that these typically millennial couples were facing over the rising costs of housing, childcare, potentially college for kids, and so forth. The advice on learning to control feelings as a way to manage spending cannot address the financial stressors that they face. Millennials have come of age in a risk society where buying a home is a challenge, childcare is expensive, the longevity of social security is questioned, and pensions have disappeared, which means that people must fund their own retirements.[42] These material and structural realities are impervious to shifts in feeling. By treating money as a domain of emotions to be managed, these programs fail to contend with or prepare couples for the type of structural pressures they will inevitably have to face even if they are privileged enough to get married now and have money to balance.

This chapter, along with the past few, has examined the organizational, ideological, and emotional structure of marriage preparation programs' lessons on how to have a good and godly marriage. The discussion, however, has occurred from the perspective of a researcher who observed the programs, listened to the lessons, and unpacked their meaning. The time has come to turn to the people who participated in these programs to ask how they viewed them and their feelings about their experiences: What did they learn from the process? How did they feel about participating in this church requirement? The next chapter considers the couples' memories to examine what motivated them to participate in premarital counseling and how the variation in motives emerged from religious differences between how Catholics and evangelicals construct their programs. Building on themes from this chapter, the following chapter reveals how people recalled little of the content and tangible advice but instead highlighted the feelings that emerged from engaging in the process. Although specific advice may have become washed out, couples revealed that regardless of whether they always agreed with the leadership, they viewed the process as significant because it allowed them to create a special set-aside time where they could intentionally connect.

6

What Did We Learn? A Structure for Couples' (Pre)marital Emotion Work

After initially meeting Malaya and Arvin during my first set of observations at the Exploring Your Relationship Retreat, we reconnected for an interview at the coffee shop where he had spontaneously proposed a year prior.[1] By the time I met them, they had been together for five years, engaged for one, and were already living together. Based on the recommendation of another couple at their church, they had decided to sign up for the retreat. Unsure of what to expect, Malaya recalled, "[Arvin] was kind of joking around, 'Like are they gonna test us if we know each other?'" Stumbling over his own answer, Arvin replied, "I think I was expecting um . . . uh, to be able to . . . learn how to um, I guess, learn about a healthy marriage and everything and, and a lot of that had to do with uh . . . communicating to each other how we're feeling exactly." Arvin proceeded to amusingly reflect on how during the long drive to the retreat center, they got into a fight because they were both too indecisive and refused to make a decision about when or where to stop for dinner. Despite arriving at the retreat's rural location hungry and angry, feelings that were exacerbated by the fact that there was no nearby restaurant, he saw this as "the first test of that weekend" and described how by the end, "we learned arguments are okay, and it's just how you respond to them." I quietly wondered listening to their reflections whether they would report a sense of disconnection from the lessons since the retreat explicitly taught that premarital sex and cohabitation are sinful and was implicitly structured to guide newlywed couples to learn how to build a home for the first time. As it turned out, that content rarely emerged in the discussion without my prompting. Rather, Malaya and Arvin fondly and almost reverently shared memories of the emotional connection they forged during the weekend's private moments. Recollecting on their time together, Malaya explained, "I felt like it strengthened our relationship together, like it made us closer together, and there was a really emotional moment where it felt real, you know? Like, all your guards are down." Thinking back, Arvin recalled, "I think the coolest thing was being able to read our thoughts to each other because that made it . . . super intimate." Likewise, Malaya "really enjoyed just being in the room and talking about certain topics, like about family or what marriage meant to us."

A year or so later, I met Max and Erica at another coffee shop hours away to discuss the marriage preparation program they had recently completed at St. Bernadette. Although she already had a teenage daughter from a previous relationship and they had been married for five years, they participated because Erica had become interested in having a "second wedding," or a convalidation, after talking with Father Jack.[2] After briefly (and it turned out incorrectly) explaining the process to her atheist husband, he easily agreed and she "freaked out" because as she stated, "I'm making this huge commitment." For a different reason than Malaya and Arvin, I wondered what insights they would take away, given their years together, from classes designed to introduce engaged couples to marriage. Yet, even Max, who shared, "I've got a lot of resentment towards Catholicism and Christianity," wished in retrospect that they had taken the parish classes earlier because it "would have been better to have all of our issues clearer." Despite joking that the workbook was a bit like a "Catholic *Cosmo* magazine" quiz, they both found it helpful to have a structure to discuss specific relational issues. Erica explained she "had a good time taking those tests and listening to what he had to say and giving my opinion or high-fiving each other because we passed or finished first." Despite their flippant descriptions, they still offered a generally positive evaluation of their participation. In fact, before we ended the interview, Erica took a moment to clarify, "I really did feel that the [marriage preparation classes] were things that I actually looked forward to . . . one, because we were doing it together and two, because it's going down a different avenue of your faith. It's just kind of like an adventure."

From the perspective of a researcher or even a religious leader, it's tempting to ask about the impact of the programs' content, such as "What did they really learn?" or "What did they think about the classes?" Such questions tend to evaluate whether the programs "work" by assessing couples' ability to recount lessons or their mastery of the presented material. As I came to realize, however, these were the wrong questions. If couples' ability to recall is used as a metric to determine the impact, then the programs would appear to be inconsequential. In interviews that regularly lasted over two hours, I found couples were the most inarticulate and brief during the section that directly asked about the marriage preparation programs. Despite some positive generalities, they often stumbled to provide concrete examples of what insights they had gained or to remember specific lessons. For example, nestled into a hip, urban coffee shop, Leticia slowly responded to one of these questions with "Yeah, I mean we learned a lot [in the programs]. But it's true that, that, I am a bit fuzzy on the details. I took away a lot of stuff but..." Paul, her fiancé, interjected, "... core concepts are there." Continuing her thought, Leticia added, "Right, but it's not on the details, which is too bad because there were really interesting ones that would be good to still have."

As it turns out, this isn't the first time that young people have been described as "inarticulate" about religious leaders' lessons. In *Soul Searching: The Religious and Spiritual Lives of American Teenagers*, sociologists Christian Smith and Melinda Lundquist Denton summarized their interviews by noting that "one finds little evidence that the agents of religious socialization in this country are being highly effective and successful with the majority of their young people."[3] Describing them as "incredibly inarticulate,"[4] they note that very few teens in any faith were able to explain the beliefs in their tradition or their possible impact on their lives. Rather, Smith and Lundquist Denton contend that teens operate from a "de facto religious viewpoint" that they call "moralistic therapeutic deism," which they describe as "centrally about feeling good, happy, secure, at peace."[5] Given the timing of my study more than a decade later, the young adults I witnessed contemplating and planning for Christian marriages were mostly millennials who could have been peers of Smith and Lundquist Denton's 2001–2005 study of American adolescents.

At first glance, it would appear that at both ages, young people are incapable of articulately speaking on lessons that their religious communities have tried to transmit and that they instead emphasize their own positive emotions. Yet, an analysis that only focuses on what their talk reveals fundamentally misses the couples' own assertion that the programs are impacting how they feel. After all, people often find it challenging to describe the ineffable quality of emotions or explain their deeply held beliefs.[6] Therefore, it's important to understand people's faith more holistically. Arguing against an overly cognitive approach to the study of religion, sociologist Meredith McGuire notes that "individual religiosity is not a mere 'mentality' or frame of mind" because "the individual is able to experience, rather than simply think or believe in, the reality of his or her religious world."[7] In other words, "being" religious is as much a state of feeling religious and engaging in the emotion work to cultivate the right internal state.

Whereas the past chapters unpacked the organizational, theological, and emotional structures to marriage preparation, this chapter shifts to evaluate the point of view of the couples who participated in the program. First, it highlights how organizational differences between Catholic and evangelical programming structure the couples' divergent motivations for why they participate and what they hope to obtain from the process. Whereas evangelicals often enroll in "premarital counseling" early to discern whether a relationship is suited for marriage, Catholics participate in "marriage preparation" to have a religious wedding. Second, it explores how evangelicals and Catholics may enroll in programs for different reasons but similarly report that they found the opportunity to connect with each other meaningful. As the opening accounts reveal, couples were expressive about how engaging in the liminal religio-therapeutic practice made them feel—about themselves, their partner, their relationship, and their future. In doing so, couples rehearsed the covenant rhetoric by doing activities that allow them to work on their relationship and prepare for their transition to marital life.

Why Do Couples Participate?
Divergent Organizational and Emotional Cultures Pattern Evangelical and Catholic Motivations

The simple answer to the question "Why do couples enroll in these programs?" is that people most often participate in premarital education because they must. In addition to picking out flowers, determining their guest list, and selecting a venue, these classes became part of the wedding planning process. Yet, couples' brief explanations that they attended the programs because the officiating clergy or church required their participation fails to capture more profound insights woven throughout their relational narratives. It also misses that this impact was felt across a range of people. Unlike the leadership of the programs, who were universally white, college educated, and typically, employed in middle-class professions, the people coming to the classes included a wider range of backgrounds in terms of race, class, relationship status, and occupation.[8] Although I regularly found myself interviewing couples in the small coffee shops that the Pacific Northwest has become famous for, the meetings included everything from speaking with a young unmarried, pregnant couple where the white man chewed tobacco between sips of his drink in a small rural town, to catching up with a professional and accomplished Black woman about her dating life over a quick cup of coffee in an eclectic urban neighborhood.

As I listened more closely to how couples situated premarital education in the stories of their relationship trajectories, I became aware that the language employed by their faith communities—evangelical premarital counseling versus Catholic marriage preparation—captures key variations about when and why people participate. Evangelicals approached these programs as a form of *counseling*, where people seek professional intervention to guide their individualized practice of relationship discernment. The organizational logic of "premarital counseling" structured everything from the greater proportion of therapists leading the programs to couples' willingness to attend before a proposal as well as to attend more than once. In contrast, Catholics more narrowly conceptualized the programs as representing *preparation* for a religious wedding, which meant that they attended only after they were engaged and as part of planning for the ceremony. The idea of turning to the Church for guidance on their relationship at an earlier stage often appeared incomprehensible to not only the engaged couples but the leadership because the practice operated under the auspices of religious education to prepare for the sacrament of marriage. As this section illuminates, the preferred language thus highlights distinct organizational and emotional cultures between the faith communities that structure how couples approach the otherwise similar premarital curriculum.

Evangelical Premarital Counseling for Relationship Discernment

The evangelical couples I spoke with not only felt comfortable approaching their religious communities for help in their relationships but expected them to offer this service. They often voluntarily sought out this intervention, at least partially, because they believed that their religious communities, or the people within them, had something valuable to offer in terms of discerning whether a partner was a good fit and how to develop skills to improve a relationship. As their preferred terminology of "counseling" would imply, the couples saw this as a resource that they could employ as necessary and as frequently as would be helpful in the journey toward marriage. Additionally, the framing of counseling bespoke the underlying anxiety that they had about making this decision in a culture where marriage is contingent. Evangelicals tended to come to the programs with a vulnerability and uncertainty that manifested in two key differences from their Catholic peers: they attended pre-engaged to discern the viability of a relationship and they participated in numerous programs. These distinctions in motivations, however, also reflected the opportunity structures within evangelical programs that created curricular programing for dating couples and conceptualized all premarital relationships as similarly in need of assessment of marriage potential.

In some cases, couples were truly *pre*-engaged and participated in the programs as a way to obtain the final confirmation that they should get engaged. In a few instances, by the time I could arrange an interview with a couple, they were no longer pre-engaged because the man had proposed. For example, after a month of failed attempts, I finally sat down with Kevin and Willa to discuss the dating class at Cosmopolitan Church. In the interim, Willa had taken a vacation to France with some friends and, coordinating with them, Kevin had flown to Paris, hid out in the backroom of a nice restaurant and surprised her by emerging to propose. Curious and not wanting to assume, I asked, "So had you been talking about it beforehand?" Kevin promptly responded, "Oh yeah, oh yeah. Immediately before taking the dating class, we had been talking about it for . . . ," pausing for a moment, he finally concluded, ". . . many months prior." Likely to explain his pause, Willa clarified that they had previously been friends and that when they finally started dating, it was under the condition that it was to explore whether the relationship should end in marriage. Although Willa had wanted to enroll in the class earlier, she noted "he wasn't ready." At a certain point, however, they "hit a rough patch . . . well, not a rough patch. We just, I don't know, [had] a fight or something [and] he suggested that we take the class, or maybe I suggested it, but he was really quick to be like 'Yeah, let's do it.' But before, that wasn't his reaction; he wasn't ready for that. I kind of knew, 'Okay, just his willingness to take this class means that he is ready.'" The significance of Kevin's participation is reminiscent of sociologist Ellen Lamont's study that found that gendered dating scripts have left even professional women hoping for egalitarian relationships looking for tangible evidence of men's willingness to commit.[9] Specifically, Lamont revealed how a belief in innate gender differences that construct men as less emotional or relational means that women rely on traditional symbolic gestures, such as paying for dates and proposing, as ways to feel any assurance in men's commitment. Within evangelicalism, where these neotraditional narratives are even more pronounced, premarital counseling not only represents a symbolic gesture of men's feelings and dedication but also a way for women to learn about and access men's internal worlds.[10] As Kevin later explained,

> Willa had been a very strong proponent of getting engaged and moving forward quickly for many months and I was still hesitant. But I think it really was the class that—[pause]—It really pushed me over the edge. It was fate. It definitely gave the opportunity for us to be a lot more open, and it created a lot of different areas of dialogue that we just hadn't been talking about and just having really honest conversations. I think through all of that I realized I have been able to bring out my concerns, [and] either way, at this point no matter what, we are going to be able to deal with them, to have open, honest dialogue and be able to get through [it] no matter what. So once I fully realized that point, 'Hands down. Let's do this.'

As with other evangelicals in dating relationships, marriage had always loomed in their relationship as something under consideration and was used as a barometer to evaluate their relationship.[11] Cosmopolitan Church's class, however, also had specifically figured in their understanding of the stages of relationship development and, in different ways, assuaged each person's gendered anxieties motivated by fears of relationship contingency. For Willa, Kevin's agreement to participate in the class indicated that he was finally ready to move forward and was a clear sign of his commitment. Whereas for Kevin, the class allowed him a structured opportunity to talk through lingering doubts, and that process instilled greater confidence that they had the relationship skills necessary for a marriage to last.

Other dating couples, however, could not envision a clear trajectory and were instead openly reflecting on the next stage in their lives. These couples were less in some anticipatory stage of engagement but rather reflexively questioning if/how marriage would fit into their lives *and* whether their current relationship had reached its expiration. In the one instance when I interviewed a woman by herself from Cosmopolitan Church's dating class, she described her relationship with her boyfriend as at a crossroad. She had been dating him for six years, had recently graduated from college, and spent a year doing AmeriCorps. After this length of time and at this stage in her life, she described how they were trying to figure out if they should move forward to marriage or if they were not meant to get married. She envisioned the class less as a stamp of approval for their relationship and more as a divining rod. In a similar case, I interviewed Teru, a woman from the Exploring Your Relationship Retreat, without her boyfriend. Unlike the first woman, however, she expressed more hesitancy about marriage itself rather than her present relationship. After having been together for four years, she explained they were searching for answers about what comes next. Teru had never thought of herself as "pre-engaged" until she attended the retreat and the leadership had used the term. Instead, she elucidated,

> We're both very cautious of this thing called marriage. [His] parents are divorced. My parents haven't had the best relationship. And so we understand it's a huge commitment. It's nothing we want to rush into. So we're reading books, going to weekends that are recommended to us, talking to couples, doing whatever research we can on not just this thing called marriage—whatever that is—but also on ourselves and each other. And what is it that we want out of marriage and what is it we want out of life. So that is where we are.

These couples, or at least the women in them, approached the programs more cautiously and with less clarity about their desired outcome. Each woman professed to loving their boyfriend but did not consider love a sufficient condition for marriage and indicated that they were still in the process of determining what they thought their futures should look like. Although neither of them left the classes with an epiphany of how to proceed, they felt it had helped structure their conversations.

The second, and more common, difference between evangelicals and Catholics was the frequency of their participation. The willingness of evangelical couples to attend early was matched only by their tendency to enroll in multiple premarital counseling programs. In fact, Leticia, the woman mentioned earlier who was disappointed that she couldn't remember the interesting concepts she learned, followed up by joking, "We can always do the class again." At the time of our interview, they had already completed both classes at Cosmopolitan Church and were in the process of meeting with one of their pastors for individualized counseling, but as their joking indicates, they were willing to continue participating in similar programs. Since the next class would take place after their wedding date, they more seriously noted that they were planning to join one of the small groups for newlyweds. In the meantime, they were continuing to meet with a few other engaged couples from their class to "just, you know, touch base with them and see how it's going." As with the other couples I spoke with during my study, evangelicals were generally motivated and interested in attending any type of program they thought may be beneficial for their relationship and could better ensure marital success.

For example, Nathan and Jaime also attended both classes and completed the individualized sessions at Cosmopolitan Church. They viewed the two organizational styles as complementary and valued the different ways that they each assuaged relational concerns. For Nathan, going to class every week and hearing from others in a similar position had helpfully normalized relationship dynamics. In contrast, he believed that the more targeted guidance of the individualized sessions helped them improve an issue that had been a perpetual strain— Jaime had a close relationship with her family, who did not get along with Nathan.

NATHAN: [Adam] was able to help us address the family stuff a little bit, which I thought was *really huge*. Actually, I saw *marked* improvement I think there. Wouldn't you agree?
JAIME: For who? Me?
NATHAN: Us. Just like how we handled your family, I just saw general changes in how *we* handled your family.
JAIME: Yeah, that's probably true. And I think I had heard that coming from my [own] counselor, but being able to go to that together and to hear the same thing makes a difference too.

The personalized sessions helped Nathan, at least, feel as if they had made traction on addressing an issue that had been a consistent point of tension by providing them tools to approach it as a team. Similar to Kevin's earlier account, participating in premarital counseling provided Nathan with an intentional and structured opportunity to discuss underlying frustrations, which allowed him to feel closer and more aligned with his partner.

Most often, couples followed this pattern of attending multiple programs by combining attendance at a collective class—such as Cosmopolitan Church or the Exploring Your Relationship Retreat—with individualized counseling with someone from their church. At Cosmopolitan Church, couples were expected to enroll in both the collective and individualized premarital counseling if they wanted to get married by one of their pastors. A reciprocal relationship, however, existed between the church's organizational structure and couples' motivations because the different classes had emerged in response to the high demand for premarital counseling that had overwhelmed the pastoral staff. In contrast, the Exploring Your Relationship Retreat program operated outside of a congregational structure, which meant attendance tended to be an "add-on" experience to whatever couples may be doing at their home church(es). Most of these couples reported enrolling based on the recommendation of someone from their church and because they had been looking for something else to supplement their premarital counseling experience. For some people coming from small churches where they had a preexisting relationship with the pastor, attending the retreat allowed for a more intimate experience as a couple in a neutral setting. Couples like Kristi and Tim, who worked at the church, or Tyler and

Hannah, whose father was the pastor, felt the retreat offered an opportunity to participate in premarital counseling without feeling guarded about what they could or should share. Regardless of the organizational logics that structured the expectations of when and what form of premarital counseling to enroll in, evangelical couples routinely *chose* to participate in multiple programs because they wanted this type of guidance and valued the opportunity.

Underlying evangelicals' consistent decision to enroll early and often in premarital counseling appears to be a pervasive apprehension about whether they were making the right choice and if the relationship would thrive in marriage. Whether enrolling in classes to prepare for marriage, to confirm their inclination to get engaged, or to help determine if a relationship may have run its course, evangelicals' worries about how to be happy and avoid divorce manifested in an emotional culture marked by relational anxiety. In fact, at the end of my interview questions, I would ask couples if there was anything else they wanted to add or if they had any questions. Some people used this time to ask me to evaluate them against all the other couples I had interviewed and wanted me to assess whether I saw any "red flags" in their relationship. Others used the time to ask me personally about my own experiences in marriage, including how we handled particular issues in our relationship or about whether I felt the first year of marriage was a difficult transition. Since I also heard evangelicals ask these types of questions to the married leadership during open question portions of the classes, these appeared to be deeply held concerns that didn't emerge exclusively from the experience of an interview that required them to reflect on their relationship and views on marriage. I did not recognize the extent to which this relational anxiety permeated the evangelical programs and motivated their participation until I began to attend the Catholic classes and spoke with couples who enrolled for different reasons.

Catholic Marriage Preparation for Sacramental Education and a Religious Wedding

For the Catholics I encountered, marriage preparation was tightly coupled with wedding planning. Specifically, their attendance was motivated by someone, most often the woman's, desire to have a church wedding *and* to receive the sacrament. When I spoke with couples who participated in Catholic programs, they generally did not expect it to lead to epiphanies about their relationship and seemed pleasantly surprised if it did. Instead, marriage preparation was more narrowly conceptualized as a requirement for a wedding, which meant they approached the programs from a different vantage point. Marriage preparation existed as one of the numerous items on their wedding to-do list along with selecting flowers, finding the dress, and finalizing the guest list. For example, Jennifer and Riley enrolled in their local parish's marriage preparation a full year in advance of their wedding date, as she explained, to "get this check marked off." In fact, selecting a program was often associated with the wedding venue. When I asked Sarah and Tom why they drove an hour to participate in marriage preparation at St. Sebastian, they instead described why they had selected that church for the wedding.[12]

For Catholics, the selection of the wedding venue holds greater religious significance than among evangelicals because it shapes whether the ceremony and marriage can be sacramental. The Catholic Church has strict guidelines that must be followed about where a wedding can be held (church) and who can officiate it (priest).[13] For many couples, before they considered whether they would turn to their religious community for premarital education, they first had to determine whether they would have a Catholic wedding. For Jennifer and Riley, this conversation occurred prior to their engagement as something that had to be negotiated because Riley was not religious and had not realized the extent of Jennifer's faith. As she explained, "I think before we were engaged, we talked about Catholic versus non-Catholic wedding. And of course at that point of time, I wasn't going to church again." After a frustrating year of teaching the RCIC (Rite for Christian Initiation for Children) at her local parish to a "*terrible* class" of twenty seven- to sixteen-year-olds who were "just disruptive and rowdy," she decided "I need a break. I can't deal with this." As she elaborated,

> So I wasn't going to church much, and he was like, "You only want to get married 'cause your parents are Catholic." I was like, "You know, that's not really the reason. I do go to the church. I do believe in the Church. You know that's part of my upbringing. I can still say yes to every one of my baptismal vows. Like, that's part of who I am." So then I started—I still

don't go all the time—but I started volunteering again at the church. To just be like, "Ha, ha! I am Catholic." (Laughs). So I think that's when he was like, "Oh yeah, you actually do go and you do participate. You are a Sunday school teacher."

The decision to get married in the Catholic Church—and by extension, whether to participate in marriage preparation—rested mainly on Jennifer. Although raised vaguely Methodist, faith held no personal significance for Riley, who described himself as "not a very religious person." However, once he realized the importance of her faith, he was willing "to get *Catholic married*," as Jennifer referred to it. From his perspective, "we're in this together. And obviously, whether or not I have the same views, I have complete respect for her views."

Most couples I met during my observations of Catholic marriage preparation similarly consisted of a Catholic engaged to a non-Catholic. In fact, of the ten couples I formally interviewed across the two parish programs, seven of them followed this pattern. Since in most of the cases, the women tended to be the Catholic partner, "their" decision to participate in these programs resulted from the woman's desire to be married in the Catholic Church. For these women, being married in the Catholic Church held significance for them personally and for their family. Yet, the women did not often expect it to be meaningful to their non-Catholic partner and regularly worried about their fiancé's feelings when the programming was overtly religious. As a result, they tended to make decisions that distanced themselves and their relationships from the Catholic Church through the process. In selecting which form of marriage preparation for them to participate in, Jennifer noted that she had opted for the weekly program in the parish instead of the diocesan weekend retreat because "I was thinking for him, it would just be a little bit at a time, instead of *shove you* into the Catholic Church." Even in the shorter classes, however, she still worried about him when it became "too churchy" and indicated that it sometimes inhibited her appreciation or learning. Erica, mentioned at the start of the chapter, had also chosen to attend the weekly parish programs over the retreat and echoed similar concerns, noting, "I didn't want [Max] to feel like he was having my faith stuffed down his throat" and thought that he wouldn't appreciate that the retreat would have meant "not sleeping together." In each case, the women sought to balance their personal motivations for participating with a relational awareness of how their irreligious partner would feel during the programs. In contrast, Sophie appreciated that the class was able to showcase a different side of Catholicism to her non-Catholic partner: "The class was great, like at least for him, it was a great introduction to the Catholic Church because you have these ideas about it. You have heard all about the scandals and the uptight gay [attitudes] or whatever. And then you go and meet some people and kind of begin to get introduced to the ideas and that 'this is what it really is; it isn't like a news headline.'"

The location of the Pacific Northwest likely contributes to the high proportion of Catholics marrying non-Catholics, but even when marrying another Catholic, the women tended to be the ones deciding to have a religious wedding. For example, in an interview with Javier and Sofia after an evening Mass one Sunday, he commented that he mostly attends church because of her. Although they had recently made this a regular part of their relationship, he claimed, "I wouldn't go at all at first." After establishing that in the past, he didn't care about church, I asked what had changed. In response, Sofia described how she didn't want to "just get together" but "always envisioned getting married in a church." After trying to "put myself in her shoes," Javier began to imagine the future positive feelings and memories that a church wedding could provide: "I kinda envision our pictures and our family all being there and where we're going to go on our wedding day." Their recent effort to be more religiously involved, therefore, was deeply connected to the type of relationship Sofia wanted, and she set the tone by making it clear she would not move in with him unless they were married. Likewise, their narrative again reveals the centrality of the wedding as a religious ceremony that structures Catholics' motivations for participating in marriage preparation and the timing of when they approach their religious communities.

Couples' emphasis on weddings as the primary explanation for participating in marriage preparation, in fact, organizationally emerges from the Catholic Church's authority over the Sacrament of Matrimony. Unlike most Protestant denominations, Catholicism maintains a clear distinction between a civil wedding and a church ("valid") wedding. Thus, the timeline for when Catholics participate differed from evangelicals not only because Catholic couples never attend prior to engagement but because they did sometimes participate (civilly) married. Any couple who didn't originally perform their marital vows within an approved Catholic setting may seek a convalidation to make their wedding "valid" within the Church. The parish leaders I spoke with regularly reported a sizable but consistent minority of approximately 20–25 percent of the couples participate in their programs for this reason.[14] The presence of civilly married couples alongside the engaged couples indicates yet another way that organizational structures pattern people's motivations. During my study, I formally conducted three interviews with civilly married couples seeking a convalidation. In each case, the couples involved a Catholic woman married to a non-Catholic partner. Although their reasons for not originally trying for a Catholic wedding varied, each woman eventually realized it was important to her to have her relationship validated by her religious community and her nonreligious husband agreed to support her in this.

By the time I met Nathalia at a local coffee shop, she had been married to her husband, Brian, for six years. The couple had met and started dating while she was an exchange student from Mexico. As a result of this circumstance, he had proposed within six months and they married shortly thereafter. Even though they had always planned to have a big Catholic wedding in Mexico, they had prioritized buying a house, and the years had slipped by. As Nathalia explained, she felt that after all these years, it had finally reached a point of "now or never [because] if not, we're not going to do it anymore." In contrast, Sophie and Nathan had discovered that they were pregnant during their engagement and opted to quickly marry because they worried about medical decision making if there were complications during labor. Although they had considered obtaining a parental affidavit, it turned out that the civil wedding with a justice of the peace was the cheaper and easier option. Their convalidation appears to have been unusual not because the couple was pregnant but because they were seeking to make their marriage "valid" within a short period of the wedding. Although Sophie shared that she had been pleasantly surprised by the lack of judgment that they were living together and pregnant, my conversations with the parish leadership indicated that they thought the couple had been married much longer and was returning because of the pregnancy.

In contrast to their evangelical peers, Catholics attend marriage preparation only once and possibly after years of being married. Often, Catholic couples walked away with personal and relational insights, but they did not enroll in these programs for relationship discernment or counseling. Rather, as a form of sacramental preparation, it connected people to what should be a once-in-a-lifetime ritual in their faith community. The narrower motivation for Catholic participation emerges from an organizational context where couples are expected to be permanently transformed through the sacrament of marriage. The seriousness of the meaning of the ritual also contributed to the divergent emotional culture, where couples were less enthusiastic but also less anxious during the classes. Since the programs weren't conceptualized as a form of discernment, couples were less concerned about determining if they were ready for marriage because they had already individually come to this decision beforehand. While these differences in why and when couples chose to enroll in marriage preparation programs led to variation in the intensity and anxiety of couples' pursuit of a good marriage, as we will see, they often used this time to similarly deepen an emotional connection.

What Do Couples Learn?
Searching for Authentic Advice and Embracing the Liminal Process

From my initial interviews with couples from the Exploring Your Relationship Retreat to the final ones at the Catholic parishes, I encountered people who routinely described enjoying programs that they struggled to recall in much detail. Many echoed David's assessment: "I thought [the class] was excellent. I would 100 percent and strongly recommend it to any Christian dating couple or even non[-Christians] probably." While others wondered whether non-Christians would be distracted by the religious lessons, the irreligious partners who attended the Catholic programs tended to report also enjoying their experiences and would similarly recommend that other couples attend. In the formal and informal interviews, I sometimes heard an evangelical quibble over the theological presentation of a concept, an extroverted person wish for more structured interaction with other couples, or someone express a "personality conflict" with a member of the leadership team. Yet, for the most part, people shared positive memories of their time, even if they held different religious, political, or social views than the premarital counselors.

Yet, despite what their generally favorable assessments of the programs may indicate, attending couples were not indiscriminatory about the lessons or the people teaching them. Willa, for example, confessed, "I don't think I am prone to trust people and what they say about relationships." But despite her tendency to be skeptical about other people's advice, she found "that [in] the class, I did trust what they said." Elaborating, she explained, "They were really honest. They were very, you know, humble in regards of what they go through [and] that it is not all a bed of roses." In fact, people regularly responded supportively to the leadership's revealing narratives of relational challenges and conflicts. Kristi likewise commented, "I loved how open and honest each couple was in sharing. They just really showed how things can affect your marriage, and each one had something different that made their marriage hard." As discussed earlier, couples attending these programs learned personal and in-depth details about the married lives of the leaders, ranging from the mundane challenges of parenting and in-laws to more intimate difficulties caused by affairs and miscarriages. Even though confessions of relationship conflict could have potentially undermined the authority of the leadership to counsel on marriage, most of the couples I spoke with saw it as a sign of authenticity that established credibility for their advice. In other words, it was easier to trust the recommendations on relationship skills when it appeared that the leaders had used them to work on maintaining or perhaps even repairing their marriages. The attending couples, in turn, not only learned the covenant rhetoric lessons that a good marriage is characterized by self-reflexivity and a marital work ethic but thus were using it to assess the leadership.

In reflecting on their experiences, couples employed language such as "honest" and "real" to evaluate premarital counselors. Amanda, for example, specifically appreciated how the leadership at Cosmopolitan Church discussed the theme of sexual shame and their struggles to transition sexually in marriage: "I liked how they were super honest too about it; that it was hard. . . . I just thought it was sweet that they were that transparent about things in front of people they don't necessarily know." The willingness to share about the sexual negotiations in one's marriage also stood out to Gwendolyn during the Exploring Your Relationship Retreat: "I was a little surprised just the way [Joseph] could openly tell his business like that. I thought that was a pleasant surprise but that [it] was good for them to be transparent in their life and their relationship with each other." Evangelicals were the most likely to share these assessments, probably because these programs tended to be more confessional and couples had more sustained time with the leadership. Nonetheless, Catholic couples usually could identify one of the rotating married leaders whom they connected with. For example, Erica noted that there was one couple that if they had led the full program, her response would have been "I don't want to do this if they're teaching this," but the rotation of the leadership meant she was comfortable returning because she knew there would be someone new the next week. Later, she encountered couples whom she felt "were just real" and "would give us examples of their personal lives that they didn't have to give us." In addition to revealing personal details, Sophie and Nathan commented that the leadership whom they found "relatable" were not only "pretty open" but also included relationship skills "that we could apply to everyday life."

In fact, most of the frustrations that people expressed about the leadership and the programs resulted from a sense that they could have done *more*—more topics, more depth, and more engagement. Sophie wished the leadership had "challenged us a little bit more maybe." Others noted elements they believed had been too shallow or insufficient. For example, many evangelicals felt the brief discussion of finances was not enough and that there should have been a whole session; several Catholics wished the programs had offered more thoughtful attention to the topic of interfaith couples. As these examples illustrate, however, people were not rejecting lessons because they didn't agree with them but because they wished for more or better content on a particular topic.

Initially, I was perplexed by how people maintained a generally positive assessment of programs that they could not always recall with much detail and that sometimes espoused views so different than their own. It wasn't until I decided to *participate* in the Exploring Your Relationship Retreat, and not simply observe it, that I comprehended the themes of emotional significance, ineffability, and the emphasis on the process.[15] Whereas in my initial observations at the retreat I had operated as an analytical and critical outsider who could pick up on small details, participating with my partner allowed me to adopt the perspective of wanting it to be personally useful. Preoccupied with determining how best to express myself and looking forward to hearing how my partner would respond to the prompts, I found myself reacting differently to the material. The content, as my interviewees shared, became something to sift through for what was meaningful, useful, and practical. I found myself disregarding lessons I didn't agree with because they weren't personally applicable but also discovering new relevance in ideas that I had previously dismissed. Indeed, the parts of the programs couples found most memorable and meaningful were the opportunities to cultivate the covenant rhetoric in their relationships—learning to better articulate qualities of the self and discover more about their partner as they did the same.

Covenant Rhetoric in Action: Practicing Self-Reflexivity and Rehearsing a (Pre)marital Work Ethic

As I asked couples to recall their experiences attending the programs, their memories tended to focus on the time that they spent together. For example, when I inquired about what Shawn and Gwendolyn had most enjoyed during the Exploring Your Relationship Retreat, she quickly responded with "the discussion times, because that's when we came together." Elaborating, she reflected, "The discussion time just let me know that we are on the right track and that we can pretty much discuss topics and be good. And, you know, pretty much be in the same place about it." Others stumbled more over their answers but ultimately described the "intimacy" of the process. For example, Malaya said, "My favorite part [was] where we can just write how we feel, you know, without someone . . . I don't know, without . . . without any guards or without . . . I don't know how else to say it, but it just felt really intimate and real to me, and it kind of strengthened our idea to get married, you know?" Perhaps because of the underlying marital anxiety in the evangelical programs, these couples tended to more often share that the discussions served as a way to affirm that they know each other and that they are entering into marriage with a clear understanding of the other person and their relationship. In contrast, Catholics also mentioned that attending the classes together, connecting over the material, and learning about each other was what made the programs worthwhile, but as we have seen, they used it less as a discernment tool for the relationship. For example, when I interviewed Erica and Max, she mentioned multiple times that their weekly class attendance became a special time as a couple that she looked forward to and that they had made a routine of going out for a drink afterward to reflect on or even joke about the class. As a Catholic woman already married to an irreligious husband, however, she found a different type of confirmation by attending the programs: "It kind of just made me also see him in a different, you know, light. Like, oh my God, he's really doing all this for me. Like, wow. I'm so worth that. You know? But he's doing that for me, so I appreciate it."

It would be a mistake, however, to interpret couples' emphasis on the intimacy of their shared time as evidence that the programs only operate in the background. Although many people emphasized their own discussions over the presented lessons, they recognized that the programs structured and directed these conversations. Amanda, for example, commented, "I enjoyed the chance, the space that [Cosmopolitan Church leaders] gave to talk as couples" because even though "a lot of these conversations we [had] have come up [already]," she appreciated "the way that they framed them and the support they gave for that was really encouraging." Likewise, reflecting on his experience with fiancée Kristi at the Exploring Your Relationship Retreat, Tim shared,

> I think one of the things that we both really liked was the communication—the openness and the honesty that we both were able to have with each other. A lot of stuff that we talked about [over] that weekend we already had discussed, but there were some things that came up that we both were kinda like, "Whoa! Okay, that's something I didn't know." It opened up more discussion in other areas.

As Amanda and Tim's accounts reveal, people often found that even if the topics were not new, their conversations about them could be deeper. Given that most couples had been together for at least a year and sometimes up to six, the programs rarely unearthed hidden dimensions to relationships. After all, the main topics covered by these programs—faith, sex, finances, communication, family of origin, conflict management, career aspirations, and so forth—do not only emerge in marriage but can also structure dating relationships. From going on dates to buying each other presents to visiting someone's family, all represent opportunities that can lead to emergent conversations about people's views on money, their families, and more. It's possible, however, that any organic discussion of these topics could be because of a misunderstanding, result in conflict, or be interrupted by other demands. Unlike the type of exchange that occurs in daily life, the liminal structure of marriage preparation facilitated deep dialogue and self-reflexivity. Specifically, couples' discussion of sensitive matters occurred at a time when people are seeking to engage in emotion work that allows them to learn about and connect with their partner. The premarital counselors' guiding lessons and prompts also create a context for emotion management that encourages people to cultivate a sense of openness and mitigate any tendency to be defensive.

In fact, there were a number of people who expressed that engaging in this process had "forced" them to discuss important issues that were uncomfortable, difficult to approach in everyday life, or that they hadn't felt capable of sharing previously. Sofia and Javier, for example, found the class at St. Bernadette to be "*super* helpful" for this reason. Sofia confessed that "there's stuff that would come up in the class that I *really* didn't want to talk about or that I *really* tried to avoid, but we had to talk about it." In particular, the class on communication had challenged her to be more open with Javier and not withdraw when something bothered her. In contrast, the Exploring Your Relationship Retreat had forced Will to realize an assumption about how he envisioned married life, which became the start of a helpful conversation with his fiancée, Gretchen.

> It asked a lot of questions that were I guess kind of uncomfortable questions, you know? Things I don't want to come out and say like, "Do you expect her to cook for you?" I don't want to be like, "Gretchen, I expect you to cook for me." But at the same time, I'm thinking, "Oh, I guess I kind of do." Like that's the picture I have in my mind is, you know, she cooks.

Will credited the process with helping him learn unknown dimensions about himself, which in turn made it possible, if not entirely easy, to reveal more to Gretchen.

Likewise, Sylvia also felt that the retreat "forced" her to recognize and confront anxieties about her upcoming wedding to Hayden. Unlike some of the other couples who relished the opportunity to write each other "love letters" at the Exploring Your Relationship Retreat, Sylvia and Hayden believed it pushed each of them outside of their comfort zone. She explained, "Just being forced in that situation where I know he's coming back and I'm gonna have to have something written and . . . yeah, it just helped me a lot. I just wrote a lot for almost everything, and it was very therapeutic for me even if it wasn't necessarily for him." Between the structure that required her to write and the questions that asked her to probe her feelings, she had to confront festering issues.

> I think some of it was surprising for him because it was like, "What do you think about marriage?" And I was like, "Scared." And he was like, "Oh, well why? That's odd." Just a lot of fear and anxiety and like sadder thoughts for a lot of things and he wasn't expecting any of those responses. It was helpful to talk about why, and, and I mean, just being honest about all that instead of just saying, "Yay! I'm happy and ready."

In contrast to her everyday experience where she felt pressured to be excited, she embraced the challenge set by the leaders to honestly own and share her anxieties about what being married would mean. Specifically, she confessed, "It was a lot to do with sex. I didn't want to have sex and I didn't want to deal with that. I didn't want to talk to anyone about it. [It was] just that unspoken fear." Through their conversations, however, she "realized it wasn't all to do with sex; it was more to do with trust and fear and preparedness." By the time I conducted the interview, they had been married for a few months, which had allowed Sylvia to reflect about how that period had been a stressful time where they were "getting in so many arguments," including one on the way there. In comparison to the unproductive conversations that they tended to have late at night with her "crying on the phone," the retreat created a different emotional space and script to discuss their feelings. Unlike issues that arose "naturally," there was a sense that the intentional and liminal quality of premarital counseling allowed couples to engage in self-reflexivity and work on their relationship under less acutely stressful conditions, such as amid an argument.

Couples' use of the word "forced" to describe their conversations indicates that they believed that participating in the programs resulted in discussions, confessions, and realizations that they may not have had on their own, or at least were unlikely to have had prior to their wedding. In fact, this led Max, the atheist husband who attended St. Bernadette, to wish in retrospect that they had been able to have these preparatory conversations earlier. After six years of marriage, he reflected, "We just kind of [thought], 'Oh, we love each other. I guess it'll all work out,' you know? So we didn't do any real planning. We just kind of, you know, threw ourselves at it. Yeah, it was one of the worst pieces of planning I've ever really done. It's probably my least well-planned move in life so far." Although it would be impossible to know what the impact would have been, Max felt that the conversations would have better prepared them for conflicts they had in the early years of marriage and allowed them to better understand what to expect for their future. Thus, from pre-engaged couples to married ones, there was a shared sense that participating in the process offered people an opportunity to feel heard by their partner, even when the program made them ask questions that resulted in surprising or difficult revelations.

Despite the feeling rules that say the wedding is supposed to be the happiest day of one's life,[16] engaged couples often appeared stressed and overwhelmed by the prospect. In attempting to arrange interviews, I regularly heard from couples that they were "too busy" until the wedding, which meant that I often conducted interviews with newlyweds who could reflect on recently having made the transition to marriage. Removed from the pressure of planning the wedding, many of these couples recalled that the programs allowed them to meet others in a similar position, which helped to normalize their sense of anxiety. For example, newlyweds Jaime and Nathan explained, "Engagement is a very stressful time in your life." Remembering how they "argued a lot," Jaime recalled Nathan worrying that "this isn't normal" and thought that "this should be a happy time." Attending Cosmopolitan Church's class helped to reassure him and alleviate some concerns, such as hearing that other couples also fought over flowers. Specifically, he found the opportunity to discuss their experiences in small group helpful because he would realize "here's someone else who's going through the same things we are. You know, they love each other, but they're still wondering about this and they're still not sure about that and they're still having trouble with this." In the end, he felt that this provided a sense that "you're, like, okay." Although lacking this relationship anxiety common among evangelicals, Catholics also believed the other couples made the requirement of marriage preparation a more enjoyable experience. Fiona disclosed that they had been "dreading" attending the classes at St. Sebastian but shared, "I think we both really enjoyed being around other couples that were getting [married] and also there were several interfaith couples." Likewise, the presence of other interfaith couples helped to assuage both Jennifer's and Erica's apprehension about making their nonreligious partners attend St. Bernadette.

A consistent critique from both evangelicals and Catholics across the various programs was actually that they wished that there had been more time to get to know the other couples. Despite their valuing the intimate discussion time as a couple, people regularly expressed a sense that there was a missed opportunity to forge connections with other people. The wish for greater "social time" with other people sometimes appeared to result from a desire to expand social networks, which was a salient concern for many of the transplants in the Pacific Northwest. Yet, there was also a programmatic dimension to this critique because people indicated that the presence of other couples enriched their ability to engage the process. In discussing the class on conflict, Javier recalled feeling that other people's contributions were "really helpful." He enjoyed having these couples around as they learned about relationships because when they "would share how they face the problems, you'd be like, 'Wow, I should have done that.'" Nathan also felt that he benefited from others asking a "good question" and "just the inputs they have." In fact, Jessica commented that "even if they gave us the curriculum and we did this all on our own, it would have gained something, but I think being in the class with other people, there's a lot more that you could gain from it."

In the end, premarital counseling doesn't get couples to do anything they wouldn't do, but it does allow them to do something they *want* to do—namely, couples want to work on their relationship and find ways to cultivate therapeutic love within it. The brief programs provide them with the space, time, and practice to rehearse a marital work ethic. The process is characterized and strengthened by its liminality—couples are able to step outside of their daily lives and busy schedules to exclusively focus on each other, their relationship, and the next phase of their lives. They regularly reported that the process emerged as a special time, but it was also one not easily replicated outside of the provided structure, which guided them in how to forge connections and organize their emotion work. Thus, the liminal quality simultaneously worked against long-term retention of ideas but also met the goal of training couples to work on their relationships. Couples may not be able to articulate the teachings, but their narratives do reflect the core lesson of the covenant rhetoric: love is not inevitable but requires individuals to be self-reflexive and engage in emotion work.

Conclusion

Couples attending marriage preparation neither reject nor accept the programs' contents. In fact, their insights rarely emerged directly from learning lessons but rather from engaging in the process, which required them to turn inward. Instead of employing an overly cognitive framework that focuses only on whether people's beliefs align with religious leaders or their reactions to the lessons, when we take a lived religion approach, we can reevaluate the question of how these programs work from their perspective. As sociologist Meredith McGuire argues, people are less invested in whether their faith is "logically coherent" and more concerned with whether it "makes sense in one's everyday life."[17] She notes that religion must "work" for people by providing some "sense of accomplishing some desired end," including "improving one's relationship with a loved one." Building on this perspective, sociologist Kathleen Jenkins challenges scholars to stop treating "religion as static background information" and suggests that "researchers should ask open-ended questions that help them unpack the processes through which religion and spirituality may inform, inspire, and limit how individuals think about families."[18] From this vantage point, the couples' practice of sifting through the lessons becomes less a case of picking and choosing what to believe and more a part of the (pre)marital emotion work required in the covenant rhetoric.

Catholic marriage preparation and evangelical premarital counseling may organizationally establish different reasons for why individuals feel compelled to enroll in the programs, but the leaders in each instruct couples that a Christian marriage requires work. This lesson, however, is more than an abstract idea that couples are expected to be able to recite. The covenant rhetoric represents something couples are expected to *do* by becoming aware of their feelings, articulating them in a way that is comprehensible, and augmenting them to align with their partner. Thus, the programming provides couples with the opportunity to rehearse a marital work ethic. Although the liminality of the process may have worked against retention of the ideas, it did offer a time and space set aside from the everyday pressures and distractions for this practice. As couples' narratives of their experience indicate, they believed that the programs "worked" when it facilitated a sense of transcendence where the couples could *feel their togetherness*.

Yet, despite this shared view that engaging in the process helped to unite couples, the broader patterns of gendered scripts for emotion work that structure heterosexual relationships were present. While researchers argue that emotion work contributes to marital satisfaction and can mediate against marital burnout,[19] the active management of feelings is gendered and can contribute to inequities in marital power. Reflecting studies that find that women are more likely to initiate marriage counseling,[20] the couples' narratives regularly revealed women's central role in enrolling in the programs. For the Catholics, this was most readily apparent because they were more likely the religious person in the couple. But even among evangelicals, it was clear that women were pushing their partners to attend as part of an effort to learn more about him and to move their relationship to the next phase. Even though women valued how the programs allowed them access to men's internal, emotional worlds, they were also often the vocal ones about how the programs could have done more, covered additional material, or gone deeper in a particular dimension. In contrast, men tended to participate at the request of their girlfriend or a religious leader. Yet, men reported appreciating how these programs structured emotion work for them by guiding their interactions in ways that allowed them to express their feelings and feel heard by their partner. In other words, the programs were able to open the gendered scripts of emotion work for men but reinscribed them for women. The narratives revealed women's greater responsibility in monitoring and inculcating intimate feelings by ensuring that men participated. Once there, men were able to engage in the process in a manner that ensured that their needs were met. This follows sociologists Tristan Bridges and C. J. Pascoe's insights that new forms of masculinities have emerged that allow men to challenge hegemonic discourses, including that men cannot be emotional, but that ultimately these new forms of masculinities "reify gender inequality even as they obscure it."[21] In the end, the programs provided couples an opportunity to also rehearse the gendered dimensions of a marital work ethic.

The couples who participated in Christian marriage preparation recognize that they are on the precipice of change. For some, this change may be greater because it may be the first time they have sex or feel that having it is "allowed." For others, it may be about moving in together, joining finances, blending their families, or the consideration of having children. Although there were some couples, more often Catholic than evangelical, that didn't anticipate that their lives would change "much," getting married in the United States alters normative expectations and the ways that people treat a person and view their relationship. Since premarital counseling is ultimately about change, the conclusion will next consider what the practice reveals about the changes to intimate relationships.

Conclusion

Working toward the Good Marriage

At around 11:00 a.m. on Sunday, I found myself helping the leadership team at the Exploring Your Relationship Retreat break down the room. While the premarital couples were off privately discussing their responses about how they could make adjustments to their lives to better include God in their upcoming marriage, I rearranged chairs and put away decorations. It seemed weird to think back that I had just met everyone on Friday evening and had spent the hours leading up to the couples' arrival helping to string up Christmas lights and place fall foliage around to personalize the space. As I moved tables out of the way, I realized that in less than seventy-two hours, I had gone from awkward introductions to knowing intimate details about the people quietly cleaning up with me.

Eventually, all that remained was a circle of chairs in the center of the room. As I was packing up another part of the room, Kelly placed a "certificate of completion" with the names of the premarital couples on the chairs. When the couples began to filter into the room and walk around the circle to find a seat, she explained, "Some pastors require couples to attend premarital counseling, and this proves you've completed it." I located the single empty chair set aside for me, sat down, and overheard the man next to me jokingly ask his fiancée in a quiet voice, "Will you hang it up on the fridge when you get home?" "No," she resoundingly but still quietly responded. "My roommate would think it's weird."

Once everyone had found their seat, Paul attempted to create the space for people to reflect by inquiring, "Are there any last comments or questions before we pray?" There was a brief silence as we stared at each other across the circle, before people began to volunteer short comments of appreciation, such as "thanks for your transparency" and for "sharing your stories." As people offered these insights, others nodded along and murmured their own agreement. One man noted, "It was nice to see how you all interacted because it's so rare to see couples who visibly love and care for each other after so many years of marriage."

Eventually, as the silence between comments lengthened, Paul shared, "The final act of the weekend is for us to pray with you." In turn, each of the three married couples on the leadership team walked around the inside of the circle, leaned into a seated premarital couple, and formed a physical connection by grasping a shoulder or holding hands. With their heads tilted in toward the younger couples, the room was filled with quiet prayers. As I sat by myself, I caught snippets of the leaders offering personalized comments about something they appreciated or learned about the couple over the weekend. One of the young women in response to these quiet affirmations began to cry because, as I later learned, she felt such pronounced relief at hearing that "differences are okay in marriage." When the prayers were complete, the leaders moved on to the next couple in the circle and the previous one gathered their stuff to leave. And with this simple event, premarital counseling had come to an end. Yet, it ended with these couples on the threshold of a new beginning and the communities considering how to repeat it all again.

Most of the time, ethnographer's decisions to enter and exit the field represent their own choices and lives, which can create seemingly artificial narratives of a beginning and an end. As religion scholar Alyssa Maldonado-Estrada notes, "ethnographers probe the ephemeral" because "relationships, material spaces, and practices are not stable."[1] For myself, as a researcher, and the Christians whom I encountered, our time in marriage preparation was structured to be ephemeral—temporary and fixed. Unlike the more nebulous process of ethnographically learning about people's relationships and faith journeys, I observed marriage preparation programs that operate as a therapeutic intervention, which is distinguished by its liminality—limited time, focused emotion work, and separation from daily life. In other words, I came alongside a rotating cast of couples during their crucible of preparing for a Christian marriage and then repeated this process in new communities and with new couples.

Whereas past work has investigated how religious leaders' views about family life manifest in congregational programming, small groups, and sermons,[2] I selected a specific form of ministry to unearth insights about the shifting landscape of religion and family. I build on, for example, sociologist Penny Edgell's study of how the type and variation of family ministries revealed that congregations remain predominately organized around the two-parent family with children.[3] She argued that "the 'standard package' of ministry from the 1950s and the cultural model of family on which it is based are still influential"[4] and at best have been "stretched"[5] to accommodate issues of managing gender roles, work-family conflict, and family disruption. Whereas her research comparatively investigated the type of family forms served by congregations, this book explored in depth what we can learn about the "good" marriage from one type of Christian programming that transcends time and place.

In particular, this study of premarital counseling has allowed for a nuanced deconstruction of family change by considering how cultural shifts are packaged for individuals. Existing research has examined historical changes in the meaning of marriage,[6] as well as how people negotiate the new tensions that have emerged as couples strive for therapeutic love while work and gendered structures make mutual fulfillment challenging.[7] This book has bridged these studies by exploring how local communities mediate information about marital change, transmit visions of a good marriage, and operate as systems of accountability. The social history of marriage preparation illustrates that religious communities aren't merely slowly reacting to broader cultural transitions but the ways that they have contributed to the rising therapeutic ethos and helped to broadly disseminate it. In the process of offering systematic marital advice, churches also emotionally socialize people into how they ought to feel in and about families, which in turn provides interpretive frames for understanding the broader landscape of changes to marriage. It also guides them in how to feel about what they feel by infusing being "Christian" with therapeutic competencies, such as the capacity to assess and manage one's emotional reactions.

To conclude the book, this chapter addresses three questions that have regularly emerged when speaking about my research. First, people have asked, "What's religious about marriage preparation?" For instance, a reader familiar with state-sponsored marriage education programs, marriage counseling, or other therapeutic interventions into relationships may wonder whether these programs are all that different than secular ones. To answer this question, I consider the impact of how the practice interweaves relationship education and religious education as a foundation for how to emotionally socialize people into what constitutes spiritual and marital success. Second, people are always curious about whether, or how well, these programs work. Implicit within this question is the view that enrolling in relationship education should transform couples and protect them against divorce. Even though I have argued that studying this outcome is methodologically fraught, I reflect on the type of impact I can reasonably claim that the programs do, and could, have on people's lives. Finally, the institution of marriage has undergone a major transition in the last decade that is notably absent from these pages. Although the leaders never publicly spoke with the couples on the topic of marriage equality, I take the time to investigate this silence for what it reveals about whom the covenant rhetoric is for. Finally, to finish out the book, I offer some parting thoughts on the power of emotions to shape our understanding of belonging, intimacy, and change.

Is This Practice Christian? And, What Is Catholic about Marriage Preparation and Evangelical about Premarital Counseling?

Throughout this book, we have seen how evangelical premarital counseling and Catholic marriage preparation represent a similar religio-therapeutic practice designed to advise Christians on the sanctification and success of marriage. The practice, however, is also part of a broader field of relationship education, including everything from high school students studying interpersonal dynamics to low-income couples learning relationship skills.[8] Across these settings, "experts" draw from psychology, sociology, communication, and counseling to instruct people in what sociologist Jennifer Randles has described as "skilled love," the view that romance can be rational, studied, and taught to ensure "healthy" practices.[9] The Christian programs are embedded within and contribute to this broader field of relationship education. For example, Catholics and evangelicals actively produce relationship texts and curricula, such as Christian therapists Les and Leslie Parrott's *Saving Your Marriage before It Starts* and Catholic thinker Christopher West's *Good News about Sex and Marriage*. Religious leaders were also, however, integrating secular insights, such as psychologists John Gottman and Nan

Silver's *The Seven Principles for Making Marriage Work*, into their lessons. Christian programs synthesize religious and secular relationship education as they transmit the marital work ethic to couples, yet these lessons cannot be disconnected from religious instruction within the local faith communities.

The lessons on how to have a *good* marriage were inextricably interwoven with the religious teachings on God's vision for the union. Christians esteem marriage to the point that it often becomes an implicit marker of adulthood within faith communities,[10] which resulted in a distinctively religious understanding that getting married is part of a process of spiritual development. Preparing for marriage, therefore, is also a form of religious education where faith communities transmit theological and scriptural lessons. In addition to impacting individuals' spiritual formation, getting married is more broadly tied to religious communities. Sociologist Mark Chaves describes the "core" feature of faith communities as "expressing and transmitting religious meaning through ritual and religious education."[11] For Christians, marriage is a ritual that transforms relationships and the people within them. As with the Eucharist (or Communion), another Christian ritual, something mundane becomes sacred. For a ritual to be transformative, a person must first be formed through religious education, where they learn why it is important, what it means to participate in it, and how it will make them feel.

In addition to the ineffable spiritual transformation that the ritual of marriage generates, for Christians, becoming a husband and wife means acquiring social statuses that include new rights, privileges, and expectations. In the domain of daily life, once couples are married, they are not only expected but also encouraged to engage in activities that had once been forbidden, including having sex, living together, sharing finances, and raising children. By transforming what actions are permissible, Christians also find themselves navigating a new emotional terrain for how they should feel personally and how others will feel about their behaviors. As with the case of sexual intimacy, this may sometimes require that people unlearn feelings of shame and avoidance to instead learn how to cultivate pleasure.[12]

We have considered thus far this practice as "Christian" and highlighted the ways a shared faith commitment has imprinted on relationship education to both distinguish it from similar secular initiatives and to forge community connection to other believers. Despite sharing the Bible as a scriptural text, a belief in premarital abstinence, an opinion that God views marriages as heterosexual, and a theology that elevates marriage for laity, Catholics and evangelical Protestants differ in key ways that emerged throughout the book. Simply put, the faith traditions may share this Christian religio-therapeutic practice, but they accentuated different dimensions of it. Catholic "marriage preparation" placed a greater emphasis on its religious education and evangelical "premarital counseling" on how it operates a form of relationship therapy. These differences, in turn, became part of the organizational structure and emotional culture that influenced when and why couples turned to their faith communities and the lessons they encountered.

As we saw, Pre-Cana, the earliest form of Catholic marriage preparation, emerged during the postwar era over concerns about the spiritual lives of the laity. Initially, it represented one strategy among Catholic family movements that sought to mobilize against secularism by better educating what they viewed as an illiterate laity. Predating the wide-sweeping changes that would come with Vatican II, clergy and laity worked together to develop a religious understanding that elevated the vocation of marriage and provided frameworks for how faith could permeate the daily activities of the home. Thus, since its inception, Catholic programs have been equal parts sacramental preparation and marriage education, which narrowed the focus to forming and assessing couples as they come to the Church for a wedding. The engaged couples I spoke with understood that marriage preparation is part of the requirement to be "Catholic married" and approached the parishes because it was important (to at least one person) that their union be recognized and that they maintain their belonging. They didn't expect this process to be a therapeutic intervention, and this low-key energy was matched by the rotating leadership that imparted what they know relationally but assured everyone that they would need to figure out what worked for their marriage. Thus, marriage, and the people within it, were often presented as malleable and works in progress, which cast "preparation" as a process of learning what you can and developing helpful habits to enable awareness about when life changes.

Evangelicals, in contrast, have always offered "premarital counseling" as a therapeutic practice for discernment. Although initially slower to embrace counseling because of its connection to secular psychology, their extensive media network of publishers and radio shows quickly became saturated with "experts" offering relationship advice and sharing confessional stories to illustrate the romantic challenges that evangelicals face. For evangelicals, premarital counseling has never been tied to preparing for a single ritual, but rather, it helps to address the cultural dilemma of living a Christian life within a secular world. Evangelicals approached the process with a series of questions—"How far is too far?" "How do you know when you're ready for marriage?" "How can you be sure that someone is right for you?"—that belied this anxiety about how best to live a faithful life. Looking to their religious communities for support and guidance, counseling became something that people could enroll in as necessary and that served as part of their ongoing effort of monitoring, assessing, and pivoting to ensure that they meet the evangelical call to "live in the world" without becoming "of the world." As a form of counseling, the process was predicated on self-discovery that required constant and serious work to learn about one's true self, whether one is ready for marriage, and if this is the right relationship, all of which raised the stakes of the process for the couples and leadership.

Despite Catholics' greater emphasis on religious education and evangelicals on therapeutic intervention, their programs generally offer similar content and pursue analogous outcomes. In an effort to prepare couples for both the mundane realities of married life and God's calling for the institution, leaders across the faith traditions selected the same topics as important: conflict, communication, the meaning of marriage, finances, family of origin, love languages, sex, and of course, the covenant rhetoric. Couples across the programs heard lessons that infused personal and therapeutic insights, had assigned homework and readings to complete on their own time, and were given assessments that asked them to explore their "compatibility" in these areas and to evaluate whether this marriage would be pleasing to God. As such, all couples were provided the opportunity to preemptively engage in the marital work ethic and self-reflexivity that they learn is part of a good and godly marriage. Yet, the evangelical programs were characterized by a greater intensity that permeated the emotion work expected from the intervention by both the leaders and couples seeking these opportunities. In a therapeutic era, sociologist Eva Illouz has argued that "the capacity to listen and identify with others" and the ability "to monitor relationships and emotions" has become part of a broader "emotional competence" that operates as a new form of capital.[13] It's possible, as she notes, that holding this type of capital allows for greater access and opportunities in both the workplace and intimate relations. Although it's conceivable that the greater demands placed on individuals in the evangelical programs may help them better cultivate this type of emotional competence, it may come at the cost of their own sense of anxiety of navigating interpersonal relationships in an insecurity culture.[14]

As an ethnographer navigating between and across the Catholic and evangelical programs, I inevitably found myself reflecting on the divergent emotional and organizational structures that I encountered. I realized that as a consequence, I walked away with a pronounced sense of difference between what I learned about marriage as an abstract concept and how I felt about being married. The evangelical programs left me with greater knowledge of relationship skills but also a more pronounced anxiety about whether I was even living up to these standards in my own marriage. In contrast, the Catholic programs left me with fewer tools but a more affable sense that marriage is doable and that I was prepared for the journey. In addition to complicating any efforts to label one approach as "better," this complexity of the impact of the program illustrates the challenges of determining how to evaluate if they "work." The next section more closely considers how we can assess the outcomes of these programs and whether couples' work during them leaves a lasting impression.

Do the Programs "Work"? Or, What Does the Program's Work Reveal?

Evangelical marriage therapist Gary Chapman, famous for *The Five Love Languages*, later wrote *Things I Wish I'd Known before We Got Married* because, as he explained, "it is my conviction that many of these struggles could have been avoided had the couple taken time to prepare more thoroughly for marriage."[15] Throughout this book, we have met people who similarly believed that it's possible to teach someone the principles of relationship success and a set of skills that will help them reach this goal. The first question that many people therefore ask when they learn about this research is, "Do these programs work?" To be able to answer this question requires first understanding what people mean by "work." Does a couple calling off or postponing a wedding count as the program working because a possibly incompatible relationship didn't make it to the altar? Or does the program work when it changes people and makes them act differently? Perhaps they work only if the marriage is different from what it would have been without the experience of participating in the program? Finally, maybe the programs work when they successfully expose couples to the challenges of marriage?

The different interpretations of how the programs might work importantly range in terms of what is knowable. From the vantage point of the leadership, couples postponing or canceling their weddings because of something that emerged during premarital counseling was always interpreted as a success because it meant that the process had effectively identified red flags. Whereas a lack of a marriage is observable, it is impossible to know how people would have interacted if they had never participated in the program. Even though someone like Max, the secular husband seeking a convalidation with his wife, Erica, may claim that the course would have been helpful because they would have handled issues differently in the early years of their marriage, this is purely hypothetical. If the programs cannot work in this manner, then what can we expect from them? And how can we be confident in our ability to know whether they have met this standard? Given the methodological challenges of studying the long-term impact of a short-term practice noted earlier in the book, I argue that the last question about exposure to marital challenges is the best way to assess these programs.

In fact, assessing the programs on this dimension of exposing couples to relevant material aligns with leaders' own concerns. While many of them would ideally like to believe that the programs could stem the tide of divorce, they more pragmatically realized that couples at this stage may wear rose-colored glasses or feel they have too many sunk costs in the relationship. Instead, many expressed a more modest goal of establishing a foundation of knowledge and tools that couples could return to when marital conflict inevitably emerged. Whether conceptualized as "preparation" or "counseling," therefore, the goal centers on ensuring that couples gain exposure to the type of stressors that inhibit communication and intimacy. In identifying these relevant topics, leadership tended to highlight individual and interpersonal factors, such as money, sex, in-laws, love languages, communication styles, personality types, and so forth. By doing so, the curriculum implicitly constructs relational strains as emerging from within the home and not external to it. The problem is that this foundation occurs in a divorce culture in which relationship success cannot be guaranteed,[16] even for Christians, and an economy in which young people's relational futures are dependent on complex structural factors.[17]

The teachings blend of neoliberal messages, which emphasize that people can control their life outcomes, and Christian views that God rewards hard work coalesce into an implicit worldview that knowing oneself, a marital work ethic, and faith can help to withstand relational tensions.[18] This process individualizes success as something couples can control and doesn't address the threats to marital stability, which stem from ignoring marital power,[19] economic pressures from a tumultuous economy,[20] or workplaces impinging on people's lives.[21] A consequence of an individualized marriage which operates as a "capstone"[22] that people work toward has meant that marriage has fallen victim to the meritocracy trap in American society. In other words, both getting married and staying married are seen as individual accomplishments that indicate worthiness. The ethos of hard work and emphasis on emotion management strategies misrepresents the "good marriage" as something entirely within a person's control. The problem, however, is that by individualizing discussions of marital problems or stressors, the programs fail to fully prepare people for the embedded challenges of a marriage.

In fact, helping couples to learn to see these forms of structural inequality would further cultivate awareness and better ensure they are prepared for future sources of conflict. For example, programs could help people identify how their choices are patterned and constrained by structures, such as work, which could potentially deescalate internal conflicts in the household and help couples make mutually beneficial decisions as partners. In particular, the gender-blind programs could be a space to challenge ideas of gendered power by facilitating awareness about how gender socialization of desires, stressors, and pressures can create differential and unequal experiences in heterosexual marriages. Cultural and interactional expectations exist for women to relinquish their desires for a career,[23] to intensively monitor the emotional states of their partner and children,[24] and to defer or mask their ambitions as for other people.[25] The attempts to bracket the contexts and pressures that surround decisions in an effort to focus people's attention on the internal exploration of an individual's desire obfuscates the ways that how someone is positioned in society shapes what desires they feel they ought to (not) have. The silence on these issues means that the programs do not fully prepare young couples for the likely challenges they'll face in their marriages. It also limits the possible effect these programs could have by better sensitizing people to structural pressures that may create unequal and undesired patterns of interaction.

Since these programs cannot change the external challenges couples will face, they will never be able to *ensure* relationship success. Those who want the programs to "work" by divorce-proofing marriages are often disappointed by this conclusion and subsequently question whether people should even participate. Reducing their worth to a set of unknowable outcomes, however, fails to acknowledge the other ways that people throughout the book have articulated the meaning of engaging in this work. For example, congregations use the programs as a form of religious education, a spiritual intervention into people's intimate lives, and a tool to forge community and connect congregants to co-religionists. Both the married couples leading the programs and the premarital ones attending enjoyed carving out time from their daily stresses and routines to foster moments of deep intimacy. After all, as sociologist Robert Bellah and colleagues note, "therapy helps us translate our experiences of this society into personal meaning, and then back into social action."[26] Christian premarital counseling thus represents a collective form of therapy where people come together to negotiate the meaning of marriage and faith. Scholars can therefore examine what this work reveals at different times and in various communities, because within these liminal moments people engage in interpersonal emotion management to instill and guide feelings in themselves and others about what makes a marriage good, happy, healthy, and holy. The next and final section builds on this insight to consider how the meaning of Christian marriage has changed.

(How) Will Christian Marriages Change? And, What Impact Has Marriage Equality Had on Christian Marriages?

Sociologists Nancy Ammerman and Wade Clark Roof once argued that churches "were not paying attention as family life changed around them."[27] Although I agree with their claim that "programming and the image they projected reinforced the notion that 'family' (meaning a married couple with children) and 'religion' go together,"[28] I also found that if we look closely, we can see that the meaning of a *Christian* marriage has changed alongside of the shifts in the meaning of marriage in the United States. In tracing the history of premarital counseling, we saw the same transition from the companionate marriage that emphasized fulfilling gender roles within a heterosexual institution to the predominance of the individualized marriage, which calls people to enter the union as a fully formed person.[29] This has meant that Christians, along with other Americans, are looking for more than someone who is merely "good enough"; they want a "soulmate."[30] The high expectations mean that the premarital trajectory of locating the right person requires "significant emotional investment"[31] and that this effort will only become intensified by the "marital work ethic"[32] that requires people to engage in constant emotion work once they have committed to the person. In other words, Christian communities' view of the good marriage has changed in tandem with the rest of the United States.

I would be remiss, however, if I did not acknowledge one of the most significant changes to the institution: marriage equality. On June 26, 2015, the Supreme Court's decision of *Obergefell vs. Hodges* granted same-sex couples the opportunity to marry across the United States. President Barack Obama issued a statement that day describing their decision as recognizing that "the Constitution guarantees marriage equality" and noting that "in doing so, they've reaffirmed that all Americans are entitled to the equal protection of the law."[33] Marriage equality was a major legal victory for LGBTQ+ Americans because it dismantled some of the heteronormative privilege embedded within the institution. Unlike the other changes to marriage that have been about how intimacy is structured within the relationship, this did not change its meaning. Instead, it altered who could enter the contract of marriage. Or as President Obama's speech elaborates, the legal decision confirmed "that all people should be treated equally, regardless of who they are or who they love." The question therefore becomes to what extent has a change to the contract of who can enter marriage in secular society impacted the Christian view of the covenant of marriage?

Since my fieldwork occurred as states were voting to allow same-sex marriage and eventually marriage equality spread across the United States, I cannot comment on what has happened over the past few years. Yet, the timing meant the topic couldn't fade to the background, and religious leaders across the programs were confronted with questions about "what is marriage?" and "who is marriage for?" The clergy, lay couples, and therapists with whom I spoke held a range of views from those who resolutely viewed marriage as a heterosexual union, to those who believed the institution should be available to same-sex couples, and finally, to those who were ambivalent and conflicted. In the last two cases in particular, people recognized that these were their *personal* views and not representative of their religious tradition.

At Cosmopolitan Church, one of the leaders mentioned while we were waiting for the couples to arrive that they had been approached by a nonheterosexual couple that wanted to enroll in the program. Although personally supportive of them learning relationship skills, the leader recognized that they couldn't ensure the space would be safe from comments by other attending couples especially since the church wasn't officially "open and affirming." They also interestingly continued by arguing that their program was not designed with queer couples in mind, a point that seemed contradictory to their gender-blind curriculum focusing on therapeutic principles. In contrast, while I was conducting observations at the Exploring Your Relationship Retreat, a retired clergy couple visited one day to suggest that if the leadership felt moved by the Holy Spirit, then they should consider reminding couples about the importance of protecting the sanctity of marriage. During one of the subsequent "prayer huddles" that preceded each session, the leadership discussed their commitment to a heterosexual marriage and, as with other times, asked God to work in the hearts of the couples to be open to His view on marriage, which they believed to be "countercultural." Yet, during their talk, there was no mention about the political debates on marriage, and instead, they read their scripted religio-therapeutic content as normal.

Perhaps knowing that there is an authoritative Catholic position that espouses "marriage exists solely between a man and a woman," Catholic leaders of the programs I observed were silent on the politics of marriage and even refrained from sharing their personal views of marriage equality in our interviews.[34] This is reminiscent of the "silent disagreement" that sociologist Rachel Ellis found in the RCIA (Rite of Christian Initiation of Adults) classes, another spiritual formation ministry in the Catholic Church.[35] In her study of programming for Catholic converts, she found that even though nearly everyone disagreed with some element of Church teaching, the initiates and leaders in the classes employed a variety of strategies to avoid outright conflict and disagreement. As she notes, "a substantial proportion of laypersons who disagree with religious teachings manage dissent individually, through everyday interactions in a specific institutional context."[36] In fact, the overwhelming silence made it more noticeable in the very few instances where I observed a lay religious leader explicitly restate the Catholic position that marriage is exclusively for heterosexuals because it's for procreation. Although typically brief, the comments were often jarring and met with silence from the people attending (many of whom I know disagreed with Catholic teachings on homosexuality and/or birth control).[37]

While my fieldwork and interviews provided opportunities to learn about premarital counselors' personal views on marriage equality, these insights were unavailable to the engaged couples attending the programs. Part of the reason is rooted in sociologist Dawne Moon's finding that many Christians thought "politics was the opposite of Church, God, and the spiritual."[38] Thus, when discussing politicized issues, including homosexuality, congregants would take care to not invoke references to any "structural exclusions and hierarchies associated with the fallen, secular world."[39] In constructing lessons and designing activities, the leaders of these programs recognized that they have a limited amount of time to impart marital advice and chose to not prioritize political issues that they saw as external to the lives of the engaged couples. Operating within these time constraints, the leaders focused on matters that they deemed relevant to individual relationship success and only shared personal views within the confessional framework that could normalize marital dynamics. From the perspective of guiding couples toward good and godly marriages, political discussions about other people's (possible) marriages appeared to be seen as detracting from the more pressing issue impending on these couples: divorce.

Divorce has its own long history of mobilizing Americans that has led to public claims-making about the naturalness and necessity of marriage.[40] Although the covenant rhetoric's implicit construction against contract marriage implies that divorce is a structural problem, for the most part, leaders narrowed their attention to how it posed an immediate and pervasive threat to couples in their community. Similar to other issues like gender and money, discussions of divorce became individualized and rested on claims about whether couples are prepared or work hard enough. In contrast, when they treated same-sex marriage as a "social problem," it only operated at the macro level; leaders didn't imagine it as being pertinent for couples' future relational success. If the emphasis was on providing tools to couples at the individual level and serving their religious community at the organizational level, in each case, marriage equality was deemed too irrelevant and treated as external. Notably, this approach reveals how religious leaders implicitly construct "Christian" as a heterosexual identity and positioned the covenant rhetoric as outside of the debate on same-sex marriage.[41]

Religious leaders I observed generally maintained a clear sense that *the* good (heterosexual) marriage is in fact the Christian marriage. By situating God as the creator of guidelines to ensure that people are not only moral but happy, they constructed the authority of churches to speak on marriage. Of course, the ways Christian leaders used this authority has been paradoxical on the topic of love and marriage. Turned inward to their own communities, as this book has examined through the practice of marriage preparation, Christians have sought to guide couples to create a union, which they find personally meaningful and rewarding. This advice is found in the covenant rhetoric, which argues that marriage is a place of sanctification and that people will be rewarded in their relationships by being oriented toward serving their partner. The covenant rhetoric, however, always exists as a discursive boundary with the secular world, which religious leaders argue holds a different view of marriage. In contrast to the relational emphasis, they located a contract marriage in secular culture and described it as a union where people are selfish, which makes it more fragile. Interestingly, over the past few decades when the topic of marriage has emerged external from the community, the symbolic boundaries have been nearly inverted. For example, in the debates about marriage equality that led up to its passage, arguments about love dominated the call to open the institution to queer couples. Against claims that "love is love," some Christian leaders framed the concept of marriage in more contractual arguments that were devoid of emotions. Thus, at the same time that Christian leaders have been active producers and transmitters of therapeutic love within their communities, they have also sought to police the concept of love outside of them.

Concluding Thoughts on Emotions

A central theme throughout this book has been examining the social and moral structure of feelings. Thus, from my vantage point, the only way to end is by briefly thinking about emotions. Although people often discuss emotions possessively as something that "belongs" to them, the understanding of any emotion and the ability to recognize it comes from our relationship with others. By participating in social groups, we learn how to identify our feelings, and in the process, we learn to feel as others do, which connects us to them and can cultivate belonging. To fully understand our own inner world therefore requires recognizing how it is constructed, enabled, and constrained by the cultural systems and structures surrounding us. Whereas therapeutic culture would teach us to locate our problems and solutions by turning inward, this structural awareness requires us to recognize what our feelings may be telling us about how our self is embedded within our world.

To help render visible the social power of emotions, this book has explored the consequences of the normative turn inward for how people understand themselves and their relationships. It has showcased how a deep anxiety and reverence for one emotion—love—has mobilized Christian communities for generations to intervene in the domestic lives of their members. Despite this collective enterprise, the therapeutic ethos permeating the practice structures people's efforts to search for the source of their feelings in their biographies and to practice sharing this narrative interpersonally with their partner. In a way, the book offers a sociological intervention into this therapeutic intervention. Rather than locate the source of feelings in people's personalities or upbringing, it consistently asked us to consider, *who* gets to feel? Instead of offering relationship skills as a way to manage emotions, it regularly explored the question, what *ought* people feel? Finally, as an alternative to promoting a covenant marriage as an inherently healthier setting for intimacy, it repeatedly invited inquiry into, what do our feelings *mean*?

By turning externally for answers to questions about emotions, it quickly becomes apparent that many of our personal conflicts emerge from paradoxes of how we culturally understand feelings. For example, broadly speaking, emotions are simultaneously seen as "irrational" and not a legitimate explanation for behavior but also as the core representation of our authentic self. Contradictory views on emotions therefore leave people uncertain about how to feel and subsequently unsure about how to act. In considering one's future, people often experience this tension about how to make the right decision: Does one follow one's passion or select a safer, more reasonable path? Perhaps no other emotions better encapsulate these cultural tensions than love. Throughout the book, we've encountered endless love paradoxes. Love has been presented as being oriented toward another but only discovered in oneself. It has been cast as one's greatest possible pleasure but also a potential for deep pain. It has been treated as something easy and fun but also as requiring hard work.

Perhaps surprisingly, I believe the covenant rhetoric offers an illustrative way to rethink the individualistic tension in these paradoxes. In attempting to distinguish the Christian vision for marriage from what they viewed as the secular model of a contract, religious leaders argued that emotions are what makes us human. At its core, this view helps remind us that emotions aren't irrational or merely subjective but offer people a way to be human and see and connect with the humanity in others. Perhaps one of the greatest lessons to be learned from Christian premarital education is that just as with religion itself, emotions offer a way to be part of a greater social power larger than just our individual selves.[42] Rather than employ this point to construct non-Christian marriages as "less than" or use the discourse as a tool to discipline intimacy, it could be used to call people to critical empathy if we extend this entreaty to be other-oriented beyond marriage. From my vantage point, this stance can help challenge the individualistic approach that dominates our neoliberal society and encourages people to focus only on themselves. After all, there is much more to learn about how emotions connect us to others.

ACKNOWLEDGMENTS

My awareness of acknowledgment sections and sociological interest in religion both emerged in an undergraduate seminar on American religious movements with Jennifer McKinney. Whereas as a student, I was accustomed to reading the pages assigned to me (and nothing more), for multiple of the books, I can recall her taking the time to point out members of our faculty in the acknowledgment section. I suspect this was one of my earliest introductions to the fact that research is produced not only by an actual person but that their work occurs within a complex set of relationships. It's fitting, therefore, that my first words of appreciation should go to Jennifer, who ignited my sociological interest in American religion, made the world of social research visible, and whose guidance set me on this journey.

Thanks to the community I found at Loyola University Chicago, I discovered my sociological voice and the confidence to use it. I learned to better articulate my ideas by constantly engaging in stimulating and enjoyable conversations with Jessica Barron, Solly Chacko, Beth Dougherty, Todd Fuist, Melissa Gesbeck, Thomas Josephsohn, Patrick Polasek, Gwendolyn Purifoye, Cesraéa Rumpf, Joseph Renow, Tim Sacco, Lucas Sharma, and Annmarie van Altena. My coursework with Japonica Brown-Saracino, Anne Figert, Fred Kniss, and Judith Wittner ensured I had the methodological training and theoretical background to conduct this research. In the dissertation phase of the project, I was fortunate to receive further guidance from Rhys H. Williams, Orit Avishai, and Edward Flores. The experience of working and publishing with Rhys and Orit on other projects has also been instrumental in developing my thinking about religion and supported my growth as a scholar.

The research for this book would not have been possible without the support of fellowships from Loyola University Chicago, including the Arthur J. Schmitt dissertation fellowship and the Women and Leadership Archives Research fellowship. The archivist at the Women and

Leadership Archives at the time was also instrumental in acclimating me to archival research and informing me of the rich history of Catholic marriage preparation programs. A grant from the Society for the Scientific Study of Religion allowed me to expand my historical understanding by supporting travel to the Maryville University Archives, Midwest Jesuit Archives, Catholic University of America Archives, and Archives of the University of Notre Dame. Along with those at the Archdiocese of Chicago, I am grateful to all the archivists who answered questions and introduced me to new sources of data. The Association for the Sociology of Religion's Joseph H. Fichter grant further supported my early fieldwork with the "Exploring Your Relationship Retreat" and allowed me to launch the overall study. Of course, the project would not have occurred without the gracious time, cooperation, and support of those who allowed me to witness their special time. The leaders at "Cosmopolitan Church," "Exploring Your Relationship Retreat," "St. Bernadette," and "St. Sebastian" kindly made sure my project was successful by answering all my questions, connecting me to participants, and so much more. Although I often approached their programs as an academic, I appreciate that they always engaged with me as a whole person—wife, mother, and someone simply trying to make sense of their place in the world.

My ability to conduct and, later, write about the research for this book was possible because of a community that graciously ensured I had the time and energy to do so. My family—Don Irby, Beth Irby, Anneliese Irby, and Erica Irby—has seen me through each stage of this process. In particular, I am grateful for the number of times that they showed their love for me by being the one present to lovingly watch my children while I collected data and later (re)wrote all of this. Upon arriving at Illinois Wesleyan University, I was blessed to have Meghan Burke as my chair, colleague, and friend. I learned a lot about how to be a teacher-scholar by watching her commitment to setting aside time to write amid her dedication to our students. I was also lucky enough to find an amazing group of colleagues, that happened to also have children, that graciously helped with playdates, after-school care, and childcare during the global pandemic. In particular, I would have never found the time to write without the support of Abigail Kerr, Ryan Kerr, Molly Robey, and Robert Erlewine.

While writing this book, I have benefited from an extensive network of people that helped me pull all the pieces together. Undergraduates at both Loyola University Chicago and Illinois Wesleyan University were instrumental in transcribing interviews, organizing data, locating sources, and more: Rosie Abraham, Alicia Cherry, Marissa Irelan, Colleen Palczynski, Jorri Poindexter, Callie Short, Lea Spiers, and especially Amanda Scheller, who read the full manuscript multiple times. Although I've had countless meaningful conversations about this work over the years, Tia Pratt and Cesraéa Rumpf offered consistent insights. Lucas Sharma also provided detailed and thoughtful advice in the final stages of writing the book. Jennifer Hammer and a series of anonymous reviewers always offered penetrating feedback that improved the manuscript with each round of revisions.

I have also been blessed to participate in a number of scholarly communities that helped me refine my ideas and improve how I wrote up this story. In the dissertation stage, I participated in The American Parish Project under the guidance of Gary Adler, Tricia Bruce, and Brian Starks, which was instrumental in shaping my understanding of Catholicism. I presented an early draft of chapter 3 at Notre Dame's Younger Scholars in the Sociology of Religion where Mary Jo Neitz kindly offered instructive feedback. Participating in the Young Scholars of American Religion program has been one of the highlights of my academic career and ensured that I completed this book. Penny Edgell and Jonathan Walton exceeded their role as mentors with their thoughtful feedback and suggestions. My thinking about religion is now richer and more interdisciplinary thanks to conversations I had with them and with my fellow "young scholars": Tazeen Ali, Phillip Gollner, Darrius Hill, Emily Johnson, Alyssa Maldonado-Estrada, Max Mueller, Sam Perry, Ansley Quiros, and Leslie Ribovich. Finally and most important, I am deeply indebted to Todd Fuist, who has listened to and helped me process all my thoughts on marriage preparation since I first began conceptualizing this project. I would not have made it to this stage without your support and dedication to our family.

NOTES

INTRODUCTION

1. Although not everyone is formally or professionally a counselor, I use the term "premarital counselors" to succinctly describe the people who conduct and facilitate marriage preparation.
2. Celello (2009).
3. Cherlin (2009).
4. Celello (2009); Hackstaff (1999).
5. Hochschild (1983).
6. Jenkins (2016:220).
7. Barkan (2006); Burdette and Hill (2009); Hull et al. (2011); Rostosky, Regnerus, and Wright (2003).
8. Brown, Orbuch, and Bauermeister (2008); Call and Heaton (1997).
9. Regnerus (2007).
10. Bartkowski (2007); Manning (2015); Wilcox (2004).
11. Beaman (2001); Nason-Clark (1997).
12. Wilcox (2006:98).
13. Jenkins (2016:219).
14. Spillman (2002:1).
15. Edgell (2012).
16. Ibid.
17. Edgell (2011:636).
18. Gerson (2010:9).
19. Coltrane and Adams (2008); Pahl (1989); Thorne (1982); Wong (2017).
20. Bernard (1972/1982).
21. Kolb (2014:30); see also Moon (2004); Wolkomir (2001).
22. Riis and Woodhead (2010).
23. Harris (2015). Sometimes sociologists' efforts to showcase the social dimensions of emotions are misinterpreted as arguing that emotions are not also physiological. Instead, the goal is to highlight the way bodies experience emotions are not merely biological or neurological but require identification and meaning making (Harris 2015; Hochschild 1997; Lois 2012). In other words, tears are not self-interpreting but require people to determine if they're feeling sad, angry, or even relieved.
24. Illouz (2012); Ingraham (2008); Randles (2017); Swidler (2001).

25　Hochschild (1983, 1997). Her initial analysis of this account appeared in *The Managed Heart*, but she later reanalyzed the ethnographic scene in a chapter titled "The Sociology of Emotion as a Way of Feeling."
26　Hochschild (1997:4).
27　Harris (2015).
28　Hochschild (1997:7).
29　Moon (2005); Riis and Woodhead (2010).
30　Coontz (2005).
31　Coltrane and Adams (2008); Landry (2000).
32　Landry (2000).
33　Coontz (1992).
34　Ibid.
35　Jackson (1993:202).
36　Ingraham (2008:124).
37　See Cancian (1987); Giddens (1992); Illouz (2012).
38　Swidler (2001).
39　Randles (2017).
40　Randles (2016).
41　Illouz (2008); see also McGee (2005); Rakow (2013); Wright (2008).
42　Aubry and Travis (2015:1).
43　Cabanas and Illouz (2017) note that neoliberalism is more of a theory than a set of actual political-economic practices. In particular, they see the therapeutic ethos as consolidating and sharpening the cultural expectations that people are personally responsible not only for their economic condition but also their emotional states. Silva (2013) has described this outcome as a "mood economy" that has privatized happiness.
44　Rakow (2013:487).
45　Part of the problem, as Rakow (2013) details, is that much of the writing on therapeutic culture, especially the more critical assessments, never studied religious groups or how they employ therapeutic approaches for their own purposes. Instead, whether classic examples, such as Rieff (1966) or Lasch (1979) to more recent work by Moskowitz (2001) or Furedi (2004), the discussion of religion has largely been suppositional at the macro level and lacked empirical data on how religion (or religious authority) operates in the lives of individuals or communities.
46　Hochschild (1983:74).
47　Many of these terms are gendered and reflect the long-standing heteronormativity in intimate relationships, but the language is often still used by nonheterosexuals.
48　Coontz (2005:1).
49　Chapman (2010:11).
50　Celello and Kholoussy (2016); Coontz (2005); Cherlin (2009).
51　Coontz (2005:1).
52　Celello (2009); Coltrane and Adams (2008).
53　Celello (2009).

54 Celello (2009); Davis (2010).
55 Celello (2009:75).
56 Celello (2009).
57 Davis (2010).
58 Cancian (1987).
59 Fischer and Hout (2005:130).
60 Hackstaff (1999).
61 Ibid.
62 Coltrane and Adams (2008).
63 Davis (2010:7).
64 Ibid., 8.
65 Coontz (2005:5).
66 Cherlin (2004).
67 Furstenberg et al. (2004).
68 Furstenberg et al. (2004); Ruggles (2015).
69 Cherlin (2004, 2009).
70 Cherlin (2009:88).
71 Ansari and Klinenberg (2015); Cherlin (2004); Giddens (1992); Illouz (2012).
72 Cherlin (2004:855).
73 Ibid.
74 Pugh (2017).
75 Randles (2017).
76 Dalessandro (2021); Edin and Kefalas (2005); Pew Research Center (2019); Schneider, Harknett, and Stimpson (2018). For the past few decades, scholars have noted that those living in poverty are less likely to get married (Edin and Kefalas 2005; Randles 2016) and that people increasingly have espoused views that financial stability is a prerequisite for getting married (Dalessandro 2021; Furstenberg et al. 2004). People sometimes conflate these classed patterns in access to marriage with racial variations by assuming that class-advantaged people are white and class-disadvantaged people are not. It's important to recognize how the racialized legacy of slavery, segregation, redlining, and lack of access to veterans benefits after World War II have patterned economic benefits in the United States and consolidated them into the present racial wealth gap (Coontz 1992; Oliver and Shapiro 1997). Schneider, Harknett, and Stimpson (2018) found that economic circumstances and incarceration both helped to explain the decline in first marriages over the past forty-five years. Specifically, marriage rates have been impacted by the decreased economic contributions and stability for both Black and white men and the rise of mass incarceration of predominately Black men. It's also imperative to not erase low-income whites or class-advantaged people of color when discussing aggregate patterns. In fact, when it comes to the romantic market, scholars have identified a number of other noneconomic ways that produce racial disadvantage and reduce the marital options for people of color, including homophily norms (dating someone from one's own group), colorblind

racism, ambivalence about interracial relationships, and privileging of whiteness disadvantage people of color, especially African Americans, in locating a partner (Curington, Lundquist, and Lin 2021; Dalessandro 2021).

77 Randles (2017:9).
78 Corse and Silva (2017:300).
79 Cabanas and Illouz (2017:25).
80 Cherlin (2009); Coltrane and Adams (2008); Coontz (2005); Davis (2010); Hackstaff (1999); Randles (2017); Silva (2013).
81 Aune (2002); Gaddini (2022); Irby (2014b).
82 Cott (2000); Du Mez (2020); Heath (2012).
83 The "marriage movement," which consists of "a coalition of religious and civic leaders, public officials, family therapists, researchers, and others" (Heath 2009:27), has promoted this type of marital advice about a good marriage. Starting with President George W. Bush's Healthy Marriage Initiative, marriage promotion proponents have successfully ensured that more than a billion dollars have been spent on efforts to publicly advertise marriage, promote responsible fatherhood, and offer marriage education courses (Randles 2012). Included among the approved activities were premarital education programming, which could make use of TANF (Temporary Assistance to Needy Families) federal funds that typically support low-income families. Scholars have critiqued these programs on a number of dimensions ranging from the efficacy of the programming to address the challenges of those living in poverty (Avishai, Heath, and Randles 2012; Halpern-Meekin 2019; Randles 2016) to the ways the programs are used to promote a white, heterosexual, Christian understanding of marriage (Coltrane 2001; Heath 2008, 2012). While often operating outside of congregational structures, critics have specifically highlighted the Christian foundation of the "marriage movement" by identifying the connection of these efforts to the Religious Right, the prominent position of Christians, and the use of religious rhetoric about "traditional marriages" (Coltrane 2001; Coontz 2008; Heath 2008, 2012).
84 Emerson, Fretz, and Shaw (1995:1).
85 Paulsen (2009:510).
86 I often use the terms "premarital counseling" and "marriage preparation" interchangeably. In practice, I found that evangelicals tended to prefer the former and Catholics the latter. Chapter 1 historically contextualize this distinction, and chapter 6 discusses how the discursive difference resulted in varied organizational logics for when and why couples are motivated to participate in the programs.
87 I am indebted to the archivists at the Women and Leadership Archives at Loyola University Chicago for introducing me to the lifework of Pat and Patty Crowley and inspiring me to wonder about the historical background of marriage preparation. In addition to helping guide me in their own collections, they directed me to secondary sources that allowed me to further identify relevant archives. In particular, I found Burns's (1999) history of the Christian Family Movement and Johnson's (2001) work on the Cana Conference Movement helpful in the early

stages of learning about the history of Catholic marriage preparation and each facilitated my efforts to locate archival documentation. In the end, I visited archives that provided insights into key members who helped establish the movements and set the ideological vision for them, as well as the organizational structure of programming: Fr. Edward Dowling's collections at Maryville University Archives and Midwest Jesuit Archives; Dr. Alphonse H. Clemens collection at Catholic University of America's Archives; Christian Family Movement and Cana Conference Movement Collections at the Archives of the University of Notre Dame; and Cana Conference Chicago and family ministries at Archdiocese of Chicago Archives.

88 Irby (2019).
89 Khan (2011:201).
90 Emerson, Fretz, and Shaw (1995); Lofland et al. (2006).
91 Silk (2005); Wellman (2008).
92 According to Pew Research Center's (2008) Religious Landscape Survey, the broader category of the "West" is approximately 64 percent Christian (22 percent Catholic and 23 percent evangelical Protestant). With the exception of Idaho, which has a higher proportion of Christians, specifically Latter-day Saints, Oregon and Washington, the remaining key states in the Pacific Northwest, have 61 percent of Christians (15 percent evangelical and 17 percent Catholic in Washington and 29 percent evangelical and 12 percent Catholic in Oregon). Despite Christians collectively doubling the overall number of religious "nones" (31 percent in Oregon and 32 percent in Washington), the category of the religious unaffiliated does account for more of the population than any specific Christian tradition, including Catholics and evangelical Protestants.
93 Avishai (2008).
94 Of the thirty-nine interviews, thirteen were with the leadership of the programs where I conducted observations and twenty-six were with other communities that offered more individualized sessions. Since I opted to interview the "unit" that facilitated premarital counseling this means that sometimes an interview occurred with one person, such as a clergy or therapist, and other times with a married couple. Fifteen of the interviews performed individualized premarital counseling in congregational contexts (six Catholic and nine evangelical Protestant) and eleven interviewees were associated with an evangelical graduate therapy program that included an emphasis on premarital counseling. Of the pastoral premarital counselors, all six of the Catholic individuals were laity for whom marriage preparation entailed one of their obligations as parish staff (most often serving in positions such as religious director). In contrast, the sample of evangelical premarital counselors working in congregations included pastors (some of whom also had professional backgrounds in counseling) and lay couples who volunteered as marriage mentors.
95 All names of people and organizations are pseudonyms.
96 Lofland et al. (2006:88) describes "informal interviewing" as "asking questions *in situ*, during the course of naturally occurring activities," which involves "asking questions

much more frequently than ordinary participants in the setting would do." I used the "naturally occurring" breaks in the programming—group meals at the retreat, waiting for sessions to start, walking to the parking lot with other couples, after the conclusion of an activity, and so forth—to ask leaders and couples emergent questions. Sometimes I inquired about similar content as the in-depth interviews, which focused on personal background, relationship history, aspirations for marriage, views on Christian marriage, and premarital counseling experiences (training for leaders and programming for couples). At other times, however, the informal interviews were less of a way to understand people's background but offered opportunities to discuss social processes relevant to the moment. In comparison to the in-depth interviews, these field interviews tended to have more back-and-forth as I sought to understand what was happening and people's feelings about it. In return, leaders and couples often used these moments as an opportunity to ask me about my work and to inquire about how other programs were structured, which resulted in clarifying questions about unspoken assumptions. All these conversations are captured in the ethnographic vignettes, whereas when I reference an interview in the chapters, it indicates the more structured ones that occurred after the end of the program.
97 Although marriage equality did not pass at the federal level until 2015, it passed earlier in parts of the Pacific Northwest (2012 in Washington State and 2014 in Oregon and Idaho).
98 Randles (2017).
99 The majority-white racial composition of the participants likely can be partially attributed to the racial divide in marriage (Pew Research Center 2019) and the whiteness of the Pacific Northwest where I conducted research. For example, according to the census, approximately 77 percent of Washington, 86 percent of Oregon, and 93 percent of Idaho identify as white. These factors may have been compounded by my emphasis on evangelicals since only about 25 percent of Black Christians identify with this religious identity (Du Mez 2020). Another possible factor is that pro-marriage messages may have an uneven impact on people within religious communities. For example, Burdette, Haynes, and Ellison (2012) found that whereas church attendance was correlated with a reduction in perceived barriers to marriage for whites, including financial concerns, it was not statistically significant for Latinos or African Americans.
100 Riis and Woodhhead (2010:11).
101 Furedi (2004); Imber (2004); Lasch (1979); Rieff (1966).
102 Edgell (2012).

1. HISTORICAL SHIFTS IN CHRISTIAN LESSONS ON MARITAL SUCCESS

1 University of Notre Dame Archives (UNDA), PMRH, The opening vignette is pulled from a recording of a Pre-Cana talk.
2 Celello (2009); Davis (2010).
3 Celello (2009).
4 Lofton (2015:40).

5   Celello (2009); Moskowitz (2001).
6   Davis (2010).
7   Coontz (2005); May (2017); Tentler (2004).
8   Burns (1999); Johnson (2001); Tentler (2004).
9   Celello (2009); Davis (2010).
10 Burns (1999).
11 Ibid.
12 The statistics come from a study conducted by Clemens (1953), who surveyed dioceses across the United States about their programming of Pre-Cana and Cana Conferences. Overall, more diocese offered Cana Conferences for married couples. Specifically, he found that the 47 dioceses that reported their numbers had collectively offered 619 Cana Conferences or an average of more than 13 conferences for each diocese. He estimated that in 1950, the number of people attending these conferences in the 47 dioceses exceeded 56,000, with individual conferences ranging from 24 to 700 and a mean of 91. In contrast, only 31 dioceses reporting Pre-Cana activities had a total attendance of 27,500 with a mean of 131 persons per conference and a range of 12–650.
13 Archive of Archdiocese of Chicago (ADC), Cana Conference of Chicago, "The History of the Cana Conference of Chicago."
14 Tentler (2004) also discusses how premarital instruction among postwar Catholics emerged as part of a perceived crisis in families but focuses more specifically on the contested discussion of contraception.
15 Clemens, A. H. 1950. "A Larger View of Cana Content." *The Cana Conference: Proceedings of the Chicago Archdiocesan Study Week on the Cana Conference, June 28–30 1949*. Chicago: Cana Conference. Pg. 7.
16 Celello (2009); Davis (2010); Moskowitz (2001); Tentler (2004).
17 Tentler (2004) points out that Pre-Cana was not the first time that marriage was presented as a means of sanctification but that this theme had not been significant among American Catholics prior to World War II.
18 Catholic University of America (CUA), Clemens, 4/4 "Pre-Cana Lectures."
19 Delaney, John. 1951. "The Need for Cana." *The Cana Conference: Proceedings of the Chicago Archdiocesan Study Week on the Cana Conference December 27–29, 1950*. Chicago: Cana Conference. Pg. 20.
20 Egan, John. 1959. "Education for Marriage: The Cana Conference." *Religious Education* 54(3):344–48. Pg. 344.
21 UNDA PMRH 129/06, "The Cana Conference: A Practical, Up-to-Date Plan for Lasting Happiness in Marriage." Chicago: Cana Conference of Chicago.
22 Fischer, Matthias. 1951. "Approach and Content in the Pre-Cana Conference." *The Cana Conference: Proceedings of the Chicago Archdiocesan Study Week on the Cana Conference December 27–29, 1950*. Chicago: Cana Conference. Pg. 48.
23 CUA Clemens 4/4, Director's Outline for Pre-Cana Conference.
24 Imbiorski, Walter, ed. 1957. *The New Cana Manual*. Chicago: Delaney Publications. Pg. 72.

25 Ibid.
26 Archdiocese of Chicago. 1950. "Pre-Cana Conference Outline." *The Cana Conference: Proceedings of the Chicago Archdiocesan Study Week on the Cana Conference, June 28–30 1949*. Chicago: Cana Conference. Pg. 102.
27 CUA, Clemens, "Pre-Cana Conference Outline."
28 Imbiorski, Walter, ed. 1957. *The New Cana Manual*. Chicago: Delaney Publications. Pg. 80.
29 CUA, Alphonse H. Clemens Collection 4/4, "Pre-Cana Conference Outline."
30 Ibid.
31 Imbiorski, Walter, ed. 1957. *The New Cana Manual*. Chicago: Delaney Publications. Pg. 85.
32 Archdiocese of Chicago. 1950. "Pre-Cana Conference Outline." *The Cana Conference: Proceedings of the Chicago Archdiocesan Study Week on the Cana Conference, June 28–30 1949*. Chicago: Cana Conference. Pg. 107.
33 Imbiorski, Walter, ed. 1957. *The New Cana Manual*. Chicago: Delaney Publications. Pg. 100.
34 Ibid., 91.
35 UNDA, PMRH 120/06, "This Is Cana."
36 CUA, Alphonse H. Clemens Collection 4/4, "Rationale of the Pre-Cana Program."
37 Imbiorski, Walter, ed. 1957. *The New Cana Manual*. Chicago: Delaney Publications. Pg. 110.
38 Ibid., 109.
39 UNDA, PMRH 120/06, "This Is Cana."
40 Despite some ambivalence on the part of priests and lay Catholics, the rhythm method was popular during the postwar era. For more information on the rhythm method and Pre-Cana and Christian Family Movements, see Tentler (2004).
41 Davis (2010).
42 Ibid.
43 Moskowitz (2001).
44 Davis (2010) identified that *Christian Century* published this letter that had originally appeared in *Pastoral Psychology*.
45 Myers-Shirk (2000, 2009).
46 Ibid.
47 Westberg, Granger. 1958. *Premarital Counseling: A Manual for Ministers*. New York: Department of Family Life.
48 Ibid., 5.
49 Davis (2010).
50 Noll (2000); Smith and Woodberry (1998).
51 Moslener (2015); Noll (2000).
52 Smith et al. (1998).
53 Marsden (1982); Schafer (2011); Smith et al. (1998).
54 Watt (1991:164); see also Du Mez (2020).

55 Lofton (2015); Myers-Shirk (2009).
56 Oates, Wayne E. 1958. *Premarital Pastoral Care and Counseling*. Nashville: Broadman Press.
57 Ibid., 5.
58 Ibid., 14–15.
59 Moslener (2015).
60 Narramore, Clyde. 1956. *Life and Love: A Christian View on Sex*. Grand Rapids: Zondervan. Narramore, Clyde. 1960. *The Psychology of Counseling*. Grand Rapids: Zondervan.
61 These questions are listed on the front cover of the 1956 edition of *Life and Love*.
62 Ibid., 82.
63 Ibid., 60.
64 Stephens and Giberson (2011).
65 Moslener (2015) and Myers-Shirk (2000, 2009) explain how evangelical counselors at this time sought to distinguish themselves from both secular therapy and the field of pastoral counseling, which was dominated by liberal Protestants. In particular, evangelicals disagreed with the situational ethics that presented morality as contextual. While they embraced psychological work, their views continued to assert the authority of scripture and its ability to provide absolute truths and moral claims.
66 The recommendations and strategies in Protestant counseling, however, reflected their different conceptions of the self. As Lofton (2015:40) notes, at this time "liberals emphasized the importance of social progress and the good found in each individual, while evangelicals directed their energies toward the identification of social ills and the need to change the self by rooting out individual sin."
67 Cherlin (2009); Coltrane and Adams (2008); Hackstaff (1999).
68 Cherlin (2009:89).
69 Cherlin (2009).
70 Coltrane and Adams (2008); Celello (2009); McGee (2005).
71 McGee (2005).
72 Ibid.
73 ADC, Cana Conference of Chicago, "The History of the Cana Conference of Chicago."
74 ADC, Cana Conference of Chicago, Report: "Implications for Total Program": Sub-Committee of Pre Cana Think Tank Committee.
75 Ibid.
76 ADC, Cana Conference of Chicago, "The History of the Cana Conference of Chicago."
77 National Marriage Encounter. 1976. *Engaged Encounter Manual*. St. Paul: National Marriage Encounter.
78 ADC, Pastoral Notes, The Cana Conference of Chicago, circa 1978.
79 Ibid.
80 ADC, Pastoral Guidelines for Marriage Preparation, 1979.

81 ADC, Pastoral Notes, The Cana Conference of Chicago, circa 1979.
82 Ibid.
83 O'Rourke, David, Andrew Thompson, Steven Preisler, John Lewis, and Mary Feldman. 1983. "Preparing for Marriage: A Study in Marriage Preparation in American Catholic Dioceses." St. Meinrad, IN: Abbey Press.
84 ADC, Cana Conference of Chicago. Cana Newsletter, Spring/Summer 1982; ADC, Cana Conference of Chicago. "50 Years Later."
85 ADC, Family Ministries Office—Cana Conference. 1991. *Pastoral Guidelines for Marriage Preparation*. Chicago: Archdiocese of Chicago.
86 ADC, "Cana's 50 Years."
87 ADC, "Outline—Marriage in the Lord."
88 Narramore, Bruce. 1973. "Perspectives on the Integration of Psychology and Theology." *Journal of Psychology and Theology* 1(1):3–18.
89 Ibid., 3, 13.
90 Lofton (2015). Moslener (2015) discusses Carl F. H. Henry's opposition to therapeutic culture and his concerns that Christian psychologists' embrace of it would further serve to undermine views that goodness comes from obedience and moral absolutes.
91 Lofton (2015:41).
92 Watt (1991) notes that the importance of the family to evangelicals in the 1960s and 1970s cannot be exaggerated. From conferences to publications, the topic of family began to even be subordinated to the church.
93 Following Myer-Shirk's (2009) example, I use the term "Christian counselors" in this section because it is consistent with how this population identified themselves.
94 Myers-Shirk (2009).
95 Marsden (1987).
96 Myers-Shirk (2009).
97 Ibid.
98 Davis (2010).
99 Wright, H. Norman. 1977/1981. *Premarital Counseling: A Guidebook for Counselors*. Chicago: Moody.
100 Chapman, Gary. 1992/1995. *The Five Love Languages: How to Express Heartfelt Commitment to Your Mate*. Chicago: Northfield Publishing; Hillerstrom, P. Roger. 1989. *Intimate Deception: Escaping the Trap of Sexual Impurity*. Portland, OR: Multnomah Press; Parrott, Les, and Leslie Parrott. 1995. *Saving Your Marriage before It Starts: Seven Questions to Ask before (and after) You Marry*. Grand Rapids: Zondervan.
101 DeRogatis (2005); Jorstad (1993); Lofton (2015).
102 DeRogatis (2005).
103 LaHaye, Tim, and Beverly LaHaye. 1976. *The Act of Marriage: A Christian Guide to Sexual Love*. Grand Rapids: Zondervan.
104 DeRogatis (2005); Du Mez (2020); Jorstad (1993). Numerous scholars have noted the central role that consumer goods have played in the construction and

maintenance of a religious identity for evangelicals (Du Mez 2020; Hendershot 2004; Jorstad 1993). In particular, Du Mez (2020:12) highlights how the evangelical popular culture industry has served to intertwine a Christian identity with embattled "family values"—teaching "evangelicals how to raise children, how to have sex, and whom to fear."

105 There has been significant research on evangelicals' role in abstinence movements and their efforts to control adolescent sexuality with the promotion of purity culture (DeRogatis 2015; Gardner 2011; Hendershot 2004; Moslener 2015). Additionally, Slominski (2021) published an important history about how liberal Protestants' earlier concerns with purity and sex education served as important conversation partners with evangelical efforts throughout the decades.

106 Du Mez (2020); Irby (2013); Harris, Joshua. 1997. *I Kissed Dating Goodbye: A New Attitude toward Romance and Relationships*. Sisters, OR: Multnomah Books.

107 Du Mez (2020:171) describes *I Kissed Dating Goodbye* as "the bible of the purity movement," and in past work, I found that young evangelicals referred to themselves as the "Joshua Harris generation" (Irby 2013). In recent years, however, Harris has reconsidered and recanted many of these views. In 2018, he published an op-ed in *USA Today* where he wrote, "My ideas reshaped how many Christians practiced relationships and viewed sex. However, 20 years later, many of them look back with deep regret that they ever read it. . . . After listening to the stories and conducting a lengthy and sometimes painful process of reevaluation, I reached the conclusion that the ideas in my book weren't just naïve, they often caused harm." The realization even motivated his decision to ask his publisher to cease any further copies of his best-selling book (https://www.usatoday.com).

108 Irby (2013).
109 DeRogatis (2015:35).
110 Cherlin (2009:114), emphasis original.
111 Ibid.
112 Cherlin (2009).
113 Davis (2010); Randles (2016).
114 Furedi (2004); Imber (2004); Rieff (1966).
115 In a review of core works on therapeutic culture, Loss (2002) notes that scholars "must stop acting as though religion does not matter when it clearly does." Likewise, Lofton (2015) highlights how the argument that therapeutic culture and secularization occurred concurrently is too neat a claim that misses the many connections between the two. From early scholars such as Rieff (1966) and Lasch (1979) to more recent ones such as Moskowitz (2001), Furedi (2004), Imber (2004), and Aubry and Travis (2015), there has been a tendency to conceptualize therapeutic ideas as in competition with those put forward by religious authorities. In some cases, critics have used "religious descriptors to insult the power of therapy" (Lofton 2015:35), and in other cases, scholars have presented therapeutic culture as a new form of "secularized religion" (McGee 2005). In either case, "religion" tends to be limited to formal authority structures and doctrinal beliefs but

fails to recognize "lived religion," which calls researchers to study not only beliefs but also "their everyday spiritual practices, involving their bodily and emotional, as well as religious, experiences and expressions" (McGuire 2008:17).
116 Bellah et al. (1985); Roof (1999).

2. WHAT IS CHRISTIAN PREMARITAL COUNSELING?

1 Jenkins (2014:4).
2 Celello (2009); Hackstaff (1999).
3 Furedi (2004); Imber (2004); Moskowitz (2001); Rieff (1966).
4 Jenkins (2014:4).
5 Aubry and Travis (2015); Illouz (2008); Jenkins (2014).
6 Celello (2009); Davis (2010); Farrell (1999).
7 Davis (2010).
8 Ibid.
9 Avishai, Heath, and Randles (2012:35).
10 See Adams and Coltrane (2006); Heath (2012); Randles (2016).
11 One of the early surprises in my fieldwork was that the congregational premarital counseling programs were intellectually, organizationally, and by all accounts, politically disconnected from the marriage movement. I had entered the field having read Heath's (2009) research on the marriage movement, which included observations of Christian premarital counseling programs, and Coltrane's (2001:288) broader critique of the "hybrid political-religious" intellectual structure in marriage promotion efforts. In contrast to Coltrane's (2001) analysis of public discourses, Heath's (2009, 2012) ethnographic research that started by accessing informants at an annual conference of the marriage movement, or even Randles's (2016) entrée into becoming a Healthy Marriage educator by sampling programs that had obtained federal funding, I identified premarital counselors through congregations and paraministry groups. As such, I learned that these programs operated as localized religious ministries with a different set of interlocutors and intended audience.
12 Coltrane (2001); Heath (2012).
13 Although collective programs did not include formal assessment, often couples' participation in these classes was only one part of their premarital counseling process. At all the sites, couples were encouraged to supplement the collective programming with individualized sessions, which tended to be structured around completing and interpreting an assessment. It's possible the use of informal assessment found in workbook quizzes, discussion prompts, and writing exercises were employed to reduce redundancy with the other programming that couples were anticipated to take part in.
14 Chapman, Gary. 1992/1995. *The Five Love Languages: How to Express Heartfelt Commitment to Your Mate.* Chicago: Northfield Publishing; Gottman, John, and Nan Silver. 1999. *The Seven Principles for Making Marriage Work.* New York: Harmony Books; Gray, John. 1992. *Men Are from Mars, Women Are from Venus: The Classic Guide to Understanding the Opposite Sex.* New York: Harper Paperbacks.

15 The quote and image both come from my field notes. I copied down the diagram that the leaders drew on the whiteboard during class. Any misrepresentation of the ideas would reflect a combination of the ways the information was translated for couples' understanding and my jottings of the explanation.
16 Irvine (1999:2).
17 Furedi (2004).
18 Wright (2008).
19 Avishai, Heath, and Randles (2012).
20 Aubry and Travis (2015); Furedi (2004); McGee (2005).
21 My sense was that leadership was often more concerned with relational diversity rather than racial or economic diversity. Perhaps because of their own collective anxiety about divorce, a number of programs commented that the leadership teams didn't consist of any blended families or remarriages. Occasionally, a younger couple on the team acknowledged the whiteness of the leadership but tended to end with a statement that it would be nice to have more representation.
22 Amato et al. (2007); Ansari and Klinenberg (2015).
23 Studies of religion and the life course consistently find that involvement in churches declines during young adult years (Barry and Nelson 2005; Pearce and Lundquist Denton 2011; Smith and Snell 2009) with marriage or childbearing sometimes linked to increased attendance (Edgell 2006). Whereas evangelicals are among those more likely to marry at a younger age (Uecker and Stokes 2008), the average age of marriage has continued to rise over the past couple of decades (Amato et al. 2007). A report by Pew Research Center (2010) estimates that men and women are both increasingly waiting until their late twenties to get married for the first time.
24 Randles (2016) found in her study of Healthy Marriage Initiative programs that FOCCUS and Prepare/Enrich were among the top ten curricula cited nationwide. They were the two inventories specifically designed for premarital assessment, whereas the rest of the ones in her study were developed to assess relationship skills more broadly or for other specialized populations, such as unmarried, low-income parents.
25 Prepare/Enrich was developed in the late 1970s and early 1980s by sociologist David Olson (Davis 2010), whereas FOCCUS was created in 1985 by marriage and family therapists (FOCCUS. 2016. "Why FOCCUS?" http://www.foccusinc.com).
26 FOCCUS. 2016. "Why FOCCUS?" http://www.foccusinc.com.
27 Prepare/Enrich. 2016. "About the Assessment." https://www.prepare-enrich.com.
28 FOCCUS. 2016. "Why FOCCUS?" http://www.foccusinc.com.
29 Prepare/Enrich. 2016. "About the Assessment." https://www.prepare-enrich.com.
30 Davis (2010).
31 Latour (1987).
32 Randles (2016); see also Heath (2012).
33 The sizable portion of convalidations was mentioned at all the Catholic parishes where I conducted observations and spoke with people facilitating marriage

preparation. Unlike evangelicals who do not view marriage as a sacrament and make no distinction about who can marry a couple or where a wedding can take place, the Catholics have clear guidelines about what makes a wedding and by extension a marriage officially Catholic.
34 Ammerman (1997); Chaves (2004); Warner (1994).
35 Avishai, Heath, and Randles (2012); Coltrane (2001); Heath (2012); Randles (2016).
36 Bodovski (2020); Lareau (2003).

3. CONSTRUCTING A GOOD AND GODLY MARRIAGE

1 I use the language of "rhetoric" to capture the discursive meaning making that Christians engaged in to denote how a Christian marriage should differ from secular culture. Since the discussion of covenant marriage contains everyday religious views as well as official doctrines, I opted to not use "theology" because it would inaccurately imply a more official and formalized belief system. Another possibility could have been "ideology," which Platt and Williams (2002) argue captures how people think the world should be based on how they understand it and what they need to do to get there. Yet, ideology felt too expansive and broad as well as lacked the active quality of convincing people to view the world from a particular cultural framework. In defining "rhetoric" as the "study of persuasion," Best (2017:25) notes that "whenever people make claims, they are trying to convince others that something is a problem." The term "rhetoric" also better captures the intentional appeal to emotions (Best 2017) where people are convinced not only what to think but also how to feel.
2 The usage of "covenant" empirically emerged from how the groups utilized the term to theologically describe their belief that God calls all people (but especially Christians) to form marriages. It is not connected to the legal option of "covenant marriage" that a number of southern states passed starting in 1997 (Nock, Sanchez, and Wright 2004). Likewise, they did not use the term "contract" and "covenant" according to its more historical or political connotations (Williams 1994).
3 Williams (1994).
4 Kolb (2014).
5 Irby (2019).
6 Cherlin (2004); Hackstaff (1999); Silva (2013).
7 Hackstaff (1999).
8 Aubry and Travis (2015); Jenkins (2014); Silva (2012).
9 Bartel and Grabowski (2018); USCCB (2009). According to Catholic Canon Law, "the matrimonial covenant, by which a man and a woman establish between themselves a partnership of the whole of life, is by its nature ordered toward the good of the spouses and the procreation and education of offspring; this covenant between baptized persons has been raised by Christ the Lord to the dignity of a sacrament" (Code of Canon Law 1055 §1). Catholics also argue that the Sacrament of Matrimony can never be dissolved (Code of Canon Law 1141).

10 Jorstad (1993:96).
11 Harris (2015).
12 Avishai (2008).
13 Kniss (1996).
14 Lamont and Molnar (2002).
15 Zerubavel (1991).
16 I am not certain which translation he used in class, but I have quoted the New Standard Revised Version.
17 Zerubavel (1991).
18 In addition to discussing Cosmopolitan Church's views on sex in greater depth in chapter 5, I have published elsewhere on the how variations in evangelical conceptions of sexuality shape leaders' recommendations for managing shame (Irby 2019).
19 Hackstaff (1999:2).
20 Hackstaff (1999).
21 Despite the tendency to regularly note that divorce rates are "rising" or that "half of marriages end in divorce," neither of these claims are quite empirically accurate. In fact, scholars find that divorce rates have stabilized and even declined among some populations in recent years (Cohen 2019).
22 Jenkins (2014) notes that despite religious leaders' assertions that divorce has little impact in their community, they have developed extensive ways to minister to people through this process. Her book offers a compelling analysis of how different religious traditions, including Christians, engage in "divorce work." Building on many of the similar theoretical frameworks of therapeutic culture and religious emotion regimes, her study explores ministries that seek to transition couples out of marriage (as opposed to mine, which examines how they transition into the institution).
23 Celello (2009); Farrell (1999); Hackstaff (1999).
24 Celello (2009:3).
25 Hackstaff (1999:21), emphasis original.
26 Randles (2017).
27 Hochschild (1989/2003:48).
28 Hackstaff (1999).
29 Jenkins (2014:11).
30 Pugh (2017).
31 Illouz (2012); Randles (2016).
32 Giddens (1992:30).
33 Aubry and Travis (2015:5).
34 Silva (2012:507).
35 *Perspectives in Marriage*. 2012/1998. Chicago: Acta Publications. Pgs. 29–32.
36 These ideas are explored in more detailed in Gottman and Silver (1999).
37 Richardson, Ronald. 2011. *Family Ties That Bind: A Self-Help Guide to Change through Family of Origin Therapy*. Bellingham: Self-Counsel Press.

38 Furedi (2004).
39 Furedi (2004); Illouz (2008); Jenkins (2014).
40 Hackstaff (1999).
41 Edgell (2012).
42 Ansari and Klinenberg (2015).
43 Ibid., 24.
44 Wilkins (2008).
45 Garland (2001); Silva (2013).
46 Coontz (2005); Silva (2013).
47 Corse and Silva (2017).
48 Gerson (2017:172).

4. TEACHING GENDER (AND) DIFFERENCES IN MARRIAGE

1 Italics and capitalization originally included on the printed worksheet.
2 Davis (2010:253), emphasis original.
3 Cherlin (2009:88).
4 Silva (2012).
5 Illouz (2008); McGee (2005).
6 Dalessandro (2021); Gerson (2010); Lamont (2020).
7 Gerson (2010:11).
8 Ibid., 10.
9 Burke (2012:122).
10 Gottman and Silver (1999).
11 I have written elsewhere about how the most common topic for scholars of gender and religion has been to explore women's experiences in conservative faith traditions (Avishai and Irby 2017) and how this work has been largely situated within the dynamics in the home as a wife and mother (Irby 2014b). In particular, scholars have evaluated the tension between religious belief systems that normalize the white middle-class family structure of a homemaker-breadwinner and the everyday challenges and resistances as men and women attempt to live out this ideology (Barkowski 2001; Brasher 1998; Chong 2006; Davidman 1991; Gallagher 2003; Gallagher and Smith 1999; Griffith 1997). The gender complementarian view that emphasizes women's domesticity and men's leadership thus amounts to a form of "religious familism" (Edgell 2011) that denotes the appropriate behaviors within homes, churches, and the public sphere. In recent years, another thread of research has emerged to illustrate how the power of gender complementarianism also operates as part of the formation of premarital intimate relationships in a purity culture where women are expected to guard their sexuality and men to pursue the relationships (Freitas 2008; Gaddini 2022; Irby 2013; Sharma 2011). The extent body of literature thus has overwhelmingly found that religious teachings and informal expectations explicitly structure intimate relationships as a site where people must manage gender differences.
12 Cott (2000:3), emphasis original.

13 Although "gender roles" has always been prescriptive for how men and women should act, in the past, it used to more accurately describe men and women's behavior (Bailey 1989; Gerson 2010; Lamont 2020). Despite the term's tendency to dominate everyday discussions on gender, scholars have argued that "roles" has become less empirically accurate, too imprecise, and normatively describes how men and women ought to act within the bounds of heterosexual relationships (Connell 2009; Gerson 2010; Lorber 1994; Risman 1998). Lamont (2014:191) notes that despite these changes, courtship remains patterned by "scripts" that "enshrine the behavior of white, middle-class heterosexuals" which are "highly gendered." The language of roles thus contributes to treating gender as an "operation of heterosexuality" (Ingraham 1996:169) by defining men and women by the expectations for how they act within a heterosexual couple (e.g., division of labor, homemaker versus breadwinner, etc.).
14 Gerson (2002:10).
15 West and Zimmerman (1987).
16 Gerson (2010).
17 Connell (2009:9).
18 Bartkowski (2001); Beaman (2001); Burke (2012); Brasher (1998); Du Mez (2020); Gallagher (2003); Griffith (1997).
19 Bartkowski (2001:41).
20 Farrel, Bill, and Pam Farrel. 2001. *Men Are like Waffles, Women Are like Spaghetti: Understanding and Delighting in Your Differences.* Eugene: Harvest House.
21 Hochschild (1989).
22 Gray, John. 1992. *Men Are from Mars, Women Are from Venus: The Classic Guide to Understanding the Opposite Sex.* New York: Harper Paperbacks.
23 Randles (2016:250).
24 Bartkowski (2001).
25 Informal conversations with the leadership at the Exploring Your Relationship Retreat revealed that they were well aware of the evangelical debates on headship and submission analyzed by Bartkowski (2001). Over my multiple visits to observe this program, the leadership became more concerned that trying to speak to these debates dated their lessons and was irrelevant. From their vantage point, the couples seemed unconcerned about who would be head of the household and accepted the idea that both partners needed to submit in marriage. As evidenced in this section, their acceptance of core tenets of both sides didn't negate the leadership's belief in gender essentialism or complementarianism, but it does illustrate the malleability of these views as new generations infuse them with other ideas (including popular interpretation of secular views on neuroscience).
26 Pope John Paul II. 2006. *Man and Woman He Created Them: A Theology of the Body.* Boston: Pauline Books.
27 Pope Francis. 2015. "'Laudato Si.' Encyclical Letter of the Holy Father Francis on Care for Our Common Home." http://w2.vatican.va/.

28 Starting in the 1970s, scholars began to distinguish "sex" from "gender" (Connell 2009; Fausto-Sterling 2000). Whereas "sex" referred to the biological or physiological differences between male and female bodies, "gender" was used to account for the social dimensions that provide different expectations for how men act (masculinity) from how women act (femininity) (Coltrane and Adams 2008; Lorber 1994). Although this distinction is still commonly used and often appears in sociological textbooks, feminists have noted that it minimizes the complexity and agency of bodies in its efforts to deconstruct the sociopolitical arrangements of gender (Connell 2009; Fausto-Sterling 2000).
29 Bartkowski (2001); Burke (2012); Irby (2014b); Konieczny (2013).
30 The ideas come from the Gottman Institute and their associated publications, including Gottman and Silver (1999).
31 I believe he started with Ephesians 5:22 and ended around 5:30. I don't know which translation he read from, but I have quoted the English Standard Version.
32 Edgell (2011).
33 Bulanda (2011); Burke (2012); Irby (2014b).
34 Davis (2010).
35 Burke (2012); Irby (2014b).
36 Connell (2009:10).
37 Jenkins (2014:11).
38 Cancian and Gordon (1988); Hackstaff (1999); Pfeffer (2010).
39 Hochschild (1997); DeVault (1991); Pfeffer (2010).
40 Hackstaff (1999); Lamont (2014); McGee (2005).
41 McGee (2005).
42 Damaske (2011).
43 Illouz (2012); Ingraham (2008).
44 Lamont (2014).
45 England and Kilbourne (1990).
46 Wong (2017:192).
47 Randles (2016:258).

5. HOW DO YOU FEEL ABOUT SEX AND MONEY?

1 Jenkins (2014).
2 Hochschild (1983:74).
3 Harris (2015).
4 Hochschild (1983).
5 Berger and Kellner (1968:10).
6 Ocobock (2013); Sassler and Miller (2017).
7 The Catholic emphasis on financial preparation and the evangelical privileging of sexual preparation were inductive findings about the groups and it's uncertain how much this pattern would appear more broadly. The interviews with premarital counselors from other congregations, however, do indicate that sexual intimacy was a greater concern for evangelicals and that Catholics were more reticent on the issue.

8   Ansari and Klinenberg (2015).
9   Gallagher and Smith (1999:217).
10 Lundquist Denton (2004).
11 Dalessandro (2021); Gerson (2010); Lamont (2020).
12 Plante (2006:102).
13 Gansen (2017).
14 Lois (2012).
15 Pollak and Thoits (1989).
16 Ghaziani (2017:16).
17 Scholars dating back to Engels (1884/1978) have observed that the institution of marriage has exerted legal control over sexual activity, especially women's sexuality. In the American context, Cott (2000:11) documents how the legal system was initially built on the English common law, which "turned the married pair legally into one person—the husband." This legal oneness reflected Christian doctrine of the time that emphasized teachings of sexual exclusivity. In early years, this doctrine of *coverture* also meant that women could not have their own assets or enter into contracts. Although much of the legal features of coverture had been dismantled by the twentieth century, it wasn't until 1984 that the last vestige that granted a husband the right to his wife's body was struck down by a New York appellate court that overturned the marital rape exemption. Struening (2010) further argues that historically, marriage served as the legal precedent to establish fatherhood because paternity was less knowable and it protected a married man's estate from claims of extramarital sexual relations.
18 Even though the "anti-sex" reputation appears to be popularly held, there has been numerous important empirical challenges by researchers studying the intersection of religion and sexuality (Avishai and Burke 2016; Burke 2016; DeRogatis 2015; Fuist 2017; Irby 2019). Specifically, scholars challenge the tendency to treat "religion" as inherently oppositional to "sexuality" by noting that neither institution is monolithic (Ellingson 2002; Fuist 2017; Page and Shipley 2016) to illustrating that official mandates don't fully capture individuals' religious or sexual lives (Avishai 2012; Burke 2016; Fuist 2017). As I have argued elsewhere (Irby 2019), an underlying theme in this body of work has been the attempt to offer a more nuanced understanding of the divergent ways that religious cultures shape how people feel about sex(uality) in their lives.
19 In previous work (Irby 2019), I have unpacked the evangelical Christian view that sex represents a gift from God. Specifically, I traced how different understandings of whether sex is a behavior or more embodied impacted the lessons on emotion management of shame. Although this chapter highlights some similar themes, the emphasis here is on emotional socialization and less about how evangelical leaders are responding to the challenges of sexual shame among their congregants.
20 DeRogatis (2015); Lewis and Brissett (1986).
21 Francis (1997).
22 DeRogatis (2015).

23 Konieczny (2013:106).
24 Harris (2015).
25 Pahl (1989:1).
26 Bartkowski (2001); Bulanda (2011); Griffith (1997); Irby (2014b).
27 Pahl (1989).
28 Historically, the United States followed the British legal foundation of common law, which argued that in marriage, the husband and wife became one person legally (Cott 2000; Pahl 1989). In addition to reflecting the Christian doctrine of sexual exclusivity (Cott 2000), common law historically resulted in "any property which a woman possessed or was entitled to at the time of her marriage . . . [becoming] her husband's to control" (Pahl 1989:12). Throughout the nineteenth and twentieth centuries, women slowly obtained the rights to own property, open savings accounts, and make other independent financial decisions. Alongside these historic changes to the legal system that allowed women to keep their own money was a rise in more women earning their own income (Coltrane and Adams 2008; McGee 2005). Scholars, however, often discuss the financial and sexual changes as disconnected. For example, research on cohabitation often focus on the rise in premarital sex more than the rise in sharing financial resources. In defining cohabitation, Coltrane and Adams (2008:82) note that the "trend involves the significant rise in the number of couples who live together in a sexually imitate relationship either before marriage or in place of it." Although they go on to describe the changes to sexual norms that altered the taboo of living together before marriage, their discussion makes very little of the financial implication of living together and how this alters the meaning of marriage.
29 Randles (2016).
30 Dalessandro (2021).
31 Zelizer (2007).
32 Pahl (1989); Zelizer (2007).
33 Harris (2005).
34 Coontz (2005:309).
35 DeRogatis (2015:43).
36 Harris (2015:50).
37 Francis (1997:153).
38 Illouz (2008).
39 Wade (2017).
40 Pahl (1989).
41 Dalessandro (2021).
42 Silva (2013).

6. WHAT DID WE LEARN?

1 Except for three cases, I interviewed the couples together. In two instances, I spoke with an evangelical woman in a dating relationship by themselves, and on one occasion, I talked with a civilly married Catholic woman independently. Although

interviewing the couples separately may have provided insights into the individual concerns or some of the gendered relational pressures, I suspect that I would have had less success hearing from men who rarely were the person to volunteer or coordinate the meetings. Additionally, I found that speaking with two people allowed the interview to adopt some focus-group qualities—people would respond, elaborate, clarify, or even recall information based on what the other person mentioned.

2   Since "Catholics who exchange vows in the presence of ministers from other religious traditions or civil officials are not considered validly married in the eyes of the Catholic Church," they are required to go through a process of "convalidation" if they would like to "bring their marriage to the Church" (Diocese of Trenton 2016). Although it would not be entirely accurate to describe this process as a "second wedding," Erica personally viewed it as having this meaning in her life. (https://dioceseoftrenton.org/convalidation)

3   Smith and Lundquist Denton (2005:27).

4   Ibid., 131.

5   Ibid., 164.

6   Harris (2015); Riis and Woodhead (2010).

7   McGuire (2008:12–13).

8   The majority of the people who attended the programs were white, but there was always a sizable minority of people of color present. My ability to report racial compositions of the classes is limited, however, since I asked about racial identification only in the formal interviews that occurred afterward. Whereas the couples who volunteered at the urban sites—Cosmopolitan Church and St. Sebastian—were mostly white, I also interviewed Black, Latino, and Asian American people during this research, especially when I recruited from the nonurban sites.

9   Lamont (2014).

10 I have published elsewhere about how the debates between "courting" have rendered dating a contentious topic (Irby 2013) and how even if women are personally okay with asking out the man that their uncertainty about how he will react often keeps them from this type of action (Irby 2014a). Thus, even for evangelical women who strive for independence or egalitarian relationships, they must navigate the neotraditional scripts within evangelicalism if they want to marry someone of a similar faith background.

11 Irby (2014a).

12 Catholics aren't required to complete a program in the parish where they'll get married, but I found that parishes that tended to hold more weddings were the ones that were also more likely to offer marriage preparation. For "transplants" who had moved to the Pacific Northwest (most often for school or work) but who planned to return home for the wedding, they had the option to locate a nearby parish to complete the marriage preparation and then have the records forwarded to the parish where the wedding would take place.

13 For the most part, a Catholic wedding must be held in a church, but there are also some other locations that qualify, such as a chapel at a Catholic university.

Unlike evangelical Protestants, however, for a wedding to be considered "valid" religiously, it must occur within sanctioned religious spaces.

14 My own observations corroborate the estimate that approximately 20–25 percent of couples in marriage preparation are seeking a convalidation. Each program I observed always included at least one to two civilly married couples of the four to six enrolled.

15 Following Emerson, Shaw, and Fretz's (1995:2) call to seek "deeper immersion in others' worlds," I opted to attend the Exploring Your Relationship Retreat with my husband to fully experience the program. In contrast to the other weekly classes where I was present for the brief couple conversations, nearly two-thirds of the time during the retreat involved activities independent of the leadership's lessons. As Emerson, Shaw, and Fretz note, "immersion in ethnographic research, then, involves both being with other people to see how they respond to events as they happen and experiencing for oneself these events and the circumstances that give rise to them" (2). Although I had met their first condition, I eventually realized that I had yet to satisfy the second when I observed the retreat independently. Since we attended while I was pregnant and expecting our first child, I found we were able to share with the premarital couples a future-oriented exploration about how our relationship might change.

16 Hochschild (1997).
17 McGuire (2008:15).
18 Jenkins (2016:234).
19 Erickson (2005); Pfeffer (2010).
20 Davis (2010).
21 Bridges and Pascoe (2014:255).

CONCLUSION

1 Maldonado-Estrada (2020:215).
2 Bartkowski (2001); Edgell (2006); Gallagher (2007); Konieczny (2013).
3 Edgell (2006).
4 Ibid., 150.
5 Ibid., 152.
6 Cherlin (2004, 2009); Celello (2009); Coontz (2005); Cott (2000); Dizard and Gadlin (1990).
7 Ansari and Klinenberg (2015); Dalessandro (2021); Damske (2011); Gerson (2010); Hackstaff (1999); Lamont (2020).
8 Avishai, Heath, and Randles (2012).
9 Randles (2017).
10 Irby (2014b).
11 Chaves (2004:5) was speaking strictly of "congregations" as the local manifestation of religious traditions. I opted for the language of "religious community" to be more inclusive of the range of religious spaces where I encountered these programs, including Christian retreat centers and colleges. Importantly, even when

premarital counseling occurred in other religious spaces, there was an expectation that individuals should be embedded within a congregation.

12 Past research has found that religious people sometimes struggle to make the transition from chastity to marital sexuality (Avishai 2012; Diefendorf 2015; Irby 2019; Sharma 2011). Whether in abstinence programming or, as seen here, in marriage education, "good sex" is often presented as the reward for waiting until marriage (DeRogatis 2015; Gardner 2011; Lewis and Brissett 1986). Yet, the move from treating sexuality as a battleground to a playground (Irby 2019) is sometimes not as simple as saying "I do" and being pronounced "husband and wife."

13 Illouz (2008:240).

14 Pugh (2017); Silva (2013).

15 Chapman (2010:11).

16 Hackstaff (1999).

17 Pugh (2017); Silva (2013).

18 Although theologically, the validity of "good works" is contested, there often remains a pervasive understanding that "God helps those who help themselves." In any case, the program emphasis on working on one's marriage supported this type of colloquialism among Christians that God will support those who are doing good work and working on the right type of matters in their lives.

19 England and Kilbourne (1990); Randles (2016).

20 Pugh (2017); Silva (2013).

21 Gerson (2010); Wong (2017).

22 Cherlin (2004).

23 Wong (2017).

24 Hochschild (1989).

25 Damaske (2011).

26 Bellah et al. (1985:127).

27 Ammerman and Clark Roof (1995:5).

28 Ibid.

29 Cherlin (2004).

30 Ansari and Klinenberg (2015).

31 Ibid.

32 Celello (2003); Hackstaff (1999).

33 Obama, Barack. 2015. "Remarks by the President on the Supreme Court Decision on Marriage Equality." June 26. https://obamawhitehouse.archives.gov/.

34 The United States Conference of Catholic Bishops has released numerous documents over the years reiterating a position against same-sex marriage. For example, in *Ministry to Persons with a Homosexual Inclination: Guidelines for Pastoral Care*, they state, "Homosexuality poses challenges that can only be met with the help of a clear understanding of the place of sexuality within God's plan for humanity" (2). It describes the Catholic view that marital love is expressed in the procreation and education of children, as well as that sexual activity outside of marriage doesn't fulfill proper purposes of the act.

35 Ellis (2017) studied RCIA (Rite of Christian Initiation of Adult) which is a ministry for Catholic converts. Similar to marriage preparation programs, it's typically taught by priests or devoted congregants with weekly meetings leading up to an important Catholic ritual. Specifically, both programs represent sacramental education (baptism or confirmation for RCIA and wedding for marriage preparation).

36 Ibid., 395.

37 The "silent disagreement" (Ellis 2017), in fact, was so pronounced at one parish that one couple was unaware of the Catholic teaching on birth control despite having attended the marriage preparation program and both partners identifying as Catholic. My interview instruments did not directly ask about religious teachings that people agreed or disagreed with, but the issue of homosexuality, birth control, and necessity of having children emerged as points of contention. Yet, as Ellis (2017) notes, people were individually consenting without necessarily openly critiquing the positions in the classes or withdrawing from the religious community. In my research, I witnessed public silence and private dissent. One interviewee, however, mentioned that in the session that they had attended (but I didn't observe other than one day to recruit participants), there was a young woman who told the lay leadership she disagreed with the teaching on birth control and planned to use it.

38 Moon (2004:124).

39 Ibid., 143.

40 Celello (2009); Coltrane and Adams (2003).

41 Importantly, same-sex marriage is not inherently antithetical to all Christian views of marriage. Christian religious leaders of other traditions and even some religious believers within Catholicism and evangelicalism see the possibility of nonheterosexual Christian marriages. In fact, Pew Research Center (2019) found that the majority of Catholics and white nonevangelical Protestants reported same-sex marriage has either been "somewhat good" or "very good" for our society. Likewise, in 2018, the Seventy-Ninth Convention for the Episcopal Church authorized "The Witnessing and Blessing of a Lifelong Covenant" for same-sex couples. Yet, the official Catholic position and many evangelical leaders continue to assert the heterosexual foundation of a Christian marriage and speak out against marriage equality. As recently as December 2022, Bishop Robert Barron, chairman of the U.S. Conference of Catholic Bishops, issued a statement against what he saw as the "misnamed" Respect for Marriage Act, which includes protections for same-sex couples. Likewise, a year earlier, the Southern Baptist Convention issued "On the Equality Act," a document in which they stated that they "strongly oppose" the legislation that prohibits discrimination based on sex, sexual, and gender identities in areas of public accommodations, such as jury and housing. Most of these declarations, however, operate at the level of defining marriage and are distinct from the concern about how to have a good marriage, which motivated the religious leaders throughout this book.

42 I am grateful to an anonymous reviewer for helping me to articulate this point.

BIBLIOGRAPHY

Adams, Michele, and Scott Coltrane. 2006. "Framing Divorce Reform: Media, Morality, and the Politics of the Family." *Family Process* 46(1):17–34.

Amato, Paul, Alan Booth, David Johnson, and Stacy Rogers. 2007. *Alone Together: How Marriage in America is Changing.* Cambridge, MA: Harvard University Press.

Ammerman, Nancy. 1997. *Congregation and Community.* New Brunswick, NJ: Rutgers University Press.

Ammerman, Nancy, and Wade Clark Roof. 1995. *Work, Family, and Religion in Contemporary Society.* New York: Routledge.

Ansari, Aziz, and Eric Klinenberg. 2015. *Modern Romance.* New York: Penguin.

Aubry, Timothy, and Trysh Travis. 2015. *Rethinking Therapeutic Culture.* Chicago: University of Chicago Press.

Aune, Kristin. 2002. *Single Women: Challenge to the Church?* Waynesboro, GA: Paternoster Press.

Avishai, Orit. 2008. "'Doing Religion' in a Secular World: Women in Conservative Religions and the Question of Agency." *Gender & Society* 22:409–33.

———. 2012. "What to Do with the Problem of the Flesh? Negotiating Orthodox Jewish Sexual Anxieties." *Fieldwork in Religion* 7(2):148–62.

Avishai, Orit, and Kelsy Burke. 2016. "God's Case for Sex." *Contexts* 15(4):30–35.

Avishai, Orit, Melanie Heath, and Jennifer Randles. 2012. "Marriage Goes to School." *Contexts* 11(3):34–39.

Avishai, Orit, and Courtney Ann Irby. 2017. "Bifurcated Conversations in Sociological Studies of Religion and Gender." *Gender & Society* 31(5):647–76.

Bailey, Beth. 1989. *From the Front Porch to the Backseat.* Baltimore: Johns Hopkins University Press.

Barkan, Steven. 2006. "Religiosity and Premarital Sex in Adulthood." *Journal for the Scientific Study of Religion* 45(3):407–17.

Barry, Carolyn, and Barry Nelson. 2005. "The Role of Religion in the Transition to Adulthood for Young Emerging Adults." *Journal of Youth and Adolescence* 34:245–55.

Bartel, Sarah, and John Grabowski. 2018. *A Catechism for Family Life.* Washington, DC: Catholic University of America Press.

Bartkowski, John. 2001. *Remaking the Godly Marriage: Gender Negotiation in Evangelical Families.* New Brunswick, NJ: Rutgers University Press.

———. 2007. "Religious Socialization among American Youth: How Faith Shapes Parents, Children, and Adolescents." Pp. 511–25 in *The Sage of Handbook of the Sociology of Religion*, eds. N. J. Demerath and James Beckford. Thousand Oaks, CA: Sage.
Beaman, Lori. 2001. *Shared Beliefs, Different Lives: Women's Identities in Evangelical Context.* St. Louis: Chalice Press.
Bellah, Robert, Richard Madsen, William Sullivan, Ann Swidler, and Steven Tipton. 1985. *Habits of the Heart: Individualism and Commitment in American Life.* Berkeley: University of California Press.
Berger, Peter, and Hansgried Kellner. 1968. "Marriage and the Construction of Reality: An Exercise in the Microsociology of Knowledge." *Diogenes* 12(46):1–24.
Bernard, Jessie. 1972/1982. *The Future of Marriage.* Binghamton: Vail-Ballou Press.
Best, Joel. 2017. *Social Problems.* New York: Norton.
Bodovski, Katerina. 2020. "Parenting, Social Class, and the College Admission Scandal." *Contexts* 19(3):40–45.
Brasher, Brenda. 1998. *Godly Women: Fundamentalism & Female Power.* New Brunswick, NJ: Rutgers University Press.
Bridges, Tristan, and C. J. Pascoe. 2014. "Hybrid Masculinities: New Dimensions in the Sociology of Men and Masculinities." *Sociology Compass* 8(3):246–58.
Brown, Edna, Terri Orbuch, and Jose Bauermeister. 2008. "Religiosity and Marital Stability among Black American and White American Couples." *Family Relations* 57(2):186–97.
Bulanda, Jennifer. 2011. "Doing Family, Doing Gender, Doing Religion: Structured Ambivalence and the Religion–Family Connection." *Journal of Family Theory & Review* 3:179–97.
Burdette, Amy, Stacy Haynes, and Christopher Ellison. 2012. "Religion, Race/Ethnicity, and Perceived Barriers to Marriage among Working-Age Adults." *Sociology of Religion* 73(4):429–51.
Burdette, Amy, and Terrence Hill. 2009. "Religious Involvement and Transitions into Adolescent Sexual Activities." *Sociology of Religion* 70(1):28–48.
Burke, Kelsy. 2012. "Women's Agency in Gender-Traditional Religions: A Review of Four Approaches." *Sociology Compass* 6(2):122–33.
———. 2016. *Christians under Covers: Evangelicals and Sexual Pleasure on the Internet.* Oakland: University of California Press.
Burns, Jeffrey. 1999. *Disturbing the Peace: A History of the Christian Family Movement, 1949–1974.* South Bend: University of Notre Dame Press.
Cabanas, Edgar, and Eva Illouz. 2017. "The Making to a 'Happy Worker': Positive Psychology in Neoliberal Organizations." Pp. 25–49 in *Beyond the Cubicle: Job Insecurity, Intimacy, and the Flexible Self*, ed. Allison Pugh. New York: Oxford University Press.
Call, Vaugh, and Tim Heaton. 1997. "Religious Influence on Marital Stability." *Journal for the Scientific Study of Religion* 36(3):382–92.
Cancian, Francesca. 1987. *Love in America: Gender and Self-Development.* New York: Cambridge University Press.

Cancian, Francesca, and Steven Gordon. 1988. "Changing Emotion Norms in Marriage: Love and Anger in U.S. Women's Magazines since 1900." *Gender & Society* 2(3):308–42.
Celello, Kristin. 2009. *Making Marriage Work: A History of Marriage and Divorce in the Twentieth-Century United States*. Chapel Hill: University of North Carolina Press.
Celello, Kristin, and Hanan Kholoussy. 2016. *Domestic Tensions, National Anxieties: Global Perspectives on Marriage, Crisis, and Nation*. New York: Oxford University Press.
Chapman, Gary. 2010. *Things I Wish I'd Known before We Got Married*. Chicago: Northfield Publishing.
Chaves, Mark. 2004. *Congregations in America*. Cambridge, MA: Harvard University Press.
Cherlin, Andrew. 2004. "The Deinstitutionalization of American Marriage." *Journal of Marriage and Family* 66:848–61.
———. 2009. *The Marriage-Go-Round: The State of Marriage and Family in America Today*. New York: Knopf.
Chong, Kelly. 2006. "Negotiating Patriarchy: South Korean Evangelical Women and the Politics of Gender." *Gender & Society* 20(6):697–724.
Cohen, Phillip. 2019. "The Coming Divorce Decline." *Socius* 5. https://doi.org/10.1177/2378023119873497.
Coltrane, Scott. 2001. "Marketing the Marriage 'Solution': Misplaced Simplicity in the Politics of Fatherhood." *Sociological Perspectives* 44(4):387–417.
Coltrane, Scott, and Michele Adams. 2003. "The Social Construction of the Divorce 'Problem': Morality, Child Victims, and the Politics of Gender." *Family Relations* 52:363–72.
———. 2008. *Gender and Families*. Lanham, MD: Rowman & Littlefield.
Connell, Raewyn. 2009. *Gender*. Malden, MA: Polity.
Coontz, Stephanie. 1992. *The Way We Never Were: American Families and the Nostalgia Trap*. New York: Basic Books.
———. 2005. *Marriage, a History: From Obedience to Intimacy, or How Love Conquered Marriage*. New York: Penguin.
———. 2008. "'Traditional' Marriage or a Break with Tradition?" *Immanent Frame*, June 2. http://tif.ssrc.org.
Corse, Sarah, and Jennifer Silva. 2017. "Intimate Inequalities: Love and Work in the Twenty-First Century." Pp. 283–303 in *Beyond the Cubicle: Job Insecurity, Intimacy, and the Flexible Self*, ed. Allison Pugh. New York: Oxford University Press.
Cott, Nancy. 2000. *Public Vows: A History of Marriage and the Nation*. Cambridge, MA: Harvard University Press.
Curington, Celeste, Jennifer Linquist, and Ken-Hou Lin. 2021. *The Dating Divide: Race and Desire in the Era of Online Romance*. Oakland: University of California Press.
Dalessandro, Cristen. 2021. *Intimate Inequalities: Millennials' Romantic Relationships in Contemporary Times*. New Brunswick, NJ: Rutgers University Press.
Damaske, Sarah. 2011. *For the Family? How Class and Gender Shape Women's Work*. New York: Oxford University Press.

Davidman, Lynn. 1991. *Tradition in a Rootless World: Women Turn to Orthodox Judaism*. Berkeley: University of California Press.
Davis, Rebecca. 2010. *More Perfect Unions: The American Search for Marital Bliss*. Cambridge, MA: Harvard University Press.
DeRogatis, Amy. 2005. "What Would Jesus Do? Sexuality and Salvation in Protestant Evangelical Sex Manuals, 1950 to the Present." *Journal of Church History* 74(1):97–137.
———. 2015. *Saving Sex: Sexuality and Salvation in American Evangelicalism*. New York: Oxford University Press.
Devault, Marjorie. 1991. *Feeding the Family: The Social Organization of Caring as Gendered Work*. Chicago: University of Chicago Press.
Diefendorf, Sarah. 2015. "After the Wedding Night: Sexual Abstinence and Masculinities over the Life Course." *Gender & Society* 29(5):647–99.
Dizard, Jan, and Howard Gadlin. 1990. *The Minimal Family*. Amherst: University of Massachusetts Press.
Du Mez, Kristin Kobes. 2020. *Jesus and John Wayne: How White Evangelicals Corrupted a Faith and Fractured a Nation*. New York: Liveright.
Edgell, Penny. 2006. *Religion and Family in a Changing Society*. Princeton: Princeton University Press.
———. 2011. "Religion and Family." Pp. 635–50 in *The Oxford Handbook for the Sociology of Religion*, ed. Peter Clarke. New York: Oxford University Press.
———. 2012. "A Cultural Sociology of Religion: New Directions." *Annual Review of Sociology* 38:247–65.
Edin, Kathryn, and Maria Kefalas. 2005. *Promises I Can Keep: Why Poor Women Put Motherhood before Marriage*. Berkeley: University of California Press.
Ellingson, Stephen. 2002. "Introduction." Pp. 1–18 in *Religion and Sexuality in Cross-Cultural Perspective*, eds. Stephen Ellingson and M. Christian Green. New York: Routledge.
Ellis, Rachel. 2017. "Silent Disagreement: Microinteractional Solutions to Moral Dissent among Catholic Converts." *Journal for the Scientific Study of Religion* 56(2):383–97.
Emerson, Robert, Rachel Fretz, and Linda Shaw. 1995. *Writing Ethnographic Fieldnotes*. Chicago: University of Chicago Press.
England, Paula, and Barbara Kilbourne. 1990. "Markets, Marriages, and Other Mates: The Problem of Power." Pp. 163–88 in *Beyond the Marketplace: Rethinking Economy and Society*, eds. Roger Friedland and A. F. Robertson. New York: Aldine de Gruyter.
Engels, Friedrich. 1884/1978. "The Origin of the Family, Private Property, and the State." Pp.734–59 in *The Marx-Engels Reader*, ed. Robert Tucker. New York: Norton.
Erickson, Rebecca. 2005. "Why Emotion Work Matters: Sex, Gender, and the Division of Household Labor." *Journal of Marriage and Family* 67(2):337–51.
Farrell, Betty. 1999. *Family: The Making of an Idea, an Institution, and a Controversy in American Culture*. Boulder: Westview.

Fausto-Sterling, Anne. 2000. *Sexing the Body: Gender Politics and the Construction of Sexuality*. New York: Basic Books.
Fischer, Claude, and Michael Hout. 2005. "The Family in Trouble: Since When? For Whom?" Pp. 120–40 in *Family Transformed: Religion, Values, and Society in American Life*, eds. Steven Tipton and John Witte Jr. Washington, DC: Georgetown University Press.
Francis, Linda. 1997. "Ideology and Interpersonal Management: Redefining Identity in Two Support Groups." *Social Psychology Quarterly* 60(2):153–77.
Freitas, Donna. 2008. *Sex and the Soul: Juggling Sexuality, Spirituality, Romance, and Religion on America's College Campuses*. Oxford: Oxford University Press.
Fuist, Todd Nicholas. 2017. "'It Just Always Seemed Like It Wasn't a Big Deal, yet I Know for Some People They Really Struggle with It': LGBT Religious Identities in Context." *Journal for the Scientific Study of Religion* 55(4):770–86.
Furedi, Frank. 2004. *Therapy Culture: Cultivating Vulnerability in an Uncertain Age*. New York: Routledge.
Furstenberg, Frank, Sheela Kennedy, Vonnie McLoyd, Rubén Rumbaut, and Richard Settersten. 2004. "Growing Up Is Harder to Do." *Contexts* 3(3):33–41.
Gaddini, Katie. 2022. *The Struggle to Stay: Why Single Evangelical Women Are Leaving the Church*. New York: Columbia University Press.
Gallagher, Sally. 2003. *Evangelical Identity and Gendered Family Life*. New Brunswick, NJ: Rutgers University Press.
———. 2007. "Children as Religious Resources: The Role of Children in the Social Reformation of Class, Culture and Religious Identity." *Journal for the Scientific Study of Religion* 46(2):169–83.
Gallagher, Sally, and Christian Smith. 1999. "Symbolic Traditionalism and Pragmatic Egalitarianism: Contemporary Evangelicals, Families, and Gender." *Gender & Society* 13(2):211–33.
Gansen, Heidi. 2017. "Reproducing (and Disrupting) Heteronormativity: Gendered Sexual Socialization in Preschool Classrooms." *Sociology of Education* 90(3):255–72.
Gardner, Christine. 2011. *Making Chastity Sexy: The Rhetoric of Evangelical Abstinence Campaigns*. Berkeley: University of California Press.
Garland, David. 2001. *The Culture of Control: Crime and Social Order in Contemporary Society*, Chicago: University of Chicago Press.
Gerson, Kathleen. 2002. "Moral Dilemmas, Moral Strategies, and the Transformation of Gender: Lessons from Two Generations of Work and Family Change." *Gender & Society* 16(1):8–28.
———. 2010. *The Unfinished Revolution: How a New Generation Is Reshaping Family, Work and Gender*. New York: Oxford University Press.
———. 2017. "Different Ways of *Not* Having It All: Work, Care, and Shifting Gender Arrangements in the New Economy." Pp. 155–77 in *Beyond the Cubicle: Job Insecurity, Intimacy, and the Flexible Self*, ed. Allison Pugh. New York: Oxford University Press.

Ghaziani, Amin. 2017. *Sex Cultures*. Malden, MA: Polity.
Giddens, Anthony. 1992. *The Transformation of Intimacy: Sexuality, Love & Eroticism in Modern Societies*. Stanford: Stanford University Press.
Gottman, John, and Nan Silver. 1999. *The Seven Principles for Making Marriage Work*. New York: Harmony Books.
Griffith, R. Marie. 1997. *God's Daughters: Evangelical Women and the Power of Submission*. Berkeley: University of California Press.
Hackstaff, Karla. 1999. *Marriage in a Culture of Divorce*. Philadelphia: Temple University Press.
Halpern-Meekin, Sarah. 2019. *Social Poverty: Low-Income Parents and the Struggle for Family and Community Ties*. New York: New York University Press.
Harris, Scott. 2015. *An Invitation to the Sociology of Emotion*. New York: Routledge.
Heath, Melanie. 2008. "Promoting Marriage and Christianity in America." *Immanent Frame*, July 2. http://tif.ssrc.org.
———. 2009. "State of Our Unions: Marriage Promotion and the Contested Power of Heterosexuality." *Gender & Society* 23(1):27–48.
———. 2012. *One Marriage under God: The Campaign to Promote Marriage in America*. New York: New York University Press.
Hendershot, Heather. 2004. *Shaking the World for Jesus: Media and Conservative Evangelical Culture*. Chicago: University of Chicago Press.
Hochschild, Arlie. 1983. *The Managed Heart: Commercialization of Human Feeling*. Berkeley: University of California Press.
———. 1989/2003. *The Second Shift*. New York: Penguin.
———. 1997. "Sociology of Emotion as a Way of Seeing." Pp. 3–15 in *Emotions in Social Life: Critical Themes and Contemporary Issues*, eds. Gillian Bendelow and Simon Williams. New York: Routledge.
Hull, Shawnika, Michael Hennessy, Amy Bleakley, Martin Fishbbein, and Amy Jordan. 2011. "Identifying the Causal Pathways from Religiosity to Delayed Adolescent Sexual Behavior." *Journal of Sex Research* 48(6):543–53.
Illouz, Eva. 2008. *Saving the Modern Soul: Therapy, Emotions, and the Culture of Self-Help*. Berkeley: University of California Press.
———. 2012. *Why Love Hurts: A Sociological Explanation*. Malden, MA: Polity.
Imber, Jonathan. 2004. *Therapeutic Culture: Triumph and Defeat*. New Brunswick, NJ: Transaction.
Ingraham, Chrys. 1996. "The Heterosexual Imaginary: Feminist Sociology and Theories of Gender." Pp.168–98 in *Queer Theory/Sociology*, ed. Steven. Seidman. Cambridge, MA: Blackwell.
———. 2008. *White Wedding: Romancing Heterosexuality in Popular Culture*. New York: Routledge.
Irby, Courtney Ann. 2013. "'We Didn't Call It Dating': The Disrupted Landscape of Relationship Advice for Evangelical Protestant Youth." *Critical Research on Religion* 1(2):177–94.

———. 2014a. "Dating in Light of Christ: Young Evangelicals Negotiating Gender in the Context of Religious and Secular American Culture." *Sociology of Religion* 75(2):208–33.

———. 2014b. "Moving beyond Agency: A Review of Gender and Relationships in Conservative Religions." *Sociology Compass* 8(11):1269–80.

———. 2019. "Instructions for God's Gift: Emotional Management in the Cultural Transmission of Evangelical Sexuality." *Journal of Contemporary Ethnography* 48(5):645–73.

Irvine, Leslie. 1999. *Codependent Forevermore: The Invention of Self in a Twelve Step Group*. Chicago: University of Chicago Press.

Jackson, Stevi. 1993. "Even Sociologists Fall in Love: An Exploration in the Sociology of Emotions." *Sociology* 27(2):201–20.

Jenkins, Kathleen. 2014. *Sacred Divorce: Religion, Therapeutic Culture, and Ending Life Partnerships*. New Brunswick, NJ: Rutgers University Press.

———. 2016. "Family." Pp. 219–39 in *Handbook of Religion and Society*, ed. David Yamane. New York: Springer.

Johnson, Kathryn. 2001. "Taking Marriage 'One Day at a Time': The Cana Conference Movement and the Creation of a Catholic Mentality." *CUSHWA Center for the Study of American Catholicism*, Working Paper Series 33:1.

Jorstad, Erling. 1993. *Popular Religion in America: The Evangelical Voice*. Westport, CT: Greenwood.

Khan, Shamus Rahman. 2011. *Privilege: The Making of an Adolescent Elite at St. Paul's School*. Princeton: Princeton University Press.

Kniss, Fred. 1996. "Ideas and Symbols as Resources in Intrareligious Conflict: The Case of American Mennonites." *Sociology of Religion* 57:7–23.

Kolb, Kenneth. 2014. "Emotional Subcultures." *Sociology Compass* 8(11):1229–41.

Konieczny, Mary Ellen. 2013. *The Spirit's Tether: Family, Work, and Religion among American Catholics*. New York: Oxford University Press.

Lamont, Ellen. 2014. "Negotiating Courtship: Reconciling Egalitarian Ideals with Traditional Gender Norms." *Gender & Society* 28(2):189–211.

———. 2020. *The Mating Game: How Gender Still Shapes How We Date*. Oakland: University of California Press.

Lamont, Michele, and Virag Molnar. 2002. "The Study of Boundaries in Social Sciences." *Annual Review of Sociology* 28:167–95.

Landry, Bart. 2000. *Black Working Wives: Pioneers of the American Family Revolution*. Berkeley: University of California Press.

Lareau, Annette. 2003. *Unequal Childhoods: Race, Class, and Family Life*. Berkeley: University of California Press.

Lasch, Christopher. 1979. *The Culture of Narcissism: American Life in an Age of Diminishing Expectations*. New York: Norton.

Latour, Bruno. 1987. *Science in Action: How to Follow Scientists and Engineers through Society*. Cambridge, MA: Harvard University Press.

Lewis, Lionel, and Dennis Brisset. 1986. "Sex as God's Work." *Culture and Society* 23(3):67–75.
Lofland, John, David Snow, Leon Anderson, and Lyn Lofland. 2006. *Analyzing Social Settings: A Guide to Qualitative Observation and Analysis*. Belmont, CA: Thomson & Wadsworth.
Lofton, Kathryn. 2015. "Gospel." Pp. 34–45 in *Rethinking Therapeutic Culture*, eds. Timothy Aubry and Trysh Travis. Chicago: University of Chicago Press.
Lois, Jennifer. 2012. *Home Is Where the School Is: The Logic of Homeschooling and the Emotional Labor of Mothering*. New York: New York University Press.
Lorber, Judith. 1994. *Paradoxes of Gender*. New Haven: Yale University Press.
Loss, Christopher. 2002. "Review: Religion and the Therapeutic Ethos in Twentieth-Century American History." *American Studies International* 40(3):61–76.
Lundquist Denton, Melinda. 2004. "Gender and Marital Decision Making: Negotiating Religious Ideology and Practice." *Social Forces* 82(3):1151–80.
Maldonado-Estrada, Alyssa. 2020. *Lifeblood of the Parish: Men and Catholic Devotion in Williamsburg, Brooklyn*. New York: New York University Press.
Manning, Christel. 2015. *Losing Our Religion: How Unaffiliated Parents Are Raising Their Children*. New York: New York University Press.
Marsden, George. 1982. *Fundamentalism and American Culture: The Shaping of Twentieth Century Evangelicalism, 1870–1925*. New York: Oxford University Press.
———. 1987. *Reforming Fundamentalism: Fuller Seminary and the New Evangelicalism*. Grand Rapids: Eerdmans.
May, Elaine. 2017. *Homeward Bound: American Families in the Cold War Era*. New York: Basic Books.
McGee, Micki. 2005. *Self-Help, Inc.: Makeover Culture in American Life*. New York: Oxford University Press.
McGuire, Meredith. 2008. *Lived Religion*. New York: Oxford University Press.
Moon, Dawne. 2004. *God, Sex, & Politics: Homosexuality and Everyday Theologies*. Chicago: University of Chicago Press.
———. 2005. "Emotion Language and Social Power: Homosexuality and Narratives of Pain in Church." *Qualitative Sociology* 24(4):327–49.
Moskowitz, Eva. 2001. *In Therapy We Trust: America's Obsession with Self Fulfillment*. Baltimore: Johns Hopkins University Press.
Moslener, Sara. 2015. *Virgin Nation: Sexual Purity and American Adolescence*. New York: Oxford University Press.
Myers-Shirk, Susan. 2000. "'To Be Fully Human': U.S. Protestant Psychotherapeutic Culture and the Subversion of the Domestic Ideal, 1945–1965." *Journal of Women's History* 12(1):112–36.
———. 2009. *Helping the Good Shepherd: Pastoral Counselors in a Psychotherapeutic Culture, 1925–1975*. Baltimore: Johns Hopkins University Press.
Nason-Clark, Nancy. 1997. *The Battered Wife: How Christians Confront Family Violence*. Louisville: Westminster John Knox Press.

Nock, Steven, Laura Sanchez, and James Wright. 2004. *Covenant Marriage: The Movement to Reclaim Tradition in America*. Piscataway, NJ: Rutgers University Press.
Noll, Mark. 2000. *Protestants in America*. New York: Oxford University Press.
Ocobock, Abigail. 2013. "The Power and Limits of Marriage: Married Gay Men's Family Relationships." *Journal of Marriage and Family* 75:191–205.
Oliver, Melvin, and Thomas Shapiro. 1997. *Black Wealth/White Wealth: A New Perspective on Racial Inequality*. New York: Routledge.
Page, Sarah-Jane, and Heather Shipley. 2016. "Sexuality." Pp. 395–419 in *Handbook of Religion and Society*, ed. David Yamane. New York: Springer.
Pahl, Jan. 1989. *Money and Marriage*. New York: St. Martin's.
Paulsen, Krista. 2009. "Ethnography of the Ephemeral: Studying Temporary Scenes through Individual and Collective Approaches." *Social Identities* 15(4):509–24.
Pearce, Lisa, and Melinda Lundquist Denton. 2011. *A Faith of Their Own: Stability and Change in the Religiosity of America's Adolescents*. New York: Oxford University Press.
Pew Research Center. 2008. "U.S. Religious Landscape Survey: Religious Beliefs and Practices." http://pewresearch.org.
———. 2010. "The Decline of Marriage and Rise of New Families." http://pewresearch.org.
———. 2019. "Marriage and Cohabitation in the U.S." http://pewresearch.org.
Pfeffer, Carla. 2010. "'Women's Work'? Women Partners of Transgender Men Doing Housework and Emotion Work." *Journal of Marriage and Family* 72(1):165–83.
Plante, Rebecca. 2006. *Sexualities in Context: A Social Perspective*. Boulder: Westview.
Platt, Gerald, and Rhys H. Williams. 2002. "Ideological Language and Social Movement Mobilization: A Sociolinguistic Analysis of Segregationists' Ideologies." *Sociological Theory* 20(3):328–59.
Pollak, Lauren, and Peggy Thoits. 1989. "Processes in Emotional Socialization." *Social Psychology Quarterly* 52(1):22–34.
Pugh, Alison. 2017. "Introduction." Pp. 1–21 in *Beyond the Cubicle: Job Insecurity, Intimacy, and the Flexible Self*, ed. Allison Pugh. New York: Oxford University Press.
Rakow, Katja. 2013. "Therapeutic Culture and Religion in America." *Religion Compass* 7(11):485–97.
Randles, Jennifer. 2012. "Marriage Promotion Policy and Family Inequality." *Sociology Compass* 6(8):671–83.
———. 2016. "Redefining the Marital Power Struggle through Relationship Skills: How U.S. Marriage Education Programs Challenge and Reproduce Gender Inequality." *Gender & Society* 30(2):240–64.
———. 2017. *Proposing Prosperity? Marriage Education Policy and Inequality in America*. New York: Columbia University Press.
Regnerus, Mark. 2007. *Forbidden Fruit: Sex and Religion in the Lives of American Teenagers*. New York: Oxford University Press.
Rieff, Philip. 1966. *The Triumph of the Therapeutic: Uses of Faith after Freud*. New York: Harper & Row.

Riis, Ole, and Linda Woodhead. 2010. *A Sociology of Religious Emotion*. New York: Oxford University Press.

Risman, Barbara. 1998. *Gender Vertigo: American Families in Transition*. New Haven: Yale University Press.

Roof, Wade Clark. 1999. *Spiritual Marketplace: Baby Boomers and the Remaking of American Religion*. Princeton: Princeton University Press.

Rostosky, Sharon Scales, Mark Regnerus, and Margaret Laurie Comer Wright. 2003. "Coital Debut: The Role of Religiosity and Sex Attitudes in the Add Health Survey." *Journal of Sex Research* 40(4):358–67.

Ruggles, Steven. 2015. "Patriarchy, Power, and Pay: The Transformation of American Families, 1800–2015." *Demography* 52(6):1797–823.

Sassler, Sharon, and Amanda Miller. 2017. *Cohabitation Nation: Gender, Class, and the Remaking of Relationships*. Oakland: University of California Press.

Schafer, Axel. 2011. *Countercultural Conservatives: American Evangelicalism from the Postwar Revival to the New Christian Right*. Madison: University of Wisconsin Press.

Schneider, Daniel, Kristen Harknett, and Matthew Stimpson. 2018. "What Explains the Decline in First Marriage in the United States? Evidence from the Panel Study of Income Dynamics, 1969 to 2013." *Journal of Marriage and Family* 80(4):791–811.

Sharma, Sonya. 2011. *Good Girls, Good Sex: Women Talk about Church and Sexuality*. Winnipeg: Fernwood.

Silk, Mark. 2005. "Religion and Region in American Public Life." *Journal for the Scientific Study of Religion* 44(3):265–70.

Silva, Jennifer. 2012. "Constructing Adulthood in an Age of Uncertainty." *American Sociological Review* 77(4):505–22.

———. 2013. *Coming Up Short: Working-Class Adulthood in an Age of Uncertainty*. New York: Oxford University Press.

Slominski, Kristy. 2021. *Teaching Moral Sex: A History of Religion and Sex Education in the United States*. New York: Oxford University Press.

Smith, Christian, Michael Emerson, Sally Gallagher, Paul Kennedy, and David Sikkink. 1998. *American Evangelicalism: Embattled and Thriving*. Chicago: University of Chicago Press.

Smith, Christian, and Melinda Lundquist Denton. 2005. *Soul Searching: The Religious and Spiritual Lives of American Teenagers*. New York: Oxford University Press.

Smith, Christian, and Patricia Snell. 2009. *Souls in Transition: The Religious and Spiritual Lives of Emerging Adults*. New York: Oxford University Press.

Smith, Christian, and Robert Woodberry. 1998. "Fundamentalism et al.: Conservative Protestants in America." *Annual Review of Sociology* 24:25–56.

Spillman, Lyn. 2002. "Introduction: Culture and Cultural Sociology." Pp. 1–16 in *Cultural Sociology*, ed. Lyn Spillman. Malden, MA: Blackwell.

Stephens, Randall, and Karl Giberson. 2011. *The Anointed: Evangelical Truth in a Secular Age*. Cambridge, MA: Harvard University Press.

Struening, Karen. 2010. "Families 'in Law' and Families 'in Practice': Does the Law Recognize Families as They Really Are?" Pp.75–90 in *Families as They Really Are*, ed. Barbara Risman. New York: Norton.

Swidler, Ann. 2001. *Talk of Love: How Culture Matters*. Chicago: University of Chicago Press.

Tentler, Leslie Woodcock. 2004. *Catholics and Contraception: An American History*. Ithaca: Cornell University Press.

Thorne, Barrie. 1982. "Feminist Rethinking of the Family: An Overview." Pp. 1–24 in *Rethinking the Family: Some Feminist Questions*, eds. Barrie Thorne and Marilyn Yalom. New York: Longman.

Uecker, Jeremy, and Charles Stokes. 2008. "Early Marriage in the United States." *Journal of Marriage and Family* 70:835–46.

Wade, Lisa. 2017. *American Hookup: The New Culture of Sex on Campus*. New York: Norton.

Warner, R. Stephen. 1994. "The Place of Congregations in the Contemporary American Religious Landscape." Pp. 54–99 in *New Perspectives in the Study of Congregations*, eds. James Wind and James Lewis, vol. 2 of *American Congregations*. Chicago: University of Chicago Press.

Watt, David. 1991. "The Private Hopes of American Fundamentalists and Evangelicals, 1925–1975." *Religion and American Culture* 1(2):155–75.

Wellman, James. 2008. *Evangelical vs. Liberal: The Clash of Christian Cultures in the Pacific Northwest*. New York: Oxford University Press.

West, Candace, and Don H. Zimmerman. 1987. "Doing Gender." *Gender & Society* 1(2):125–51.

Wilcox, W. Bradford. 2004. *Soft Patriarchs, New Men: How Christianity Shapes Fathers and Husbands*. Chicago: University of Chicago Press.

———. 2006. "Family." Pp. 97–120 in *Handbook of Religion and Social Institutions*, ed. Helen Rose Ebaugh. Houston: Springer.

Wilkins, Amy. 2008. "'Happier than Non-Christians': Collective Emotions and Symbolic Boundaries among Evangelical Christians." *Social Psychology Quarterly* 71(3):281–301.

Williams, Rhys. 1994. "Covenant, Contract, and Communities: Religion and Political Culture in America." *International Issues* 37:31–50.

Wolkomir, Michelle. 2001. "Emotion Work, Commitment, and the Authentication of the Self: The Case of Gay and Ex-Gay Christian Support Groups." *Journal of Contemporary Ethnography* 30(3):305–34.

Wong, Jaclyn. 2017. "Competing Desires: How Young Adult Couples Negotiate Moving for Career Opportunities." *Gender & Society* 31(2):171–96.

Wright, Katie. 2008. "Theorizing Therapeutic Culture: Past Influences, Future Directions." *Journal of Sociology* 44(4):321–36.

Zelizer, Viviana. 2007. *The Purchase of Intimacy*. Princeton: Princeton University Press.

Zerubavel, Eviatar. 1991. *The Fine Line: Making Distinctions in Everyday Life*. New York: Free Press.

INDEX

Pages in *italics* indicate figures and tables

abstinence, 16, 33, 46, 88, 139, 142–43, 146, 194, 221n105, 233n12; abstinence education, 16. *See also* purity culture
The Act of Marriage: A Christian Guide to Sexual Love (LaHaye and LaHaye), 46
Adams, Michele, 228n28
adulthood, 3, 14, 193; transition to, 14
advice, 3, 9, 26–27, 35, 37–38, 47–48, 67, 71, 83, 91, 96, 106–7, 111–14, 116, 118, 128, 136, 140, 142, 148, 155, 157–58, 160, 176–79, 195, 203, 209, 214n83; gendered, 23, 159; marital, 11–16, 70, 106–8, 191, 202, 214n83; therapeutic, 43, 122–26
American Association for Marriage and Family Therapy, 44
American Psychological Association, 44
Ammerman, Nancy, 200
Ansari, Aziz. *See Modern Romance*
anxiety, 3–4, 11, 20, 33, 65, 91, 159, 166, 176, 182–83, 195–96, 204, 223n21; marital, 16, 179; relational, 171, 184
Archdiocese of Chicago, 29, 40, 41, 42
assessment, 17, 45, 54, 58, 74, 150, 195, 222n13; assessment tool, 45, 57, 66–71, 74–75, 223n24, 223n27, 223n29; questionnaire, 17, 35, 73, 104–5. *See also* FOCCUS; Prepare/Enrich
Aubry, Timothy, 9, 48. See also *Rethinking Therapeutic Culture*
authority, 31–33, 38, 40–41, 43–44, 48, 51, 58, 65, 74, 80, 84, 88, 174, 177, 203, 219n65, 221n115; religious, 5, 6, 10, 48–49, 53, 89, 212n45; organizational, 89; scientific, 68; spiritual, 22
autonomy, 8, 132; personal, 44, 106
Avishai, Orit, 54

Bartkowski, John, 114, 117, 227n25
Bellah, Robert, 9, 199
Berger, Peter, 136
Bernard, Jessie, 6
Bible, 37, 80, 87, 114–15, 129, 150, 194; Genesis, 105–6, *111*, 111–12, 114–15, 123–24, 129, 143; gospel, 72; New Testament, 37, 124, 140; Old Testament, 140; Ten Commandments, 121, 146. *See also* scripture
Bridges, Tristan, 187
budget, 138, 150–54, 156, 158. *See also* finances; money
Burns, Jeffrey, 17, 214n87

Cabanas, Edgar, 9, 212n43
Cana Conference Movement, 17, 25, 28–30, 32, 40–41, 45, 214n87, 217n12. *See also* Pre-Cana capitalism, 39; industrial capitalism, 8, 39
calling, 12, 16, 31–32, 78, 149, 195. *See also* vocation of marriage
Catholicism, 18, 162, 174, 203n41; Catholic Church, 17, 21, 29, 40, 72, 121, 123, 172–74, 202, 231n2
Celello, Kristin, 11–12, 91
Chapman, Gary, 10, 46, 60, 63, 100, 196. See also *The Five Love Languages*

247

chastity, 146, 193, 233n12. *See also* abstinence
Chaves, Mark, 232n11
Cherlin, Andrew, 13–15, 48
Christ, 26, 29, 38, 80, 123–24, 129, 224n9; his disciples, 111, 123–24. *See also* Jesus
Christian Century, 34
Christian Family Movement, 17, 28, 33, 214n87, 218n40
Christianity, 36–37, 43, 138, 143, 162; history of, 27
class, 7–9, 15, 21, 38, 58, 70–71, 75, 149, 152–53, 155, 159, 165, 213n76; college-educated, 19, 21, 58, 65, 165; low-income, 16, 56, 67, 192, 214n83, 222n24, 223n76; middle-class, 8, 15, 27, 39, 70–71, 76, 110–11, 165, 226n11, 227n13; working-class, 15. *See also* poverty
Clemens, Alphonse, 29, 29n12
cohabitation, 11, 14, 42, 71, 89, 121, 136, 147, 149, 161, 175, 193, 224n28, 230n28
Coltrane, Scott, 55, 121, 222n11, 228n28
commitment, 2–4, 28, 42, 52–53, 66, 81–82, 87, 94, 100, 104, 110, 143–44, 147–49, 157, 162, 167–68, 193, 201
communication, 13, 26–27, 32–33, 39, 40–41, 48, 53–54, 60, 63, 67–68, 89, 93–95, 99, 109, 112–16, 122, 124–29, 141–44, 150, 155–56, 180–81, 192, 195, 198; active listening, 68, 108, 128; and conflict management, 3, 96; listener, 94, 105, 118; skills, 48, 67, 93, 156; styles, 3, 105, 113, 115, 119, 121, 125, 198
community, 2, 10, 16–18, 21, 24–25, 27, 36, 38, 42– 43, 467, 51, 53, 55, 64–66, 71, 81, 84, 138, 176, 190–91, 194, 199, 203–4, 212n45; building, 64, 76; of faith, 6, 52, 57, 84, 101, 122, 165, 193–94; religious, 3, 4, 6, 10, 17–18, 21–22, 28, 36, 49, 56, 64, 74–76, 79, 84, 90–91, 101, 130–31, 163, 166, 172, 174–75, 191, 193, 195, 200, 202–3, 216n99, 232n11, 234n37
companionship, 26, 31, 95, 137, 157

compatibility, 9, 48, 69, 142, 150, 153, 156, 195. *See also* assessment
complementarianism, 105, 108, 110, 115–17, 121, 125, 224n25. *See also* gender
conflict, 2, 15, 30, 32, 36, 64, 69, 82, 92–93, 95, 97–98, 103, 109, 113, 122, 125–26, 128–29, 136, 176–77, 181, 183–84, 191, 195, 198, 202, 205; management, 3, 11, 89, 95–96, 181; marital, 54, 90, 128, 134–35, 138, 197; resolution, 54, 68; style, 60
congregational, 16, 18, 55, 73, 75, 88, 170, 190, 214n83, 215n94, 222n11
contraception, 3, 11, 29, 32–33, 148, 217n14; birth control, 202, 234n37; natural family planning, 118, 138, 148; rhythm method, 33, 218n40
contract, 27, 78–79, 80–83, 86, 89, 102, 138, 147, 205, 224n2, 229n17; conjugal, 159; of marriage, 200–201; contractual, 81, 85, 139, 143, 204. *See also* marriage
convalidation, 42, 72, 80, 161–62, 174–75, 197, 225n33, 230n1, 231n2, 232n14
Coontz, Stephanie, 7, 10–11, 13, 157. *See also Marriage, a History*
Corse, Sarah, 15
Cott, Nancy, 110, 138, 229n17
counseling, 18, 19, 23, 27, 36–37, 44, 49–51, 60, 85–88, 128, 165–66, 176, 192, 195, 198, 219n66; marriage, 11–12, 28, 33, 35, 131, 186, 191. *See also* pastoral counseling; therapy
covenant, 77–79, 80–82, 83, 83–86, 88, 91, 139, 142, 145, 149, 201, 223n2, 224n9; rhetoric, 4, 6, 10, 21–23, 27, 76, 78–79, 80, 82–83, 85, 88–92, 94, 96–97, 101–2, 107–8, 111, 113, 115, 124, 126, 130, 132, 136, 138–39, 143, 146–48, 157–58, 164, 177, 179–86, 192, 195, 203, 205. *See also* marriage
Crowley, Patty, 28, 54
culture/cultural, 5, 12, 49, 81, 84, 86, 142, 157, 166; anxieties, 22; approach to the study of religion, 4–6, 22–23; change,

3, 24, 48, 101, 136; context, 44, 91; emotional culture, 20, 164–65, 171, 176, 194; expectations, 7, 9, 24, 136, 142, 212n43; gender differences, *111*, 117–22, 131; insecurity culture, 15, 196; marriage culture, 4, 13, 90, 137; organizational culture, 54; popular culture, 9, 46, 220n104; reception, 19, 23; resource, 84, 101; ; subculture, 27, 37, 47, 79; transmission, 23, 49, 53, 74

Dalessandro, Cristen, 159
dating, 15, 21, 46–47, 51, 54, 68, 95, 104, 134, 139, 141, 148, 161, 165–68, 175–76, 181, 213n76, 221n107, 230n1, 231n10; date, 15, *111*, 167, 181. *See also* pre-engaged; scripts
Davis, Rebecca, 11–12, 34–35, 106, 218n44
decisions, 28, 42, 57, 92, 95, 130, 132–33, 137–38, 149, *153*, 156, 161, 166, 171, 173, 175–76, 198–99, 205, 230n28; decision-making, 6; moral, 121–22, 146, 152
DeRogatis, Amy, 158
discourse, 5, 10, 19, 23, 24, 43–44, 55, 107, 114, 123, 136, 139, 140, 143, 187, 205, 222n11; therapeutic discourse, 126
division of labor, 3, 8, 14, 28, 72, *111*, 132, 227n13; household labor, 6, 39, 124. *See also* gender
divorce, 2–6, 11–13, 23, 26–27, 30–31, 39, 56, 60, 65, 75, 89–91, 94, 101, 107, 145, 168, 171, 192, 197, 199, 203, 223n21, 225n22; divorce culture, 79, 89–91, 97, 101, 198; fear of, 11, 47; rates, 4, 22, 28, 40, 90–91, 223n21
doctors, 30, 32–33, 37, 46, 148
Du Mez, Kristin Kobes, 220n104, 221nn106–7

Edgell, Penny, 5, 191
education, 16, 21, 28, 33, 35, 58–59, 75, 80, 110, 152, 214n83, 224n9, 233n34; marriage, 11, 16, 54, 92, 191, 193–94, 202n34, 214n83, 233n12; religious, 49, 72, 74, 76–77, 110, 117, 165, 192–95, 199
egalitarian, 106, 123, 126, 137, 167, 231n10
Ellis, Rachel, 202, 234nn35, 37
emotions/emotional, 6, 7, 9, 13, 21, 23–24, 39, 43, 48, 79, 81–82, 92, 95, 98–99, 102, 132, 136, 138, 140, 145, 146–48, 156–59, 163–64, 191–92, 196, 199, 204–6, 211n23, 212n43, 216n1, 224n1; emotional bank, 94–95, 108, 124; deviance, 7; distance, 64, 93; fulfillment, 106; independence, 14, 17; intimacy, 99; management, 53, 92–93, 101, 137–39, 142, 151, 157–58, 181, 198–99, 225n19; emotion norms, 7, 136; regime, 6, 7, 21, 90, 136, 225n22; emotion work, 27, 94, 113, 128, 131–32, 136, 164, 181, 185–86, 190, 196, 200; subculture, 79; well-being, 9. *See also* happiness; love
Engels, Friedrich, 229n17
England, Paula, 132
ethnography, 16–17, 20–21, 178, 214n84, 215n90; ethnographers, 190; of the ephemeral, 16; of a practice, 17, 214n84, 215n90, 232n15
ethos, 36, 84, 198. *See also* religious familism; therapeutic
evangelicalism, 18, 43, 47, 167, 203, 231n10, 234n41; evangelical culture, 20, 46; evangelical worldview, 36, 38, 40, 45, 55, 80, 82, 109–10, 112, 139, 165, 195, 219n65, 221n105
experts, 9–12, 26–29, 33–34, 47–48, 53–54, 67, 70, 91, 106, 192, 195; expertise, 32, 48–51, 58, 62, 74–75, 106, 127; *See also* doctors; psychology; therapy

family, 4–6, 8, 12, 29, 31, 35, 37, 40–41, 43, 46, 48, 55, 62, 97, 98, 101–2, 106–7, 111, 114–16, 118–20, 127, 132, 137–38, 148, 156, 162, 169–70, 180–81, 190, 195, 200, 220n92, 220n104; Christian, 36; backgrounds, 99, 118, 122; change, 24, 191;

family (*cont.*)
   norms, 130; family of origin, 55, 98–99, 106–7, 115, 116, 118–20, 122, 127, 156, 180, 195; structure, 43, 70, 110n11; homemaker-breadwinner, 7, 110–11, 159, 226n11, 227n13; and religion, 27, 191; and work, 103, 106–7, 191
Farrel, Bill and Pam. See *Men Are like Waffles, Women Are like Spaghetti*
feeling rules, 4, 7, 136, 148, 157, 183
femininity, 121, 228n28; feminine, 33, 107, 127. *See also* gender
feminism, 2, 11, 105; feminist, 5, 8, 39, 121, 228n28
finances, 15–16, 23, 32, 54, 68, 115, 137, 149–59, 178, 180, 187, 193, 195, 213n76, 216n99, 228n7, 230n28; financial management, 68, 154; financial planning, 38. *See also* money 213
Fischer, Claude, 13
Fischer, Matthias, 25–27
The Five Love Languages (Chapman), 10, 46, 60, 63, 100, 196
FOCCUS, 67–68, 70, 223nn24–28
Francis, Linda, 158
Francis, Pope, 121, 227n27
Friedan, Betty, 12
friendship, 48, 93, 95–96, 138
Fuller's School of Psychology, 44
Furedi, Frank, 9–10, 48, 212n45, 221n115
Furstenberg, Frank, 14

Gansen, Heidi, 138
gay marriage, 2, 11; marriage equality, 2, 3, 16, 21, 192, 200–204, 216n97, 233n33, 234n41; same-sex marriage, 201–3, 233n34, 234n41. *See also* nonheterosexual; sexuality
gender, 3, 7, 9, 23, 38, 107, 111–12, 119, 121, 125, 127, 130–32, 138, 159, 203, 228n28; gender-blind, 107, *111*, 130, 132–33, 198, 201; gender complementarianism, 8, 23, 103, 107, 110, 120–23, 126, 144, 226n11, 227n25; gender differences, 23, 31, 105, 107, 110–11, 112–25, 127, 130–31, 167; gender inequality, 158, 187; gendered institution, 107, 111, 131; gender roles, 2, 29, 31–33, 35–36, 106–7, 111, 114–15, 118, 120, 124, 130–31, 137, 149, 191, 200, 227n13; gendered power, 107, 159, 198; gendered self, 106; nongendered, 116, 125, 128. *See also* division of labor; femininity; masculinity
Gerson, Kathleen, 5, 106
Ghaziani, Amin, 138
God, 3, 10, 18, 21, 26, 30–31, 38, 43–44, 47, 59, 76, 78–80, 82–85, 87–89, 91–92, 100–102, 105, 107–10, 112, 114–117, 120–21, 123, 129, 134, 138–39, 140–46, 148–49, 150, 152, 155, 157, 189, 193–95, 198, 201–3, 229n19, 233n18, 233n34
Good News about Sex and Marriage (West), 192
Gottman, John, 60, 62, 98, 128, 228n30; love labs, 60, 126. See also *The Seven Principles for Making Marriage Work*
Gray, John, 60, 113, 118. See also *Men Are from Mars, Women Are from Venus*

Hackstaff, Karla, 89, 91, 101
happiness, 9, 14, 30–31, 37–38, 48, 79, 87, 91, 101–2, 146, 212n43; happy, 3, 6–7, 18, 26, 28–31, 37–38, 49, 53, 83–84, 91, 101, 106–7, 123, 157, 163, 171, 182–83, 199, 203; marital happiness, 12, 36, 113–14
Harris, Joshua, 46–47, 221n107. See also *I Kissed Dating Goodbye*
Harris, Scott, 7
Healthy Marriage Initiative, 114, 214n83
Heath, Melanie, 54–55, 222n11
heterosexuality, 8, 16, 21, 28, 31, 36, 65, 111, 128, 130, 138–39, 186, 194, 200–203, 234n41; heterogender, 8; heteronormative 35, 111, 144, 200; heterosexual marriage, 16, 22, 47, 131–32, 199, 201

Hillerstrom, P. Roger. See *Intimate Deception*
Hochschild, Arlie, 7, 10, 136, 212n25
Hout, Michael, 13

identity, 140, 203; religious identity, 21, 216n99, 220n104
ideology, 5, 8–9, 35, 131–32, 145, 224n1, 226n11
I Kissed Dating Goodbye (Harris), 46–47, 221n107
Illouz, Eva, 9, 196, 212n43
individualism, 28, 48, 53
inequality, 9, 15, 123, 157–58, 187, 198
Ingraham, Chrys, 8
interfaith, 42, 72, 172–75, 178, 184
intimacy, 3, 12–14, 22, 24–25, 31, 33, 61–62, 65, 82, 95, 97–101, 137, 139–40, 143–44, 146, 148–49, 157, 179–80, 192–93, 198–200, 205, 228n7
Intimate Deception: Escaping the Trap of Sexual Impurity (Hillerstrom), 46, 220n100

Jenkins, Kathleen, 4, 93, 185, 225n22
Jesus, 36, 37, 47, 59, 81, *111*, 123–24, 129, 130, 150. *See also* Christ
Johari window, *61*, 61–62, 100, 223n15
John Paull II, Pope, 121, 227nn26–27; *Theology of the Body*, 121
Journal of Psychology and Theology, 43

Kellner, Hansgried, 136
Kilbourne, Barbara, 132
Klinenberg, Eric. See *Modern Romance*
Kniss, Fred, 84
Konieczny, Mary Ellen, 146

LaHaye, Beverly and Tim. See *The Act of Marriage*
Lamont, Ellen, 167, 227n13
Lasch, Christopher, 212n45, 221n115
Life and Love: A Christian View on Sex and The Psychology of Counseling— for All Who Are Engaged in the Art of Counseling, 37, 219nn60–61
liturgy, 72, 122, 146
Lofton, Kathryn, 219n66, 220n90, 221n115
Loss, Christopher, 221n115
love, 2, 7, 8–11, 13, 20–21, 25, 27, 30–33, 37, 38, 46, 51, 63–64, 78, 80, 92, 97, 100–102, 110, *111*, 114–15, 118, 124, 126, 129–32, 135, 137–39, 146, 148–49, 157, 169, 177, 182–83, 185, 190–92, 201–5, 208, 219nn60–61, 220n103, 233n34; history of, 8; therapeutic, 6, 8–10, 21, 22, 49, 53, 64, 131, 137, 143, 148, 184, 191, 204; rationalization of, 97; romantic, 7–8, 11, 13, 132; sacrificial, 30; skilled, 9, 71, 92, 192. *See also* romance
love languages, 1, 63, 100, 118, 122, 195, 198. *See also* Chapman, Gary
Lundquist Denton, Melinda. See *Soul Searching*

mainline Protestants, 22, 34, 36–38, 44–45
Maldonado-Estrada, Alyssa, 190
marriage: biblical, 86–87, 129–30; Catholic, 29, 40–41, 72, 122–23; Christian, 6, 22–23, 27, 36, 49, 59, 76, 79–80, 82, 84–89, 89–92, 101, 124, 129, 130, 186, 190, 199, 200, 203, 205, 215n96, 224n1, 234n41; covenant, 4, 23, 71, 79, 82–85, 88–89, 91, 101, 103, 106, 145, 157, 205; companionate, 11–14, 28, 39, 47, 102, 106, 137, 200; contract, 23, 79, 80, 88–89, 97, 147, 203–4; good, 3, 4, 11, 13–16, 21–22, 24, 27, 39–40, 43, 48–49, 53, 65, 73–74, 76, 84, 86, 102, 111, 142, 176–77, 189, 191, 193, 198, 200, 211n83, 234n41; healthy, 23, 60, 63, 83, 161; history of, 11, 35, 191; individualized, 14, 39, 48, 71, 106, 198, 200; gap, 15, 21, 149, 155; mentor, 18, 56–57, 65, 68, 71–73, 215n94; marital satisfaction, 4, 186; marital success, 38, 79, 84, 90–91, 106, 169, 192; marital tension, 33;

marriage: biblical (*cont.*)
    marital work ethic, 4, 11, 39, 52, 64, 75, 91–94, 101–2, 136, 142–43, 177, 179, 184, 186–87, 193, 195, 198, 200; work, 11, 23, 39, 53, 60, 63, 80, 88, 91–93, 95–97, 125, 131, 136, 193, 222n14; soulmate, 102, 137; traditional, 7, 16, 22, 101, 123, 214n83; transition to, 2, 10, 47, 85, 141, 164, 171, 177, 183, 193, 233n12
Marriage, a History (Coontz), 11, 15, 48, 51, 212nn30
marriage movement, 16, 55–56, 71, 75, 214n83, 222n11
masculinity, 113, 121, 124, 228n28; masculine, 33, 107, 127. *See also* gender
McGuire, Meredith, 164, 185
Men Are from Mars, Women Are from Venus (Gray), 60, 113–14, 118, 125
Men Are like Waffles, Women Are like Spaghetti (Farrel and Farrel), 112, 125
Modern Romance (Ansari and Klinenberg), 102, 137
Money & Marriage (Pahl), 149
ministry, 25, 27, 41, 43, 45, 47, 50, 74, 88, 102, 190, 191, 202, 202n34, 202n35; ministries, 2, 17n87, 26, 27, 43, 45n85, 55n11, 57, 90n22, 191
money, 23, 53, 68, 133, 137–38, 149, 150–59, 181, 198, 203, 230n28; management, 153, 156–57. *See also* finances
Moon, Dawne, 202
Moskowitz, Eva, 212n45, 221n115
Moslener, Sara, 219n65, 220n90
Myers-Shirk, Susan, 38n65, 44

Narramore, Clyde, 37–38, 43, 46. *See also Life and Love*
Narramore, Bruce, 43
neoliberalism, 9, 96, 102, 198, 206, 212n43
nonheterosexual, 201, 203, 212n47, 234n41; queer couples, 21, 136, 201, 204; same-sex couples, 200, 201, 234n41. *See also* gay marriage; sexuality

Oates, Wayne E. See *Premarital Pastoral Care and Counseling*
Obama, Barack, 200
oneness, 21, 23, 83, 107–9, 147, 157, 229n17

Pahl, Jan. See *Money & Marriage*
Parrott, Les and Leslie. See *Saving Your Marriage before It Starts*
partnership, 14, 15, 27, 39, 80, 83, 90, 106, 121, 126, 131, 224n9
Pascoe, C. J., 187
pastoral counseling, 22, 34, 36, 38, 44–45, 219n65
Pastoral Psychology (journal), 34
Paulsen, Krista, 16
personality, 2, 20, 54, 60–61, 98, 100, 105–6, 114–15, 118, 122, 126–27, 130–32, 176; personality type, 54, 61, 100, 127, 198
Pew Research Center, 215n92, 223n23, 234n41
Platt, Gerald, 224n1
Plante, Rebecca, 138
poverty, 15–16, 55–56, 75, 149, 213n76, 214n83; poverty reduction, 75
power, 5, 6, 21, 32, 48, 81, 88, 91, 107, 131–33, 136, 157, 159, 186, 192, 198, 204–5, 226n11
prayer, 25, 77, 86, 124, 134, 190, 201
Pre-Cana Conferences, 25–26, 28–33, 40–42, 54, 148, 194, 216n1, 217n12, 217nn17–18, 217nn 22–23, 217n26, 218nn26–40
pre-engaged scripts, 166, 168, 183. *See also* dating
Premarital Counseling: A Guidebook for Counselors (Wright), 45
Premarital Counseling: A Manual for Ministers (Westberg), 34
Premarital Pastoral Care and Counseling (Oates), 36–37
premarital sex, 4, 140, 149, 161, 230n28
postwar, 12, 22, 26–29, 31, 34, 36, 40–41, 43, 45, 54, 191, 194, 217n14, 218n40

Prepare/Enrich, 67–69, 71, 73, 223nn24–25, 223nn27, 223nn29
psychology, 4, 9, 34, 36–38, 43–44, 48–49, 61, 106–7, *111*, 122, 152, 192, 195, 218n44, 219n60, 220n88; psychological explanations, 111; psychological differences, 23, 107, 127; psychological well-being, 12. *See also* therapy, counseling
Psychology for Living (radio), 37
purity culture, 46–47, 221n105, 221n107, 226n11. *See also* abstinence, chastity

race, 7–8, 15–16, 21, 38, 41–42, 65, 70–71, 76, 120, 126, 165, 213n76, 214n83, 216n99, 223n21, 226n11, 227n13, 231n8, 234n41
Rakow, Katja, 212n45
Randles, Jennifer, 9, 54, 114, 192, 211n24
relationship education, 23, 53–54, 57, 60, 63, 75, 76, 192–93; premarital education, 27, 32, 164–65, 172, 205
relationship science, 27, 48, 60, 65, 67, 70
relationship skills, 4, 53–54, 58, 67, 74–75, 89, 92–93, 95–97, 108, 132, 136, 142, 150, 158–59, 168, 177–78, 192, 196, 201, 205, 223n24
religious familism, 5, 6, 17, 226n11
remarriage, 41–42, 73, 223n21
Rethinking Therapeutic Culture (Aubry and Travis), 9, 215
rhetoric, 3, 39, 86, 88, 91, 101, 106, 110, 112, 117, 121, 123, 127, 130, 214n83, 224n1. *See also* covenant
Rieff, Phillip, 212n45, 221n115
romance, 9, 48, 93, 96, 137, 192, 221n106; romantic, 9, 95, 138, 195, 213n76; rationalization of, 9, *See also* love
roles, 2, 8, 10–13, 28–29, 31–33, 36–37, 39, 55, 68, 106–7, 111, 114–15, 118–20, 124, 130–31, 137–38, 148–49, 159, 191, 200, 227n13; social roles, 9, 13
Roof, Wade Clark, 200

sacralization, 4, 6, 27, 33, 47, 89, 92, 100, 107–8, 124, 131, 158

sacrament, 30, 72, 77–78, 123, 171–72, 176, 194, 224n9, 234n35; of marriage, 40–42, 49, 76, 165, 174, 176; sacramental marriage, 72–73, 82, 117, 120, 122–24, 126, 146–47, 172, 223n33; sacramental education, 171, 234n35
sacrifice, 31, 126
sanctification, 3–4, 13–14, 27, 29–31, 47, 49, 53, 90, 100–101, 109, 129, 142, 148, 186, 192, 203
Saving Your Marriage before It Starts (Parrott and Parrott), 46, 69, 192
scripts, 3, 6, 111, 137, 149, 186, 227n13, 231n10; sexual scripts, 148; dating scripts, 167
scripture, 13, 37, 44, *111*, 114, 117, 143, 150, 152, 193–94, 213n65. *See also* Bible
secular, 3, 18, 27–29, 33, 44–45, 49, 76, 83, 86, 108, 113, 192–95, 201–3, 219n65, 221n115; culture, 23, 36, 40, 79–80, 84, 89–90, 97, 101, 105, 108, 139–40, 143–44, 148, 204; unaffiliated, 18, 211n92; people, 3, 83; other, 18, 83; secularism, 22, 28–29, 33, 38, 47, 194, 221n115; marriage, 33, 81–82, 85, 147, 205; secularization, 221n115
self, 8–10, 13, 23, 27, 38–39, 43, 48, 62–63, 78, 80, 97–98, 100–102, 104, 106, 109–10, 116, 135–36, 141, 143, 179, 195, 204, 205; self-help, 2, 9, 17, 38, 46, 47, 60, 98, 106, 112–13, 119, 125, 225n37; self-improvement, 100; selfless, 81, 124, 126; self-realization, 15, 52, 98, 100; self-reflexivity, 39, 48, 59, 63, 89, 97, 126, 143, 177, 179, 181–82, 185, 195; self-work, 9, 23, 27, 53, 55, 66, 99, 102, 132
The Seven Principles for Making Marriage Work (Gottman and Silver), 60, 125, 192–93
sex, 14, 23, 31–33, 35, 37–38, 40, 43, 45–46, 53–54, 121, 133, 137–49, 157–59, 161, 180, 182, 187, 192–93, 195, 198, 219n60, 221n104, 222n14, 222nn105–7, 225n18, 227n22, 228n28, 229nn18–19, 230n28;

sex (*cont.*)
  sex education, 32, 33, 46, 148; sexual shame, 20, 88, 140–141, 177, 225n18, 229n19. *See also* heterosexuality; premarital sex; scripts
sexuality, 1, 7, 9, 20, 23, 46, 68, 88–89, 138–46, 148, 193, 202, 221n105, 225n18, 226n11, 229nn17–18, 233n12, 233n34. *See also* gay marriage; heterosexuality; nonheterosexual
Silva, Jennifer, 15, 212n43
Silver, Nan, 125, 193
Slominski, Kristy, 221n105
Smith, Christian. *See Soul Searching*
social class, 7–9, 152; *See also* class
socialization, 4, 23, 53, 75, 93, 136, 138, 148, 163, 191; emotional socialization, 4, 23, 75, 133, 136–39, 140, 145, 148, 151, 156–57, 159, 191–92, 229n19; gender socialization, 132, 198; religious socialization, 163
Soul Searching: The Religious and Spiritual Lives of American Teenagers (Smith and Lundquist Denton), 163
spiritual, 3, 4, 22, 31–32, 43, 48, 68, 77, 93, 122–24, 126–27, 137, 142, 163, 192–94, 199, 202, 221n115; spirituality, 29, 32–33, 48, 100, 185
spouses, 12, 21, 80, 82, 85, 105, 116, 121, 126, 137, 145, 224n9
Struening, Karen, 229n17
Swidler, Ann, 8
symbolic boundaries, 79, 83–85, 90, 101–2, 136, 204

Tentler, Leslie Woodcock, 217n14, 217n17
theology, 36, 43, 72, 79–80, 121, 194, 220n1; theological, 3, 27, 29–30, 32, 44, 80, 85, 101, 117, 147–48, 164, 176, 193, 220n88, 224n2, 233n18
therapy, 10, 15, 18, 38, 44, 48, 68, 75, 98, 194, 199, 215n94, 219n64, 221n115, 225n37. *See also* counseling
therapeutic, 6, 9, 10, 13, 23, 27, 36, 38–39, 43–44, 47–49, 52, 57, 60, 62, 65, 70, 80, 83, 88–89, 100–101, 125–27, 129, 130–31, 136, 150–51, 158, 182, 195–96, 201, 212n45; culture, 9, 10, 22–23, 43, 49, 53, 63, 64, 65, 101–2, 204, 220n90, 221n115; therapeutic ethos, 10, 15, 48, 102, 132, 135, 191, 204, 212n43; intervention, 53, 190, 194–95, 205; practice 9, 12, 22, 27, 43, 55, 58–59, 65, 70, 74–76, 195; self, 23, 97, 99, 101–2, 106; skills 106, 156; religio-therapeutic, 2, 10, 52–53, 74, 79, 151, 158, 164, 192, 194, 201
Travis, Trysh, 9, 221n115

unity, 23, 32, 109, 115, 121, 143–44, 146–47, 158; unitive, 23, 87, 108, 148; *See also* oneness
Vatican, 123
Vatican II, 194
vocation of marriage, 26, 29, 30, 32, 35, 43, 48, 77–78, 194

Watt, David, 220n92
wealth, 15, 25, 150, 152, 154, 157, 158, 213n76
wedding, 7, 18, 23, 24–26, 37, 41, 50, 54, 56–57, 63, 72, 75–76, 87, 95, 129, 155, 162, 164–65, 169, 171–72, 182–83, 194, 197, 223n33, 231n2, 231nn12–13, 234n35; civil wedding, 80, 174–75; marriage ceremony, 7; wedding liturgy, 72, 122; wedding proposal, 92, 165; wedding planning, 95, 164–65, 171
West, Christopher, 146, 192. *See also Good News about Sex and Marriage*
Westberg, Granger, 34–35, 45. *See also Premarital Counseling: A Manual for Ministers*
Wilkins, Amy, 102
Williams, Rhys, 224n1
Wong, Jaclyn, 132
World War II, 12, 27, 48, 213n76, 217n17
Wright, H. Norman. *See Premarital Counseling: A Guidebook for Counselors*

Zerubavel, Eviatar, 85, 88

ABOUT THE AUTHOR

COURTNEY ANN IRBY is associate professor in the Department of Sociology and director of the Women's, Gender, and Sexuality Studies program at Illinois Wesleyan University.

www.ingramcontent.com/pod-product-compliance
Lightning Source LLC
Chambersburg PA
CBHW020401080526
44584CB00014B/1115